**ANDREA**

**Contemporary Critical Perspectives**

Series Editors: Jeannette Baxter, Peter Childs, Sebastian Groes and Sean Matthews

Guides in the *Contemporary Critical Perspectives* series provide companions to reading and studying major contemporary authors. They include new critical essays combining textual readings, cultural analysis and discussion of key critical and theoretical issues in a clear, accessible style. Each guide also includes a preface by a major contemporary writer, a new interview with the author, discussion of film and TV adaptation and guidance on further reading.

Titles in the series include:

# ANDREA LEVY

## Contemporary Critical Perspectives

Edited by
**Jeannette Baxter and David James**

B L O O M S B U R Y
LONDON • NEW DELHI • NEW YORK • SYDNEY

**Bloomsbury Academic**
An imprint of Bloomsbury Publishing Plc

50 Bedford Square
London
WC1B 3DP
UK

1385 Broadway
New York
NY 10018
USA

www.bloomsbury.com

**Bloomsbury is a registered trade mark of Bloomsbury Publishing Plc**

First published 2014

**British Library Cataloguing-in-Publication Data**
A catalogue record for this book is available from the British Library.

ISBN: HB: 978-1-4411-6045-4
PB: 978-1-4411-1360-3
ePub: 978-1-4411-4758-5
ePDF: 978-1-4411-2473-9

**Library of Congress Cataloging-in-Publication Data**
Andrea Levy / edited by Jeannette Baxter and David James.
pages cm – (Contemporary critical perspectives series)
Includes bibliographical references and index.
ISBN 978-1-4411-6045-4 – ISBN 978-1-4411-1360-3 (pbk.) – ISBN 978-1-4411-4758-5
(epub) – ISBN 978-1-4411-2473-9 (epdf) 1. Levy, Andrea, 1956–Criticism and
interpretation. I. Baxter, Jeannette, editor of compilation. II. James, David,
1979- editor of compilation.
PR6112.E889Z55 2013
823'.92–dc23
2013033733

Typeset by Newgen Knowledge Works (P) Ltd., Chennai, India
Printed and bound in Great Britain

# Contents

# CONTENTS

# Foreword

## Finding a Voice – Giving a Voice

### Lawrence Scott

'I'm just a North London Girl.'

(Andrea Levy)

Some years ago, when we read together at the Hornsey Library in Crouch End, Andrea Levy declared, 'I'm just a North London girl'. The context was one of those discussions concerning the question of identity and being West Indian. It was said tongue-in-cheek, followed by that inimitable laughter, which I learnt was the Levy ironic-comic-tone evident in all of her books; that thrust and sideways look which undercuts poignant moments, serious statements, in case they sound too portentous. Levy prefers to have you laughing, even if you have been angry or sad. She wants to entertain you. 'I'm a tap-dancer at heart', she said to me recently as we discussed her five novels. We began to explore how that dance became more complicated, how the steps became more intricate and its intention more deeply grounded in the histories, which would give a fuller voice to her characters.

Angela in *Every Light in the House is Burnin'*, Olive and Vivien in *Never Far from Nowhere* and Faith in *Fruit of the Lemon* are all North London girls. These characters are in search of an identity, even if they do not always immediately know it themselves. They are looking for that fuller voice: readers know it and both cry and laugh through the narrative and drama. These girls are always being asked, *Where're you from?* or, being told to, *Go back to where you've come from*. Their brothers also experience this racist interrogation and banishment. But, it is the girls who are at the centre of these fictions. In the first two books, in particular, they in turn interrogate their parents about who they are and where they are from and why they are being called *things*. Their West Indian parents tell them they should answer that they are from here, they are from England. They should ignore the racist taunts, the jibes and insults. They should find other friends. *Tell them you're English,* they advise their children.

These characters experience themselves in a place they call home. But they are being told that they are not from that place, that instead, they are from somewhere else, though they do know that place. This is the complex knot of un-belonging for the black West Indian, *Never Far from Nowhere* in these not uncommon encounters in racist Britain: on the street, in the playground and in the pub. It was true of the 1950s and 1960s, and, unfortunately, continues to be true now, though in different forms.

This experience is further complicated by the parents of these North London girls with their first-generation West Indian parents, who, in their effort to settle in Britain, communicate to their children a kind of amnesia about where they are from. They refuse to answer their questions about the West Indies. They do this in an effort for their children to assimilate, to blend. It is in the heart of the West Indian family with this struggle, this conundrum, that Levy finds her stories. It is there that the explorations of settlement, growing up, belonging, not belonging, blending and understanding, take place.

As we experience Levy finding her own voice as a writer in the early novels, we listen to the characters being given a voice. These characters, historically, have not had a voice.

Levy had to go on a journey of discovery. Her girlhood was spent in North London in the 1950s–1960s generation. She had been sometimes the only black girl in her school. This offered her the experience, the life-research, which she uses for her characters Angela, Olive, Vivien and Faith.

Levy came to her serious reading in her twenties. She first of all went to black North American writers such as Toni Morrison and Audre Lourde. She fed herself with feminist writers like Michelle Roberts and Zoe Fairbairn here in England. James Baldwin changed her life, changed how she looked at fiction, the politics of fiction.

I was particularly interested in whether Levy had been influenced by West Indian writers. My first impressions of Gilbert and Hortenses's arrival in London in *Small Island* had reminded me of *The Lonely Londoners*. She did not know any West Indian writers at that time. She discovered Sam Selvon's *The Lonely Londoners* by chance. She was attracted to the *casual delivery* of his prose, his casual humour. This was a Caribbean humour she began to recognize as her own father's tone of humour, that particular West Indian humour. The representation West Indian fathers and West Indian men was something that particularly interested me in Levy's novels. She is a destroyer of stereotypes. In the early books, fathers, even though the father has died at the beginning of *Never Far from Nowhere*, are central carers, tender and funny. This is a corrective to the theme of the absent West Indian father, the stereotype of the abusive, brutalizing man.

The style and tone of the early novels are not obviously influenced in by the writers she claims as her early mentors. She wanted to write books that she would want to read herself, she says. She needed a direct, entertaining, social realism, with no tricks, as the vehicle for her narrative and dialogue and quick-moving scenes. That is the point in our conversation when she adds, 'I am a tap-dancer at heart'.

*Fruit of the Lemon* signals a shift in the way the narrative is extended and expanded and the historical background is deepened. The first section of the novel, *England* bears some resemblance to the two earlier books in their social realism and fast-moving scenes, but the narrative is already more extensive and expansive. The structure of the novel, in the way it takes the story to Jamaica in the second part, is what boldly tells us that Levy is deepening the historical ground, digging more deeply for the detail and hinterland of her characters. Faith outs herself as black, her attempt to blend with a white England is no longer satisfactory. This takes place in a compelling scene in an English country pub. Faith is tired of being excluded, and challenges the condescending humour and superficiality of a country Englishman to own his connection to the history of enslavement. Levy argues that one of the most difficult challenges for the black person is to make themselves uncomfortable, to live as uncomfortable, in challenging people about racism.

In going to Jamaica, Faith discovers, as Levy does, when she visited Jamaica during the writing of *Fruit of the Lemon*, where she is from, and where her parents are from, is a much more complex society than anything she had formerly imagined. The novel's change in tone and structure to include a series of ancestral stories reveals a more expansive and deeper geographical and psychological hinterland. She discovers a diaspora, which stretches from Harlem to Panama, an experience of race that includes the variety of mixed-race relationships, which are founded in the colonial history of enslavement. Faith finds herself and her brother Carl to be connected to relations she had not imagined she possessed. The ancestral stories are punctuated with a series of family trees, a visible and poignant series of hieroglyphs linking Faith and Carl to their heritage. While these first three novels are all separate stories, this hinterland is a background that Angela, Olive and Vivien of the early novels might have wanted and needed in order to understand their ancestry and to aid their survival on the streets of London.

The discovery of this complex society for both Levy and her character Faith in *Fruit of the Lemon* is a life-changing experience. Levy experiences fully where she is from and Faith sees that she can blend in this new home. Levy attributes what she then began to do differently as a writer with her prose to the discovery of this deeper interrogation of her characters and their backgrounds. She saw this happening in the novels of writers like Margaret Atwood and Annie Proulx. While the earlier novels were written in the voice that she wanted at that time, she felt that now she had been skimming the surface. She wanted to give her voices that greater detail and resonance.

Over the next five years, Andrea Levy worked at bursting open the covers of the book, as she described what she wanted to now do with her writing. The directness and the social realism of the early novels and the structural changes in the second half of *Fruit of the Lemon* came to her aid, giving her the confidence to leap off, as she then decided to research

more deeply before embarking on her writing. This resulted in the novel
*Small Island.* Levy said that she wanted the book to be embracing, not
only of the West Indian story, but also of the white British story, and the
story which is the meeting of those worlds. She discovers through her
characters that people are more alike than they are different. A character like Bernard and his racism had to be understood. She wanted to
develop and show his humanity. She was confident to dramatize the
meeting of the worlds in post-war London with the history of Empire,
the arrival of West Indians to England. Her own father had arrived on
the S. S. Windrush. Her first-hand knowledge of Jamaica gave her the
detail for Hortense and Celia and Gilbert. She follows Bernard to India.
The much-praised character of Queenie shows the extent of her intention to drag characters as far away from stereotype as she possibly could
without them becoming eccentric. The result was a book that British
readers fell in love with. The novel won several major awards.

Levy had now truly found her readers. This is a unique achievement
in the history of Caribbean literature, if that is one place for Levy's work.
As a literary writer, she has found a popular audience that she speaks
to with an authentic voice that is understood both here in Britain and in
the Caribbean. She tells a story that connects both archipelagos, linking
the centre of empire to its periphery.

Having found her readers, Levy would then embark over the next six
years on a book she could never have imagined writing at the beginning
of her career. If *Fruit of the Lemon* was a development from the two earliest novels, and *Small Island* burst open the covers, *The Long Song* would
find Levy being able to leave the twentieth century to return to where
the story of colonialism and the Atlantic slave trade produced a society
which was founded on racism, the same racism which had caught up
with Angela, Viviene, Olive and Faith in North London. The story-telling voice she discovers in the second part of *Fruit of the Lemon* takes us
even further back as Levy finds narrators and plots to tell July's complex
story which begins during the last days of enslavement in Jamaica and
continues through emancipation and beyond.

I wondered if Levy had been in any way awed by her earlier men-
tor, Toni Morrison with her novel *Beloved* as she embarked on her own
enslavement story. Not at all was her response. She wanted to bring her
own directness, realism, humour and irony to a story that had stretched
for more than 300 years. She was intent on showing the strategies of
survival, which people had to use. One of those strategies would be, had
to be, humour. With the comic element in the novel and its appropriate-
ness, Levy is fully confident that the story, as she tells it, needed that
expression of humanity.

Reading Andrea Levy's five novels very closely together again before
writing this piece, and then talking with her, confirmed my original
feeling that her work is about finding a voice in order to give a voice.
Though you get a sense that the first books, in particular, come directly

out of her life, out of the life of that North London girl, they are not told as her story. They are told with the gritty realism and directness that excludes self-indulgence in the creation of characters, as she finds the voice for young black girls, West Indian first-generation parents, and the characters in the white society in which they find themselves. Finding her voice, and giving voice to her characters, is on the one hand Levy's discovery and personal survival as a black person and as a writer, as it is on the other hand the discovery and survival story of black people.

I am confident that the tap dancing Levy will now produce another story from yet another of those depths in the extended geographical and psychological hinterland she has discovered.

# Series Editors' Preface

The readership for contemporary fiction has never been greater. The explosion of reading groups and literary blogs, of university courses and school curricula, and even the apparent rude health of the literary marketplace, indicate an ever-growing appetite for new work, for writing which responds to the complex, changing and challenging times in which we live. At the same time, readers seem ever more eager to engage in conversations about their reading, to devour the review pages, to pack the sessions at literary festivals and author events. Reading is an increasingly social activity, as we seek to share and refine our experience of the book, to clarify and extend our understanding.

It is this tremendous enthusiasm for contemporary fiction to which the *Contemporary Critical Perspectives* series responds. Our ambition is to offer readers of current fiction a comprehensive critical account of each author's work, presenting original, specially commissioned analyses of all aspects of their career, from a variety of different angles and approaches, as well as directions towards further reading and research. Our brief to the contributors is to be scholarly, to draw on the latest thinking about narrative, or philosophy, or psychology, indeed whatever seemed to them most significant in drawing out the meanings and force of the texts in question, but also to focus closely on the words on the page, the stories and scenarios and forms which all of us meet first when we open a book. We insisted that these essays be accessible to that mythical beast the Common Reader, who might just as readily be spotted at the Lowdham Book Festival as in a college seminar. In this way, we hope to have presented critical assessments of our writers in such a way as to contribute something to both of those environments, and also to have done something to bring together the most important qualities of each of them.

Jeannette Baxter, Peter Childs, Sebastian Groes
and Sean Matthews

# Acknowledgements

The editors and publishers would like to thank Andrea Levy for her generous support for this book. Special thanks also to our contributors to this volume for their participation, patience and enthusiasm. Susan Fischer deserves a special mention for interviewing Andrea Levy (twice!), as does Michael Perfect for his initial help with the 'Further Reading' section of this volume. The CCP Series Editors Sebastian Groes, Sean Matthews and Peter Childs, and our commissioning editor, David Avital have, as always, provided many helpful suggestions during the preparation of this book, for which we are very grateful. Thanks to Bloomsbury for their efficiency (and forbearance) throughout the production process. Jeannette would like to thank K and W for providing much needed distractions. David would like to thank Bill Schwarz for his inimitable eleventh-hour advice.

# Contributors

**Jeannette Baxter** teaches modern and contemporary literature at Anglia Ruskin University, Cambridge. She is the author of *J. G. Ballard's Surrealist Imagination: Spectacular Authorship* (Ashgate 2009); editor of *J. G. Ballard: Contemporary Critical Perspectives* (Bloomsbury 2008); and co-editor of *Visions and Revisions: Essays on J. G. Ballard* (Palgrave 2012); *Women: A Cultural Review: Reading Jean Rhys* (Routledge 2012); and *A Literature of Restitution: Critical Essays on W. G. Sebald* (Manchester 2013). She is the Series Co-Editor of *Contemporary Critical Perspectives* (Bloomsbury), and is writing a monograph titled *Exquisite Corpse: Literature/Surrealisms/Fascisms*.

**Rachel Carroll** is Principal Lecturer in English at Teesside University where she teaches courses on contemporary fiction, feminist theory, film and television adaptations and African American writing. Her research has been published in journals including *Journal of American Studies, Journal of Gender Studies, Textual Practice* and *Women: A Cultural Review*. Her edited collection *Adaptation in Contemporary Culture: Textual Infidelities* was published by Continuum in 2009 and her monograph *Rereading Heterosexuality: Feminism, Queer Theory and Contemporary Fiction* was published by Edinburgh University Press in 2012. A co-edited collection (with Adam Hansen), *Litpop: Writing and Popular Music,* is forthcoming with Ashgate.

**Susan Alice Fischer** is Professor of English at Medgar Evers College of The City University of New York. She is Editor of the online journal *Literary London Journal* and Co-Editor of the peer-reviewed journal *Changing English: Studies in Culture and Education* (Routledge). She writes about contemporary women's London narratives and about British national identity in contemporary literature and culture. She is editing a collection of essays on Hanif Kureishi for Bloomsbury (forthcoming 2014).

**Dave Gunning** teaches contemporary English Literature at the University of Birmingham, UK, with particular interests in postcolonial and postimperial writing. He is the author of *Race and Antiracism in Black British and British Asian Literature* (Liverpool University Press 2010) and *Postcolonial Literature* (Edinburgh University Press 2013) and is working on a study of the postcolonial essay as a distinctive literary form.

**David James** is Reader in modern and contemporary literature at Queen Mary, University of London. He is author of *Contemporary British Fiction and the Artistry of Space* (Continuum 2008) and *Modernist Futures* (Cambridge University Press 2012). His journal special issues include 'Fiction since 2000: Post-Millennial Commitments' (co-edited with Andrzej Gasiorek) for *Contemporary Literature* (Winter 2012), and 'Musicality and Modernist Form' (co-edited with Nathan Waddell) for *Modernist Cultures* (May 2013). With Matthew Hart and Rebecca L. Walkowitz, he edits the book series *Literature Now* at Columbia University Press. He is currently editing *The Cambridge Companion to British Fiction since 1945*.

**Michael Perfect's** teaching and research interests include contemporary British literature and culture, modernist and postmodernist literature, and postcolonial studies. He has published articles in peer-reviewed journals on Monica Ali and Andrea Levy and, among other projects, is currently working on his first monograph. Titled *Multicultural Fictions: Diversity and the Contemporary London Novel*, this research analyses a range of literary representations of ethnic and cultural diversity in London over the last three decades. It argues that, in recent years, the most successful and engaging works of literature about the city have attempted to assert its heterogeneity as undeniable while also challenging the notion that London is an inclusive utopia which offers sanctuary and prosperity to its immigrants. Michael has taught contemporary literature and postcolonial studies at the University of Cambridge, where he completed his PhD in 2011.

**Lawrence Scott** is from Trinidad and Tobago. He was awarded a Lifetime Literary Award in 2012 by the National Library of Trinidad and Tobago for his significant contribution to the Literature of Trinidad and Tobago. His new novel *Light Falling on Bamboo* (Hdb 2012; Pbk 2013) was inspired by the paintings, life and times of Michel Jean Cazabon, Trinidad's most famous nineteenth-century painter. It received a Special Mention from the Great Prize for Caribbean Literature from the Congress of Caribbean Writers and the Council of Guadeloupe, 2013. It was shortlisted for the 2013 BOCAS Fiction Category and long-listed for the overall BOCAS Prize 2013. His second novel *Aelred's Sin* (1998) was awarded a Commonwealth Writers' Prize, Best Book in Canada and the Caribbean, (1999). His first novel *Witchbroom* (1992) was short-listed for a Commonwealth Writers' Prize (1993), Best First Book. This was followed by *Ballad for the New World* (1994), including the Tom-Gallon Award prize-winning short-story *The House of Funeral's* (1986). His novel, *Night Calypso* (2004) was also short-listed for a Commonwealth Writers' Prize, Best Book Award, long-listed for the International IMPAC Dublin Literary Award (2006) and translated into French as *Calypso de Nuit* (2005). It was the One Book One Community choice in 2005 by the National Library of Trinidad and

Tobago. He is the Editor of *Golconda: Our Voices Our Lives,* an anthology of oral-histories and other stories and poems from the sugar-belt in Trinidad (UTT Press 2009). Over the years, he has combined teaching with writing. He lives in London and Port of Spain and can be found at www.lawrencescott.co.uk.

**Matthew Taunton** is a Lecturer in the School of Literature, Drama and Creative Writing at the University of East Anglia. He is the author of *Fictions of the City: Class, Culture and Mass Housing in London and Paris* (Palgrave 2009), as well as numerous articles and book chapters on twentieth-century literature, culture and cities. His current research project examines the cultural resonances of the Russian Revolution in Britain, from 1917 to 1950. He is associate editor of *Critical Quarterly.*

**Fiona Tolan** is Senior Lecturer in English at Liverpool John Moores University. She is author of *Margaret Atwood: Feminism and Fiction* (Rodopi 2007), and co-editor of *Writers Talk: Conversations with Contemporary British Novelists* (Continuum 2008) and *Teaching Gender* (Palgrave 2012). She has recently published on Zadie Smith and Pat Barker (*Tulsa Studies in Women's Literature*) and Alice Munro (*Contemporary Women's Writing*). She is Associate Editor of the *Journal of Postcolonial Writing* and an Executive Committee member of the Contemporary Women's Writing Association. She is currently working on a monograph titled *The Good of Art in Contemporary British Fiction.*

# Chronology of Andrea Levy's Life

**1956**   Born in London, 7th March. Raised in Highbury, North London. Education: Highbury Hill Grammar; Middlesex University (Textile Design and Weaving).

**1989**   Enrols in Creative Writing programme at City Lit, Convent Garden, London.

**1994**   *Every Light in the House Burnin'* published by Headline Review.

**1996**   *Never Far from Nowhere* published by Headline Review. Judge for Saga Prize.

**1997**   Judge for Orange Prize for Fiction.

**1998**   Arts Council Writers' Award for *Fruit of the Lemon*.

**1999**   *Fruit of the Lemon* published by Headline Review.

**2001**   Judge for Orange Prize Futures.

**2004**   *Small Island* published by Headline Review. Winner of Whitbread Novel Award for *Small Island*. Winner of Whitbread Book of the Year Award for *Small Island*. Awarded Orange Prize for Fiction for *Small Island*. Awarded Costa Book of the Year (Novel) for *Small Island*.

**2005**   Shortlisted for the Romantic Novelists' Association Award for *Small Island*. Awarded Orange of Oranges Prize for *Small Island*. Shortlisted for British Book Awards (Literary Fiction) for *Small Island*. Shortlisted for British Book Awards Decibel Writer of the Year. Winner of Best Book Award for the Commonwealth Prize for *Small Island*.

**2009**   Broadcast of BBC adaptation of *Small Island*.

**2010**   *The Long Song* published by Headline Review. Shortlisted for the Man Booker Prize for *The Long Song*.

**2011**   *The Long Song* awarded Walter Scott Prize for historical fiction.

# Towards Serious Work

## JEANNETTE BAXTER AND DAVID JAMES

'I'll have to fight to get in the canon. I had this thing through the post about the classics of the future, and they wanted me to choose 15 books out of this list of a hundred books. I just looked at this list of a hundred books and I thought *Small Island*'s not on it. You've left my book off it, and there's *Captain Corelli's Mandolin* and *Birdsong*. Who chose this list of a hundred? Who's making this canon? And I wrote back saying this list is so limited. It's daft. It makes me so mad. I do think we're going to have to fight so hard to come out of this oh-that-was-lovely-dear syndrome. It's so patronizing. No, this is serious work. It's more serious than a lot of serious writing in Britain.'

(Fischer 2014: 131)

It may seem striking to think of Andrea Levy as a writer with doubts about her literary stature and potential legacy. A two-time Orange Prize judge, whose work has been successfully adapted for the screen, Levy can also lay claim to several of the most coveted literary prizes in the United Kingdom, including the Commonwealth Writers' Prize (2005) and the Whitbread and Orange Prizes for Fiction (2004) for *Small Island* (2004), and the Walter Scott Prize for Historical Fiction (2011) for her most recent novel, *The Long Song* (2010). Yet, as a black woman writer still confronting speculative lists of supposed future 'classics', Levy is taking nothing for granted. For her, the struggle for recognition and artistic self-assertion continues, mindful as she is of the fact that 'the inventiveness and creativity of black British writers', as Mike Phillips has argued, 'have traditionally been submerged in a narrative about race' (Phillips 2006: 28). Without of course sidestepping the very urgent and politically charged questions of racial identification, community and discrimination that Levy's fiction has, irrespective of its changing historical and geographical settings, addressed so purposefully, this volume of critical essays seeks nonetheless to shed new light on Levy's writing – taking quite literally her conviction that 'this is serious work' (Fischer 2014: 131) that in turn demands and deserves serious scholarly attention.

But what might we understand 'serious' to mean in the contexts of Andrea Levy's work? Clearly, her combative response to *Small Island*'s exclusion belies a certain frustration with the kind of value placed on black writing in contemporary British culture. Canon formation of any kind invariably throws into sharp relief questions of literary value, authority and authenticity, together with attendant issues of national identity and cultural belonging. As Toni Morrison put it so well: 'Canon building is Empire building. Canon defence is national defence. Canon debate, whatever the terrain, nature and range [. . .] is the clash of cultures. And *all* the interests are vested' (Morrison 1989: 8). In terms of her own aesthetic, cultural and political interests, it is important to emphasize at this point that it is seemingly not enough for Levy that her work be recognized as making a valuable contribution to a black British canon. As John McLeod notes, while the formation of a black British canon can be considered 'a significant achievement within post-war British culture as a whole', its construction remains deeply problematic for the ways in which it 'emphasise[s] inclusion and particularity on the grounds of a race or nation' (McLeod 2008: 56). As with any act of canon formation, the development of a black British canon not only runs the risk of homogenizing diverse experience and containing productive tensions, but the 'alliance of the terms "black" and "British" ' risks 'perpetuat[ing] the division of blacks from Britons, each conceived of as a racially-different homogenous group' (McLeod 2008: 56). This is a division that Levy's writings work so hard to challenge:

> All my books are about me trying to explore my British Caribbean ancestry, and to place that heritage where I think it belongs – squarely in the mainstream of British history. Britain created those societies for better or worse, and she profited enormously from them. They have been relegated to the margins or, in the case of slavery, almost forgotten. I want to give them a voice, and make that voice an accepted part of our history. (Levy in conversation with Walters 2011: no. pag.)

One of the reasons why Levy's writing should be taken so seriously, then, lies precisely in the 'extent to which it revises the nationalist understanding of the islands we name as "Britain" at the levels of both history and culture, and points the way forward to the reconceiving of the creation of British culture, if not British nationhood, in transnational terms' (McLeod 2008: 59). If it belongs anywhere, Levy's work belongs in a British literary canon. But this is a British literary canon that must be prepared to open itself up to *all* of the poetic forces, political tensions, and historical voices that shape and energize it.

In many respects, Levy's insistence on the transnational and transcultural dimensions of British literature clearly explodes previous attempts at canon formation, including T. S. Eliot's enormously influential 'Tradition and the Individual Talent' (1919). Conspicuously separatist in his approach to race, nation, class and gender, Eliot calls for a body of literature that is narrowly conceived in both geographical and ideological terms: 'The existing monuments form an ideal order amongst themselves [. . .] of European, of English literature' (Eliot 1975: 38–9). The 'universal' Western values inherent in, and perpetuated by, Eliot's canon are precisely those that Andrea Levy's work holds up for interrogation. For any move towards articulating 'universal' experience inevitably risks silencing everything that falls outside of such neat accounts of subjectivity. It is for this reason, perhaps, that we encounter such a diverse range of voices within and across Levy's novels, from black teenagers growing up in inner-city London, to Windrush migrants in post-war Britain, to slaves across the plantations of the Caribbean. As Wendy Knepper observes, it is precisely '[t]hrough multi-vocal narratives', that Levy 'creates imagined spaces where new forms of audibility and visibility are made possible' (Knepper 2012: 2). But then, difficult and complex 'stories of dislocation' can only demand a range of 'dislocating narrative techniques' in their very articulation: multiple and contrasting narrative points-of-view; generic transformations; shifts across time and space; and intertextual exchanges all work hard across Levy's narratives to 'enabl[e] a strategic representation of the past from a postcolonial vantage point' (Knepper 2012: 7).

It is ironic, of course, that Levy's dedicated examination of the relationship between the colonial past and the postcolonial present should bring her directly into dialogue with Eliot and, more specifically, his understanding of the role of the contemporary writer. The 'historical sense', Eliot writes, 'involves a perception, not only of the pastness of the past, but of its presence'; it 'is what makes a writer traditional. And it is at the same time what makes a writer most acutely conscious of his place in time, of his own contemporaneity' (Eliot 1975: 38). In her bid to reconfigure the narrative of national literary culture by introducing transnational literary forms, voices and influences, Levy is in many ways the serious contemporary writer that Eliot calls for. Her writing recognizes consistently, for instance, 'that the past should be altered by the present as much as the present is directed by the past' (Eliot 1972: 39). This is evident not only in her move to expand our understanding of British imperial history by forcing uncomfortable narrative encounters with slavery and its legacies, but also in her transnational accounting of British literary history.

Arana and Ramey observe, for instance, that one of the many challenges of black British writing resides in the 'range of works to which they can be related – indeed, to which they *actually refer*, and which form for them a sort of Eliotic "tradition" against which they playfully (but very seriously) signify' (Arana and Ramey 2004: 6). Certainly, the essays in this collection attest to the simultaneous existence in Levy's writings of European modernist influences (such as Virginia Woolf, Jean Rhys, the literary and visual modernist avant-garde), and Caribbean oral traditions (including the 'trickster' spider Anansi). But what's actually at stake in Levy's work is a far more complex 'simultaneous order' than that imagined by Eliot. That is because, in contrast to Eliot's nationalist moves to reconsolidate rather than revise literary-cultural borders, Levy's expansive transnationalist approach very valuably 'emphasises the continuity of national formations while bearing witness to the crossing of their borders' (McLeod 2008: 58).

A body of work that seeks to reconceive British literary culture by simultaneously incorporating, and reconfiguring, a range of national and transnational literatures will be inevitably rife with contradictions, tensions and ambivalences. And it is the serious work of the reader to encounter these head-on, and to develop a willingness to resist any temptation to resolve or explain them straightforwardly away. This is, indeed, part of the challenge of reading and responding to Levy's work. It is also, of course, part of the pleasure of reading and responding to Levy's work. For one of its hallmarks, as the essays and interview in this volume identify, is its consistent recourse to humour. And, if this has led some readers to dismiss Levy's work as being somehow 'light' in comparison to, say, the weighty historical imaginaries of *Captain Corelli's Mandolin* (1994) or *Birdsong* (1993), then they have missed the joke and the point. In her conversation with Susan Fischer, Levy insists, for instance, how humour is an essential part of the human condition; it therefore has a place in any story, even a neo-slave narrative such as *The Long Song*:

> It seems incredibly funny to have slaves in a room where they're serving their masters, and every time that the wine comes around, they're sticking it out the window. It's funny. And then you start to acknowledge the real *humanity* in people. People then stop becoming just the victim of a tragedy. They become real people, and you can understand how their lives would have evolved. They become like you and me. (Levy in conversation with Fischer 2014: 137)

Across Levy's five novels, humour works variously to create sites of resistance and moments of reprieve, at the same time that it moves towards articulating an ethics of empathy. Certainly Levy's unflinching engagement with the very complex and shifting issues of racial exclusion, discrimination and dislocation across hundreds of years of black experience means that her work is frequently – and appropriately – unnerving. But that doesn't mean that we don't often find ourselves laughing our way towards serious work.

While our contributors showcase a range of methodological and thematic means of engaging with the seriousness of Levy's endeavour, the aspect of her work that is perhaps most conspicuous in terms of the sustained attention it has yet to receive is her innovations in form. In the opening chapter, Dave Gunning offers a corrective to this relative neglect, by reconsidering Levy's adoption and development of the *bildungsroman*. Approaching her use of this mode as far from uncritical,

Gunning suggests that we 'question why, given the *bildungsroman*'s association with individual development and flourishing and desirable social transformation, Levy's first two novels read as examples of the form'. As he goes on to show, 'these early texts in fact portray situations of entrapment, lack of agency, and the curtailment of individual flourishing by institutional indifference or hostility'. As such Gunning takes as his premise the question of what it is that might make 'a novel a non-celebratory, or unhappy, *bildungsroman*?' In this way Gunning sheds new light on the relation of form to social and familial content, arguing that 'the bleakness of these texts, the persistence of a melancholic notion of loss, and the idea that any move forwards is countered always by a parallel step backwards demand that the concept of the black British *bildungsroman* is divorced from the sense of celebration that so often accompanies it'. Through a sequence of readings that move between structural and characterological concerns, Gunning draws the conclusion that such apparently 'unhappy texts' stage a 'desire to transcend a marginalised position', while remaining simultaneously 'sceptical about the existence of any resources that might allow young black working-class women like Angela Jacobs and Vivien Charles to exercise lasting and transformative agency'.

This reading of Levy's reworking of modes that might otherwise be employed in the service of celebratory narratives of maturation and self-determination reminds us of her commitment to uncompromising forms of social realism, an uncompromising vision of urban habitation that Matthew Taunton considers in his chapter on *Never Far from Nowhere*. Historicizing the conditions of inner-city housing figured in this narrative, Taunton reveals that the 'novel imagines a subtle and complicated relationship between race, class and the culture of the council estate'. Although a highly localized text rooted in the familiar routines and familial tensions of everyday life, *Never Far from Nowhere* nonetheless addresses a broader cluster of social dilemmas that allow the novel's ambit to expand to a national scale. For as Taunton suggests, the text 'seems delicately poised', insofar as Levy sets out to pose 'powerful questions about where the responsibilities of the individual and the family end, and those of the state begin'. This poise is matched by a doubleness at the heart of the novel's locale, as Levy offers perspectives that are by turns interrogative and affirmative towards an environment that both supports and inhibits her characters. 'Rather than a universal system', contends Taunton, 'the welfare state appears in Levy's novel as a safety net for the very poor'. And yet, this system is Janus-faced, because in 'the context of the council estate, this leads to an ever-increasing social marginalization, a spatial division of London between the owner-occupying majority and enclaves of council tenants on estates that are represented as miserable or even dangerous places to be'. As in Gunning's analysis of the way Levy appropriates the *bildungsroman* against its transformative grain, Taunton likewise reveals that an unsentimental tenor forever coincides with Levy's perception of change and opportunity.

Matters of form take centre stage once more in the following two chapters from Michael Perfect and David James. While neither assumes that social and political lines of inquiry have been exhausted, both James and Perfect nonetheless argue that greater attention needs to be devoted to structural and stylistic dimensions that have hitherto been overlooked in readings preoccupied with the sociological pertinence of Levy's fiction. For Perfect, another hurdle to cross en route to more formally acute approaches to her narrative technique is that of the supposedly biographical premise of the early works. Although *Every Light in the House Burnin'*, writes Perfect, 'should certainly be considered a foundational text in Levy's oeuvre, one which prefigured her later work, it is *not* the case that it did so simply in the sense that it saw Levy begin to turn her own experiences into literary works. Rather, it is a novel that, through a complex and nuanced structure, subtly interrogates the ways in which the past and the present give meaning to each other.' Attending to the strategies by which that interrogation is achieved, Perfect offers fresh readings of what has now become – especially in the wake of *Small Island* – Levy's celebrated rhetoric of recollection. *Every Light in the House Burnin'*, as Perfect shows, 'asserts that even though our personal memories cannot always adequately prepare us for traumatic experiences, those memories *do* help us to give meaning to traumatic experiences, and vice versa'. By rethinking the oeuvre in light of these textures of retrospection and recovery, Perfect is able to argue that the shaping of form by memory in *Every Light* is the most vital 'sense in which Levy's first novel prefigures her later work, in which the importance of engaging with the past is increasingly emphasised'.

In something of a departure from this praise of Levy's dextrous rendition of memory, James refocuses our attention upon the effects of her language. Playing devil's advocate with Levy's own strong identification with realist writing, James complicates the generic impression of *Small Island* as a purely naturalistic historical drama by a series of close readings that reveal how inventive Levy can be at the level of syntax, diction and rhythm. Here the reading experience itself enters the critical frame, as James suggests that Levy creates a sense of immediacy that leads to our intense involvement in events, a sense of involvement that is at the same time often qualified when our full sympathetic identification with characters is refused or forestalled. James thus asks to what extent Levy tries 'to have it both ways, by involving us in the experience of events in all their sensory and social detail without necessarily provoking the reader's empathy'. In offering an answer to this question, James argues that with a closer appreciation of just how emotive Levy's syntax can be – even as she gives us pause in our desire to empathize with narrators who so intimately address us – we begin to understand how 'involvement and distantiation, immersion and impartiality coexist' in crucial ways that highlight how *Small Island* cultivates ethical forms of response.

Continuing the focus on *Small Island*, Rachel Carroll offers the first in-depth critical account of the implications of the novel's 2009 BBC adaptation. Carroll points out that although the novel has been clearly 'canonized', through literary prizes and sustained attention from reading groups, the adaptation did ambiguous justice to the value of the novel's political intervention. Significant omissions and structural decisions are brought to light, as Carroll notes that the 'adaptation not only omits the narrative perspective of its most explicitly racist white British narrator, Bernard, but also introduces a voiceover which assumes the authority of an omniscient narrator'. Carroll suggests that the screen version therefore 'deploys traditional narrative and dramatic techniques in its efforts to engage a mass audience in identification with its key characters, both black and white. In so doing, it arguably underplays the representation of racist sentiment by ordinary British subjects which is given such frank and provocative expression in Levy's novel.' Offering a critically pertinent and provocative demonstration of how the methods of adaptation studies and book history can be brought to bear on contemporary fiction, Carroll demonstrates how Levy's work deserves both interpretive and contextual levels of analysis in order to reread now-prominent texts like *Small Island* in ways that are alert both to the craft of their composition and to their conditions of reception.

Developing this impulse to offer new interpretive approaches that reframe Levy's fiction, Jeannette Baxter develops a model for working comparatively across seemingly contrasting texts and concerns from different points in Levy's oeuvre. Baxter opens up the possibility of reading *Fruit of the Lemon* and *The Long Song* as exquisite corpses of sorts. Employing a methodology of 'un/folding', 'a technique integral to any practice of exquisite corpse', Baxter focuses on the complex relations between verbal and written historical accounts, together with individual and collective acts of historical storytelling as they manifest themselves across the two novels. By interpreting *Fruit of the Lemon* and *The Long Song* in relation to one another, Baxter's comparative account explores the deliberately 'non-synthesizing energies of the un/fold in order to tease out neglected textual crossings, and foreground overlooked historical and political associations, within and across both novels'.

Extending Baxter's approach to Levy's most recent novel, Fiona Tolan provides a sustained consideration of narrative authority in *The Long Song*, unpacking the gendered implications of perspective and voice. Tolan suggests that Levy 'positions July's subversive tale of trauma, rebellion and liberation as mediated and delimitated by an authoritative masculine narrative frame'. But this position is complicated by the manifold registers of a narrative that, at the level of form, begins 'with a birth myth of magical realist proportions', before 'proceeding through elements of oral tradition, satire, tragedy and farce, socio-historical treatise' and *bildungsroman*, while, at the level of character, 'encompassing multiple histories and ventriloquising a cacophony of voices', as 'July becomes a female trickster-narrator, wily and disruptive'. Tolan detects in the novel an 'irrepressible and often comic energy', juxtaposed with the tragedy of colonial violence, presenting us with 'a narrator who both demands and is assured of her own narrative authority'. From out of this complex mix of registers, Levy finds 'a means of reconstituting the lost lives' of a dispossessed people, 'reconstituting them not as victims but as survivors'. Tolan argues that it is precisely from this ethical premise – a 'lost history' 'could inspire admiration rather than pity' and 'may be salvaged from the margins of "History"' – that Levy commences a novel which nonetheless acknowledges 'the intractable psychological legacy of slavery'.

In the final exploration of Levy's latest novel, Susan Fischer examines the trope of the portrait in *The Long Song* and its attendant politics of power and identification. As Fischer observes, while July's 'presence in the portrait is meant to "add a touch of the exotic"', she in fact 'insinuates herself into the picture in such a way that she upstages the mistress, thereby showing her importance in their story, as well as the centrality of slavery and colonialism in British history'. Tracing this visual tropology of disruptive self-insertion and self-representation as July is seen 'forcing her way to the centre of the picture' at the novel's heart, Fischer focuses on July's struggle to write herself into the centre of the historical legacy of slavery. While *The Long Song* is the first novel by Levy not to focus on the Windrush Generation and its sociocultural legacy, Fischer suggests that it nonetheless indicates a continuation of Levy's preoccupation with the inextricably conjoined destinies of Britain and Jamaica – moving closer in fact to the root of that relationship through the exploration of slavery and its immediate aftermath.

Taken together, then, the essays collected here comprise the first critical companion of its kind devoted to Levy's writing, offering fresh insights into her thematic range, her formal and rhetorical inventiveness, and her commitment to reimagining personal and collective experiences of history, while never losing sight of the way she moves nimbly between tragic and comic registers. In key respects these perspectives also contribute to the important 'recuperative' task of attending to Levy's relatively neglected early work, not in isolation but in dialogue with her more recent fiction, thereby opening up new interpretative avenues for reading her novels comparatively and in conversation with different points in her development as a writer. Demonstrating how a wide range of historical, theoretical and stylistic frameworks can illuminate, and in turn be inspired by, the vitality of her prose, this book exhibits a spectrum of approaches that can begin to do justice to the poetics and politics of Levy's fiction.

# CHAPTER ONE

# Unhappy *Bildungsromane*

## DAVE GUNNING

**Chapter Summary:** One effect of the situation in which Levy's later writing receives far more critical attention than the earlier works is that her first two novels occasionally seem to be read through critical models that might be better suited to the material that comes after. Most work that interprets *Every Light in the House Burnin'* (1994) and *Never Far from Nowhere* (1996) by reading them as examples of the *bildungsroman* form can seem guilty of this, imposing a celebratory vision of individual and social transformation on novels that in fact are far more concerned to trace the constraints and lack of meaningful change in the lives of their young female protagonists. This chapter wishes to retain the idea that the *bildungsroman* offers a useful way to read these explorations of loss and limitation (often determined as much by class as by race), but to suggest that a more nuanced conception of the form, divorced from too-easily positive associations needs to be mobilized to read these unhappy texts.

In Andrea's Levy's first novel, *Every Light in the House Burnin'* (1994), the narrator Angela Jacobs presents a range of vignettes from her childhood in Highbury, North London, interspersed with an account of her father's death from cancer during her adult years. Levy's second novel, *Never Far from Nowhere* (1996) tells the stories of two sisters, Vivien and Olive Charles, as they grow up in Finsbury Park, the former eventually leaving for art college in Kent, while the latter is unhappily separated from her husband and forced to raise her daughter alone. These novels are frequently read alongside *Fruit of the Lemon* (1999) as examples of the *bildungsroman* form within which Levy worked early in her writing career. Yet, seeing these three works as a trilogy of novels of formation risks conflating them in unhelpful ways. The third book contains elements that do not feature in the first two, revealing a different way of working through the challenges of the *bildungsroman*, one that is more at ease with the transformations of personal identity captured within the form. In paying attention to the first two novels in isolation, we may get a more precise sense of exactly how Levy is able to stretch the conventions of the novel of (self-)formation, thereby avoiding in turn the danger of reading these novels only in terms of how they anticipate her later critically celebrated works.

In an important position paper that looks to distinguish a new current in black British writing of the twenty-first century, John McLeod approaches Levy in ways that set more recent work like *Small Island* apart from those texts produced in previous few decades. McLeod invokes Levy's 2004 novel as an example of writing that moves away from intense interrogation of the dilemmas caused for people negotiating the twin poles of identity signalled in the compound phrase 'black British'. Instead, *Small Island* points to alternative means of addressing questions of race and nation that are able to look outwards beyond constricting borders imposed by a narrow focus on the individual experience of racial and national belonging. He labels this new literature 'black writing *of* Britain' and finds in it an engagement with new forms of narrative, frequently based around 'cultural zygoticism': a process of twinning and doubling that is required always to search for similarities and parallels. This strategy rejects the introspection of a narrow identity politics, reflecting the fact that 'black writing of Britain is an important contributor to a broad series of debates about the identity of the nation in an international context, one that shadows a set of concerns much wider than solipsistic and exclusivist diasporic matters about "myself"' (McLeod 2010: 51). As part of McLeod's attempt to show that a new internationalist sensibility has manifested itself in innovative formal structures, he contrasts recent writing with the model set out by Mark Stein's important work on the 'black British *bildungsroman*'. McLeod argues that the *bildungsroman*'s 'key concerns' of 'subjectivity and consciousness' seem to have become dated, though he acknowledges that the particular model set out by Stein did not see the form as tracing only a 'crudely individualistic endeavour', but allowed for a 'synchronisation of private and public transformations' (McLeod 2010: 47).

Stein's account of the black British *bildungsroman* therefore seems crucial in approaching black British writing of the 1990s, especially if we accept McLeod's implication that the form's historical moment is firmly located in that decade and has been seen far less in the new century. Stein partly signals his wish to think beyond a conception of *bildungsromane* as concerned only with identity in the narrowest sense by choosing to refer to his texts not as novels of formation, but of *transformation* – the changes that occur are not confined only to the subjective development of the individual, but are equally brought about within the fabric of society of a whole. It is not just that the form allows new subject positions to come into being through the imagining and representation of ways of being that combine 'black' and 'British'; there is also an irresistible pressure on the surrounding society to change and make available locations within which these new types of selfhood can be formed and lived out: 'the black British novel of transformation [. . .] has a dual function: it is about the formation of its protagonists as well as the transformation of British society and cultural institutions' (Stein 2004: 20). Most significantly, Stein's account of this function insists on the causal links between these two spheres of change, as the developing individual within the text both figures as and initiates 'a symbolic act of carving out space':

> through the process of subject formation, the bildungsroman negotiates the formation of its protagonist or protagonists within the social world that is encountered and shaped. While the individual, then, struggles with family, education, and the experiences of society at large, this struggle is significantly not without consequences for the cultures within which it takes place. (Stein 2004: 30–1)

Stein does not, however, accept that this process results in a smoothly homogeneous new configuration of society, but rather argues that the disruptive dynamic brought into being by the irruption of new forms of selfhood into the national space may persist in forging a new society that is fluidly heterogeneous – able to preserve fragmentation rather than trying to recuperate the disparate pieces of a newly fractured culture into a unified whole. In doing so, he is able to argue against the need for an author consciously to express a particular vision of social transformation before being able to produce the unruly and disturbing subjectivities that find form in the *bildungsroman*, thereby insisting that black British authors need not be 'burdened with certain responsibilities that can curtail his or her work' (Stein 2004: 54).

Nonetheless, the *bildungsroman* is frequently seen as required to display a form of unity in its resolution. While this may not take the form of a defined social vision (and the black British *bildungsroman* discussed by Stein in fact most frequently end with moments of transition or metamorphosis, with acts of travel rather than of settling), there does nonetheless seem to be a need for correlation between the situation of the protagonist and that of the society, even if it is merely that they each remain unsettled and portray identity at the point of becoming, rather than being. Michael Perfect captures this neatly in his description of the resolution of Monica Ali's *Brick Lane* (2003), which, in its embodiment of the values of 'individuation and socialisation' he considers a paradigmatic 'multicultural bildungsroman', 'with the novel celebrating the adaptability both of its immigrant protagonist as well as that of the multicultural metropole' (Perfect 2008: 119). The *bildungsroman* can therefore seem a celebratory form, not only commending the strength of the individual protagonist for finding a way to conquer the alienation brought about by the privations of minority identity, but also applauding the new social spaces that have opened to allow for the lessening, if not quite the elimination, of prejudice.

It seems pertinent, then, to question why, given the *bildungsroman*'s association with individual development and flourishing and desirable social transformation, Levy's first two novels read as examples of the form. These books portray situations of entrapment, lack of agency and the curtailment of individual flourishing by institutional indifference or hostility. To describe either as offering a happy ending for its protagonists or a meaningful reshaping of social norms seems to involve a wilful blindness to just how bleak the plots of these stories are. In fact, although both McLeod and Stein do describe the novels as *bildungsromane*, these critics' analyses, at the level of content, are slight. McLeod sees Levy's 'preoccupation of [sic] Black British identity' in her first three novels as superseded by *Small Island*'s ability to relocate its concerns 'beyond the realm of subjective selfhood by nurturing an analogous vision of social and cultural admixture as *constituting* the veiled reality of the British nation' (McLeod 2010: 49). However, the analogous connection between the 'new' writing of a heterogeneous nation and the 'old' vision of multiplicity at the level of the individual is built only upon the example of *Fruit of the Lemon*, at the end of which Faith Jackson finally finds herself able to understand 'the inability of words like "Jamaican", "black" and "British" fully to capture her manifold filiations' ( McLeod 2010: 49). Stein's study equally finds in Faith's journey the material for an extended survey of how the black British *bildungsroman* links the development of the individual to the restructuring of social understanding. Faith perhaps falls harder than any of the other young women in Levy's early fiction, suffering a distressing nervous breakdown after witnessing an act of extreme racial violence, but she also finds redemption in a way that does not seem available to Angela Jacobs, or Vivien and Olive Charles. Her journey to Jamaica and subsequent discovery of her diverse lineage is, in Stein's words, 'a voyage of discovery' that 'is not so much a discovery of roots as a charting of routes', as she 'seeks to clarify for herself how she relates to her Jamaican and African family history', a knowledge that will 'impact on her identifications within London' (Stein 2004: 80). While Stein has nothing to say about *Never Far from Nowhere*, his brief reading of *Every Light in the House Burnin'* is far less convincing than that he gives of Levy's third novel. Here, he finds in Angela's statement that England is her 'birthright', a clear indication of Levy's 'didactic' purpose in 'contrasting an accepting and passive Mr Jacob's with a determined and therefore successful Ange' (Stein 2004: 48). Yet, as I will discuss below, this confident ascription of meaningful agency to Angela, pitted against her complacent parents, is made deeply problematic by the novel.

Perfect engages with Levy's novels in a different article to his discussion of the multicultural *bildungsroman*. Interestingly, he never actually uses the term to describe these novels, showing an awareness that the texts are often too despairing of the possibility of development to be easily associated with the label's positive connotations. However, his analysis of *Every Light in the House Burnin'* and *Never Far from Nowhere* through the lens of Edward Said's strategy of contrapuntal reading – in Perfect's words, 'reading for what remains unspoken in a text' (Perfect 2010: 32) – offers a useful perspective in understanding why these first two books are regularly connected so freely with a version of *bildungsroman* form that in fact fits only their successor. Perfect's intention is not to enact a contrapuntal *reading* of Levy's fiction, rather to demonstrate that the texts themselves have 'developed an increasingly "contrapuntal" conceptual framework, and that *Small Island* in particular can be understood as a form of contrapuntal *writing*' (Perfect 2010: 32). While this account of how Levy has become increasingly concerned with 'narrating rather than negating the imperial past', and of how her conviction to do so requires an engagement 'with a multiplicity of contrapuntal voices' (Perfect 2010: 32), seems a useful approach to *Small Island*, it is not clear that it is quite appropriate in reading her first two fictions. Indeed, Perfect's wish to trace a line of 'formal and conceptual developments in her works' (Perfect 2010: 32) risks reading the earlier novels in the light of the later ones, and ascribing an historical consciousness to the early books that does not in fact emerge until much later in her career. Perfect's reading of *Every Light in the House Burnin'* asserts that it is 'a novel that insists on the importance of where one has come from' (Perfect 2010: 33), a claim I would not dispute, though I remain unconvinced that the text suggests that this requires Angela to know anything of her parents' life in Jamaica. His reading of *Never Far from Nowhere* insists that the novel warns of the need for a better awareness of 'the importance of historicizing one's society, one's ancestry and oneself in the fight against racism, prejudice and ignorance', and that realizing the hybridity of their Caribbean roots would have helped Vivien and Olive to more productive resolutions of their situation, but it is hard to see how the novel practically demonstrates this (Perfect 2010: 34). He describes *Fruit of the Lemon* as enacting a '(re)constructive' healing for Faith (Perfect 2010: 37), but to imply that Levy intended for readers of the earlier books to imagine such a healing for the characters seems to attribute a consistency to her oeuvre that is not borne out by her actual aesthetic choices. Of course, a contrapuntal *reading* can freely suggest such an ignorance of the past is the cause of these young women's bleak situation, though such reading for what is not said is always by definition speculative; but to locate this absence as an authorial choice makes a different, and probably less sustainable, claim. Perfect's work is valuable, however, not only because its theoretical model does seem far more applicable to Levy's later novels, but also for the way it reveals through detailed analyses an assumption that is more casually made in McLeod and Stein's arguments: that because *Fruit of the Lemon* finds a recuperative version of the past that allows for a *bildungsroman*-style resolution, the earlier two books might be seen as less fully worked-through variations on the same theme, rather than operating to suggest a different message.

It may be useful briefly to figure the formulations offered by the critics discussed above in terms of Homi Bhabha's influential account of the relation between national imaginaries and the subjects who must live within them. His contention is that nations speak always with a double voice: the 'pedagogical' address that relies on a continuity of national space across time, and the 'performative' address that recognizes the diversity of national subjects at any given moment. Although their respective terms of reference may frequently contrast, each address is essential. Their 'conceptual ambivalence' brings into being what Bhabha calls 'the site of *writing the nation*' (Bhabha 1994: 145). Stein's model of subject-formation coming to create new formations of social relations within the nation seems an example of the pedagogical being necessarily re-shaped by the unruly disorder of the performative; Perfect's contrapuntal strategy as a direct challenge to the logic of the pedagogical that might make it more accountable to the realities of the performative; and McLeod's internationalization recasts the space of the performative and thus opens up a wider canvas for the pedagogical. In trying to avoid attributing an historical consciousness to Levy's first two novels which is never textually indicated as being there, it seems unwise to try to suggest that they perform a direct assault on the integrity of the pedagogical national narrative – such as Perfect finds more convincingly in her later works – and the narrowness of their spatial concerns and disavowal of analogical links to external situations seems to rule out McLeod's model (from which they are, of course, explicitly excluded). It is then perhaps to Stein's model to which we might most valuably return, but with a view to seeing why these novels do not stage a successful assault against pedagogical norms – what is it about the performative stagings of identity in *Every Light in House Burnin'* and *Never Far from Nowhere* that leaves them unable to disrupt pedagogical exclusion? What makes a novel a non-celebratory, or unhappy, *bildungsroman*?

A recent challenge to reading black British literature in terms of the *bildungsroman* has been made by Vedrana Velickovic, who questions whether the verse-novels of Bernardine Evaristo (including *Lara* (1997), which Stein reads in a pairing with *Fruit of the Lemon*) should be seen as conforming to the formal model of the novel of formation. Velickovic argues that 'as a genre of resolution [. . .] the *Bildungsroman* risks normalizing Evaristo's complex engagement with loss' (Velickovic 2012: 75–6). Her reading emphasizes the prevalence in Evaristo's books of the state of '(un)belonging' – a partial and always incomplete resolution of identity conflict – and cautions against celebratory conceptualizations of black British narratives. She does so through a focus on melancholia, here indicating the state of irrevocable loss that can be read in societies that fail to address their blighted racial histories. Velickovic is concerned to note that melancholia need not always be seen as negative, but might also generate positive strategies which look to rearticulate the injustices of the past and remind society of their continuing pernicious effects, and argues that 'the significance of (un)belonging lies precisely in what is less a melancholic "inability" in Evaristo's narratives to resolve cultural and personal conflicts, and more a melancholic obligation to resist neat resolutions as simply being about the protagonist's identity negotiation' (Velickovic 2012: 67). Her detailing of Evaristo's strategies suggest an historical consciousness at work in these novels not wholly dissimilar from that which Perfect identifies as the contrapuntal narratives of *Fruit of the Lemon* and *Small Island*, and Velickovic's model perhaps also cannot be carried across to Levy's other novels for the same reasons as Perfect's. However, the notion of melancholia does offer the basis of a useful way into reading Levy's unhappy *bildungsroman*. Although Velickovic reads Evaristo's melancholia as played out in her conscious revisiting of history, it is useful to note that the melancholic subject need not always recognize their own symptom, nor comprehend exactly what object has been lost. Indeed, melancholia may be an overdetermined condition, with no single, easily identifiable root. As in the case of the seemingly perfect Mrs Simpson in *Every Light in the House Burnin'*, who babysits the young Angela in her spotless flat, the maintenance of a particular social identity might belie a deeper disturbance. Mrs Simpson cleans her house every day: 'she wiped and dusted furiously, like she had something to hide' (Levy 1995: 134–5). It is soon revealed that this pristine woman's marriage is a torrid battlefield, despite the public faces she and her husband show. Melancholia offers a useful way into understanding how the staging of unified identity might often at best be a coping strategy for repressing deeper disturbance, or, at worst, a conscious deception of both others and oneself. A seemingly unified identity is not necessarily the sign of a happy individual. I do not agree with Velickovic that we should abandon the critical model of the *bildungsroman* so easily in reading black British writing, but there does seem to be a pressing need to expand its definition and find a way to account for its melancholic, unhappy forms.

If the sources of melancholic disaffection are overdetermined, so too of course are the constituents of identity. If Angela suffers a marginalized position within *Every Light in the House Burnin'*, then it is one rooted in discriminations based not only on race, but also on gender and, importantly, class, this last felt most keenly in the setting of the flats where she must come into maturity. That the Simpsons suffer in their own way reminds us that racial difference is not the only – nor always the most significant – way in which a social situation can frustrate people's chances of happiness. It is perhaps unhelpful to think of the various types of marginalization lived by Angela as examples of double, or triple, colonization (Rutherford and Peterson 1986), but rather we might understand any particular moment of discrimination as motivated by the divisions enacted by any of these discourses, though possibly expressed through any of the others. This process perhaps finds better expression in the insight of the authors of *Policing the Crisis* that 'race is the modality in which class is lived', and Paul Gilroy's supplementary suggestion that 'gender is the modality in which race is lived' (Hall et al. 1978: 394; Gilroy 1993: 85). These systems of oppression cannot usefully be thought of as separate from each other, or as doubled, but rather as intertwined to a degree that one may serve as the manifest expression of an attack latently motivated by another.

The chapter of *Every Light in House Burnin'* entitled 'The Game' gives some sense of how this layering may operate. Playing a game of rounders with her brother John and a group of other children from the estate, Angela struggles to join in sufficiently well, while John defends her from criticism. Eventually, they are both declared out by the boy who assumes the role of leader, but John responds by insisting that the game must end and he tries to take his bat back home. His defiance of Ronnie is a rebuttal of the usual rules of dominance justified by greater age (and contains also a challenge to the assumption that Angela's gender rules her out of full participation in the game). However, Ronnie responds by calling the siblings 'golliwogs' and 'nig-nogs' (Levy 1995: 57). The recourse to offensive racism is used to re-assert the older boy's dominance, but racism does not itself seem to be the cause of his aggression. The situation soon escalates into a prolonged campaign by the local children of racial abuse against the Jacobs siblings and they are forced to confess the situation to their parents. The response of Mr and Mrs Jacobs is interesting. Angela's mother insists to her: 'You born here. That's what matter [. . .] You're not black and you're not white' (Levy 1995: 59). This might be read as an unhealthy denial of the family's real racial difference, but it does not function differently from that within the novel. Mrs Jacobs demands the children go out among their newly hostile neighbours and thereby assert their right to belong. Her strategy seems justified when they are soon re-accepted back within their peer group. Her denial of the significance of racial identity might then be read as a utopian determination that race should not matter and that conviviality is instead better served by insisting on the ways in which the children are the same as their neighbours, not by accepting the difference imputed by the discriminatory address. This assertion can be contrasted with the response of the vicar who is forced to react to the racism Angela and a friend face from another child in Sunday School later in the novel. He mentions the abuse within his sermon and Angela gleefully anticipates the admonition of the offending child: 'now, I thought, God will show him how wrong he is, how bad he is to hate difference' (Levy 1995: 145). But it is actually Angela and her friend who are called to the front, while the congregation of children are forced to sing a hymn about how Jesus loves all children. The vicar's good intentions inadvertently serve to reinforce the supposed difference of the little black girls, suggesting that the situation is somehow (if indirectly) their fault, rather than undercutting the racist logic but emptying out the divisive significance of racial difference, in the way that Mrs Jacobs seeks to.

The novel is an attempt to read together the various identity-creating processes that have formed Angela. It focuses firmly on her home life in order to find the roots of her current identity and to explore how various types of social determinants operate in creating the adult self. This entails examination of class allegiance as much as racial filiation: the identity that will be formed is not only a reductively racial one, such as may be the focus for the type of stultifying difference forced on her in the Sunday School incident, but recognizes a plethora of connections and disconnections from those around her. The novel is a *bildungsroman* in that our adult narrator serves as the proof of development, of having reached a point of secure selfhood from which she can recount the diverse incidents that acted as her education into maturity. Yet this retrospective introspection is often carried out anxiously, revealing a concern that the developmental process has somehow been incomplete. When her parents finally leave the flat where they have lived for so much of Angela's childhood, her father expresses his joy finally to be moving on, but Angela cannot react in the same way: walking away from the block, 'I looked back' (Levy 1995: 225). This is more than just a nostalgia for her past, but an indication of a deeper concern that haunts both this novel and the one that follows it: that transformation is a form of loss, and that the gains of reaching adult subjectivity might be outweighed by the concurrent sacrifice of a more desirable type of belonging.

Mr Jacobs' pleasure at leaving his flat behind is an unusual moment for him within the novel, in which he more often acts as a point of stasis against which any transformation experienced by Angela might be contrasted. In the description given of him in the opening pages we are told that he is a man who 'seemed only to exist in one plane of time – the present' (Levy 1995: 3), and 'he did what was expected of him' as a father (Levy 1995: 2). He is seen as having decided on a particular way of being and unable to move forward from that. As a father, his role becomes increasingly irrelevant to Angela as she matures – while he is able to act effectively as protector in saving his small daughter from a vicious dog (Levy 1995: 52), by the time she is a teenager his prohibitions against boyfriends are unhelpfully draconian (Levy 1995: 209). Stein suggests that the contrast between Mr Jacobs's fixity and Angela's ability to adapt is the central trope of transformation in the novel – her confidence in asserting her 'birthright', her ability to 'kn[o]w this society' (Levy 1995: 88) as the antidote to Mr Jacobs's withdrawal from the world and failure to engage fully with British society (Stein 2004: 48). Indeed, it does seem that Angela's parents at times wish to curtail the possibilities open to her: after she is taken under the wing of her music teacher and introduced to middle-class life (including an unwanted experience of eating an avocado for the first time – 'it reminded me of the bar of Palmolive soap we use to wash with at home' (Levy 1995: 188) – and a happier

introduction to pizza), she excitedly reveals her dreams of becoming an
actress to her parents. They respond by chastizing this unrealistic wish
and insisting she instead follow a more practical, and less romantic,
path (Levy 1995: 191–2). Contra Stein, however, the novel is concerned to
show that her parents may not be entirely wrong.

The scene that follows this crushing of dreams begins with the adult
Angela eating guacamole with middle-class friends at a party – suggesting that the alien nature of avocado has confidently been dispelled for
her. Yet the middle-class milieu represented is tinged from the start by
a sense of inauthenticity and superficiality: when she raises the topic of
her father's cancer, people drift away 'in search of some real small talk
about house conveyancing or Czech beer' (Levy 1995: 193). The same
party seems to provide the revelation that her new social status will
allow her finally to address the inadequacy of medical care from which
her father is suffering; when she makes contact with a GP who informs
her of the existence of a hospice service, she is struck by how 'the charge
of the professional class cavalry' to fix her problem is made possible
because of her elevated standing in the world (Levy 1995: 195). Yet the
seeming fix that is offered by having 'made that social climb to a position where I could have influence' is revealed ultimately as a false hope
(Levy 1995: 198). Her father is to die in the hospital from which she is
unable to liberate him. As she walks along a characterless corridor in
this hospital later, she reflects on how it makes one 'feel that you were
making no progress on your journey' (Levy 1995: 215). The patronizing
attitude of the institution does not only serve to infantilize her father –
who, in a particularly distressing scene, is forced to 'shit on the floor like
a baby' (Levy 1995: 150) – but also frustrates her own sense of maturity,
making her feel 'like I was a selfish child wanting my own way' (Levy
1995: 150). The limits of transformation are consistently shown as more
keenly felt than its opportunities.

The anxieties of transformation are reinforced by the structure of the
novel, with the childhood scenes presented in non-chronological order.
Progress is refused as the need to keep looking back is continually re-
asserted. Against this, the forward-moving narrative of Mr Jacobs's
deterioration might be read as a bleak counterpoint that shows transformation happening even through painful processes – the death of a
parent operating as a key moment in a person's coming to full maturity – but even this plot is eventually marked by recursion and a return
to adolescent experience when the concluding chapter, 'The Death', does
not dwell on Angela's own process of mourning but rather melancholi-
cally returns to her father's own reaction to the death of the family cat.

Franco Moretti's crucial study of the *bildungsroman* distinguishes
between two forces at work in the form, and which can be seen variously
to take prominence in diverse examples. First, the principle of classification, which focuses on the need to settle within a particular social
role and is characterized by a sense of teleology, in which the ending

of the novel explains and justifies the process lived through within it. And secondly, the principle of transformation, which focuses on change and is best characterized by constant development, by the narrativity of the novel which might work to refuse closure. The former emphasizes happiness as the most desirable human good, the need to find a place for oneself within society; the latter instead eulogizes freedom and demands that the individual preserve autonomy and authenticity. Most importantly, Moretti counsels against seeing the principle of classification as inherently conservative and therefore diametrically opposed to the radical quest for transformation. Instead the *bildungsroman* offers acknowledgement of their co-existence and possible inseparability:

> the truly central ideologies of our world are not in the least [. . .] intolerant, normative monologic, to be wholly submitted to or rejected. Quite the opposite: they are pliant and precarious, 'weak' and 'impure'. When we remember that the *Bildungsroman* – the symbolic form that more than any other has portrayed and promoted modern socialization – is also the *most contradictory* of modern symbolic forms, we realise that in our world socialization itself consists first in the *interiorisation of contradiction*. (Moretti 1987: 10)

Moretti's work is invaluable in reminding us that the novel of formation is always as much about the return to a settled way of life as it is about transformative potential, and that the form allows for both of these drives to exist simultaneously. What may be especially interesting about Levy's unhappy *bildungsroman*, however, is that each of these seeming desiderata are characterized by loss, or even dominated by the melancholic sense that both the striving for freedom and the happiness of settled resolution are necessarily marked by dissatisfaction.

The sense of transformation of loss is even more strongly marked in *Never Far from Nowhere*. The novel can be seen as a dual *bildungsroman* tracing the development of both sisters, though it is tempting to read it as primarily the story of Vivien, whose narrative takes up far more space and both begins and ends the novel, with Olive's misadventures as bleak counterpoint to Vivien's happier tale. The reminder of the meaning of Vivien's name might seem to reinforce this sense of her prominence in this portrayal of developing identities:

> 'What does [Vivien] mean then?'
>
> 'I'm not sure . . . something . . . Alive, or something . . . Life . . . something like that'.
>
> 'That's nice. Mine means the Keeper of Riches. Well, Edward does.' (Levy 2004a: 135)

But names are deceptive in this novel: Eddie holds no riches, and the dark-skinned Olive and anything-but-rocklike Peter equally defy the names given to them. Vivien's life is not one marked by vitality and freedom, but always characterized by curtailment and the need to conform.

*Never Far from Nowhere* is much more directly interested in race than its predecessor, though the terms of this engagement are less than straightforward. Vivien's opening section of the narrative ends with her conclusion that 'the English people hated us' (Levy 2004a: 5), but her later revelation that 'I never thought we were black' suggests that this sense of separation from Englishness may not strictly depend upon an awareness of racial difference but instead be inspired by an unconscious sense of other divisions (Levy 2004a: 172). Eddie reminds her late in the novel that she is 'just a working-class girl' and this 'just' seems telling (Levy 2004a: 268), drawing attention to the fact that class might function as an equally compelling reason for the withdrawal of full human potential from an individual.

The girls' mother, Rose, refuses to consider herself as black (Levy 2004a: 8), seeming to echo Mrs Jacobs's advice to her daughter in the earlier novel, but while Mrs Jacobs also refuses whiteness, Rose seems wholly to aspire towards it. A key contrast between the two can be seen in how while Angela's mother relishes the company of other West Indian women at the hairdressing salon (Levy 1995: 166), Rose rejects any association with 'her' community. There is no sense of utopianism to her denial, just an insistence on conforming to her belief, in Olive's words, that one should 'just follow the laws and you'll never have to think about anything again' (Levy 2004a: 8). Olive responds to this by inverting her mother's logic and understanding her identity purely through the lens of race, which might ultimately seem confirmed when her fleeting sense of happiness late in the novel is crushed by her experience at the hands of racist policemen (Levy 2004a: 256–9). However, the novel equally suggests that there may be more going on than Olive is able to articulate: her silence when faced by the middle-class boy who attacks the culture of 'scroungers', indicates that she has failed fully to understand that her class position equally determines her misery (Levy 2004a: 204).

The paler-skinned Vivien, however, identifies in the first instance wholly with her class identity, seeking to belong in a gang of white working-class youths even to the extent of silently endorsing their racism (Levy 2004a: 29). The conditions of belonging within a community are cynically examined in the novel's portrayal of how one fits in. To belong requires an extinction of individual personality in the service of conformity: when her friend praises Vivien's application of make-up to her eyelashes – 'They're great [. . .] they look false' (Levy 2004a: 44) – we are reminded that staged identity is always likely to lead to greater acceptance than the pursuit of idiosyncrasy. This finds its best expression in the dancing that requires the young people to move in exactly the same way as each other and where 'free expression' is 'not allowed' (Levy 2004a: 54). The image of the teenagers enjoying themselves in strictly regimented rows might offer the reader a satirical interpretation of the idea of the novel of 'formation'.

Vivien gradually comes to recognize that the codes to which she has subscribed may not provide the best route to her ultimate success. The divisions within the post-16 education at her grammar school bring home to her the full meaning of social stratification: the 'A-stream' candidates who take A-levels are 'posh girls who came from nice homes', while 'B-stream girls' are destined for less glamorous lives (Levy 2004a: 100). Vivien chafes against the future laid out for her and becomes determined to join the more privileged group. This decision is simultaneously paralleled with, and motivated by, her recognition of just how limited life in the working-class gang is. After witnessing a brutal attack in one of the pubs they frequent, she and her friend gaze bereft at a venue where the A-stream types congregate: 'A load of hippies we'd have called them a year ago, and pulled faces. But me and Carol watched. Creatures from another planet watching humans having fun' (Levy 2004a: 111). Vivien's determination to replace her peer group and become part of an aspiring middle-class milieu, however, does not in fact provide her with access to the full humanity that seemed there from outside. Middle-class socialization is seen as just as predicated upon a set of rules as that of the group she has left, with Georgina's decision not to wear make-up as reliant on conformity to an external standard of behaviour as Carol's devotion to it (Levy 2004a: 127). The extreme affectation of the overly dramatic Victoria, with whom Vivien shares a house when at art college in Kent, equally reveals that one's social role is determined by the acceptance of particular ways of acting, even when individuality is posited as the ultimate goal.

The climactic stand-off in the novel which takes place when Olive announces her plan to return 'back' to Jamaica, 'somewhere where being black doesn't make you different' (Levy 2004a: 272), and Rose begs Vivien to tell her sister 'where you belong' (Levy 2004a: 281) sees Vivien articulating the greatest sense of her self-awareness she exhibits anywhere in the novel: 'I had grown too big for our council flat, but not sure where else I would fit [. . .] I answered my mother the only way I could. I said, "I don't know"' (Levy 2004a: 281). Vivien has not found a satisfactory way to belong anywhere; any transformation she has undergone has involved simply trying to fit in to a pre-existing set of prescribed norms, without any sense of her taking ownership of these developments. The final scene of the novel, therefore, should not be read as showing her finally coming to inhabit a confident sense of identity, but rather as a retreat from this key moment of self-knowledge. When asked by an old woman on a train back to Kent where she comes from, her reaction is to question 'what country she would want me to come from'? The answer she gives does not then seem a confident assertion of the unique individual she has become, but rather a further compromise in accepting a palatable narrative of her identity. Her answer, 'My family are from Jamaica [. . .] But I am English' (Levy 2004a: 282), is not inaccurate, but neither is it a full truth. The novel has reminded us that being English is by no means an unproblematic identity, and is subject to all kinds of gradation depending on class, gender and other factors. Whether we read this statement as indicative of Moretti's principle of settled classification, or of untrammelled and autonomous transformation, it is clear that it serves as compromise, of a (perhaps desired) loss of much of what has made her experience unique.

Levy's first two novels are undoubtedly concerned with processes involved in coming to maturity, and therefore clearly merit investigation through the optic of the *bildungsroman*. But the bleakness of these texts, the persistence of a melancholic notion of loss, and the idea that any move forward is countered always by a parallel step backwards demand that the concept of the black British *bildungsroman* is divorced from the sense of celebration that so often accompanies it. While her later works do indeed seem to trace the seeds for recuperating the denial of productive identity, *Every Light in the House Burnin'* and *Never Far from Nowhere* cannot neatly be confined to a narrative that sees black British writing of the 1990s as demonstrating a confidence in claiming the national space. Rather, these unhappy texts might better be read as giving the lie to exactly this narrative, showing the desire to transcend a marginalized position but sceptical about the existence of any resources that might allow young black working-class women like Angela Jacobs and Vivien Charles to exercise lasting and transformative agency.

# Council Housing and the Politics of the Welfare State in *Never Far from Nowhere*

## MATTHEW TAUNTON

**Chapter Summary:** This chapter explores the representation of council housing in Levy's second novel, *Never Far from Nowhere* (1996). This is a 'double *bildungsroman*' whose two protagonists grew up on a council estate in Islington in the late 1970s. Vivien and Olive follow very different trajectories, and this chapter shows how Levy uses the setting of the council estate in order to explore a number of important political issues relating to the post-war British welfare state, suggesting that the question of class is central both to understandings of council housing and to Levy's fiction. The novel depicts a time when faith in the cradle-to-grave provision set out in the Beveridge Report (1942) was under severe strain, and Levy dramatizes a renegotiation of the relationship between the individual, the family and the state. The chapter also explores the influence of writers such as Doris Lessing and Zoë Fairbairns on Levy's treatment of these issues.

## Levy's Council Estate in Context

Andrea Levy's second novel, *Never Far from Nowhere*, tells the story of two sisters, Olive and Vivien, coming of age on a council estate near Finsbury Park in North London. This location is important as the novel's characters are frequently defined by the spaces in which they live. We read that Maggie 'lived in a council house, not a very nice place' (Levy 1996: 26), that Carol 'lived in a big house, but her family only seemed to occupy a little bit of it' (Levy 1996: 41), that Georgina lived in an 'old', 'big' house with 'fitted carpets and cushions scattered around' (Levy 1996: 147), while Eddie lived in 'a block of flats made of pale concrete slabs . . . looking like the council had left it there to upset architects'

(Levy 1996: 150). These houses and flats operate as markers of class, and the council estate in particular is a symbol of poverty, crime and unemployment. But the estate is also an embodiment of the egalitarian ambitions of the British welfare state. These ambitions were central to the post-war settlement in Britain, a broad, Keynesian social-democratic consensus that was enshrined in the Beveridge report of 1942, and to which all three main political parties subscribed.

Following the economic turmoil occasioned by the Organization of the Petroleum Exporting Countries (OPEC) crisis of 1973, as Tony Judt put it, 'the British political consensus collapsed' and Margaret Thatcher's Conservative Party were 'able to seize control of public policy and wreak a radical transformation on the country's political culture' (Judt 2010: 537–8). As Thatcher herself said in 1975, 'A vital new debate is beginning, or perhaps an old debate is being renewed, about the proper role of government, the welfare state, and the attitudes on which it rests' (quoted in Timmins 1995: 356). Joseph Brooker's *Literature of the 1980s* (2010) has recently explored the literary culture of Thatcher's Britain, and, despite its publication date in 1996 and its setting in the late 1970s, I want to suggest that *Never Far from Nowhere* demands to be read in relation to the cultural politics of Thatcherism. Levy's novel engages with crucial debates of the 1980s that were part of a complex renegotiation of the relationship between individual, family and state. The council estate played an important role in such debates, which have a lasting resonance in the present.

*Never Far from Nowhere* is a 'double *bildungsroman*' (Lima 2005: 63) which alternates chapter by chapter between two narrators to explore the events described from two distinct perspectives (the device of alternating between multiple narrators is also a feature of *Small Island*). The story is told by the cynical, downtrodden Olive and her ambitious and intelligent younger sister Vivien. The estate on which the sisters grew up initially appears as a 'fairy-tale kingdom of white concrete, radiant in the sun' (Levy 1996: 3), combining the utopian ideals of architectural modernism with the 'cradle to grave' provision of the British welfare state. As Vivien puts it, however, the estate 'held the promise of decent living but didn't fulfill it' (Levy 1996: 3). Olive becomes a teenage mother who survives on benefits and 'hadn't really left the flat for years' (Levy 1996: 197), while complaining that living there is 'like being buried alive' (Levy 1996: 220). Vivien, by contrast, escapes to Art College in Canterbury where she mixes with the bohemian middle class, getting the feeling that she 'had grown too big for our council flat' (Levy 1996: 281). The flat is associated in the novel with feelings of confinement and even incarceration, feelings that complicate a picture of the welfare state as a benevolent overseer.

The trajectories of the novel's two narrators can be illuminated by being set in the context of the history of social housing in Britain after 1945. In the Labour government of 1945–51, headed by prime minister Clement Attlee, the foundation stones of the welfare state were laid. The state had made huge demands of its citizens during the two world wars, and – in the terms of the Beveridge report of 1942, the founding document of the welfare state – it now had a responsibility to tackle the 'Five Giants' of Want, Disease, Ignorance, Squalor and Idleness (Timmins 1995: 24). The Blitz, along with a wartime hiatus in house building, contributed to a severe housing shortage, and it was now increasingly seen as the state's responsibility to make up the shortfall. Council housing, then falling under the remit of minister for health and housing Aneurin Bevan, was a key part of the new social contract that was being drawn up in the post-war period. Bevan set high standards for council housing, but could not build enough to cope with demand. The Conservative government of 1951–5, with Winston Churchill as Prime Minister and Harold Macmillan as housing minister, saw a shift of emphasis from quality to quantity. Tree cottages with gardens were replaced by poky urban flats (often cheaply constructed from prefabricated slabs of concrete), and the idea that the state was ultimately responsible for providing housing for the whole community was displaced, over the following decades, by a notion of emergency housing for the poor and unemployed (Taunton 2009: 139–44). This led to a decline in the reputation of local authority housing in the press and in the popular mind such that it became the 'housing of last resort' (Beider 2009: 70). By the 1970s, the welfare state and the Keynesian social-democratic consensus that supported it started to be assailed by monetarist and neoliberal arguments drawing on the free market economics of Friedrich Hayek and Milton Friedman. These were increasingly recognized as the official line of the Conservative Party, particularly under the leadership of Margaret Thatcher and her closest advisor and chief ideologue Keith Joseph (who, ironically and to his later regret, had been responsible for much high-rise building during his stint as housing minister in the early 1960s (Timmins 1995: 186)). The perceived failure of council housing – evidenced by the concentration of unemployment, crime and drug addiction on estates – became part of a powerful argument for the withdrawal of the state from the provision of housing and other services. 'Right-to-Buy' – which enabled council tenants to buy their homes at a vastly reduced rate – became a flagship Thatcherite policy (Timmins 1995: 365–7).

Elsewhere, I have explored how the boundaries of the council estate became 'the frontier of the class divide' (Taunton 2009: 162), and how this was manifested in films set on council estates from Ken Loach's *Cathy Come Home* (1966) to Gary Oldman's *Nil by Mouth* (1997) and Michael Winterbottom's *Wonderland* (1999). The idea that the council estate, brought into being in order to improve the living conditions of working-class slum-dwellers, was now itself an oppressive institution is suggested in Levy's novel by the limited horizons of many of its characters, notably Vivien's school friends from the estate. Pam, for example, 'wanted to be as happy as her mum. Get married young and have a flat with a washing machine' (Levy 1996: 35). Vivien's narration invites the reader to view this with a certain scepticism, however, as she notes that 'Pam's mum always looked haggard to me. [. . .] I'd see her down the shops screaming at her sons, [. . .] "You get 'ere now or I'll fucking brain yer"' (Levy 1996: 35). Even the more adventurous and ambitious Vivien finds the class-associations of living on the estate heavily restrictive, as we see when Vivien and Carol witness a horrific fight in the Oak, a rough pub they frequent. A man is glassed in the face and 'scarred for life' (Levy 1996: 111), and this seems a regular night out for these girls. On the way home they witness the following scene:

> We got to the main road and found we were suddenly standing outside a pub. Music was playing, I could see the live band clearly, standing on a stage. In front of them people were dancing round. Women with long hair flying this way and that, men in T-shirts waving their arms in the air; singing, clapping, laughing. A load of hippies we'd have called them a year ago, and pulled faces. But me and Carol watched. Creatures from another planet watching humans having fun. (Levy 1996: 111)

Though they might live in the same city, this passage suggests that there is an interplanetary distance opening up between the dwindling number of council estate dwellers (making up 12% of the UK population in 2007) and the petty-bourgeois majority of owner-occupiers (72%) (Hanley 2007: 98).

## Geographies of Race and Class: The *Flâneur* in Question

*Never Far from Nowhere* has often been read (along with Levy's other work) as a novel that is primarily about race: an attempt critically to 'figure Englishness as a specific race, language, and moral authority which excludes Blacks', as Maria Helena Lima has written (2005: 70). It would be foolish to underestimate the important role played by race in the novel. Yet by placing its council estate setting in the foreground – attempting to understand Olive and Vivien as being defined as council estate dwellers as much as they are defined by being black – my reading complicates this view of the novel. The racial makeup of council estates in London was (and is) quite different from the projects in US cities such as Chicago and Miami, where public housing and racial segregation go hand in hand. In the United Kingdom estates have historically tended to be racially mixed (Beider 2009: 75). Levy's novel reflects that demographic reality, and as a result the question of race intersects problematically with that of class in her novel. The girls share a mixed heritage, including a Scottish grandfather, and a grandmother (on the other side) who was 'part Spanish, part Indian, part African' (Levy 1996: 2). Olive – described as 'darker. Black. The Caribbean legacy' – experiences extreme racism which damages her chances and holds her back. Vivien is paler skinned, ashamed of her Caribbean heritage, and can effectively pass herself off as 'Italian or Spanish' (Levy 1996: 1), and so she is able to sidestep racism to some extent. She mixes mainly with white friends. When Susan Alison Fischer put it to Levy that Olive was held back by her ethnicity, Levy was keen to insist that class, too, had played a role.

**SAF:** [. . .] In *Never Far from Nowhere*, we see Olive encountering low expectations because of her ethnicity –

**AL:** And her class.

Going on to discuss the low expectations she encountered in her own upbringing in North London, she says that 'I would have to say it was class almost more than ethnicity' (Fischer 2005: 365). Levy is certainly interested in the relation between social mobility or opportunity and race, but this is not the sole factor for our understanding of the fates of her two protagonists: her novel imagines a subtle and complicated relationship between race, class and the culture of the council estate. In the passage quoted above, Carol – who is white – feels just as excluded from the spectacle of 'humans having fun' as does Vivien. She does not live on the estate but her class origins mean that she feels comfortable there. On this estate there is considerable racial hatred, most obviously perpetrated by the menacing skinheads who say 'Fucking wogs' (Levy 1996: 14) to Olive as she passes them on the stairs. But these racist thugs are just as cut off from 'humans having fun' as are Vivien and Carol. Levy's council estate appears as a separate ecosystem, and the racism which Olive faces is a part of the reality of that ecosystem. Racism is one of the results of the separation of estate-dwellers from the rest of the city, not its cause.

In *The Fall of Public Man*, the sociologist Richard Sennett has analysed the ways in which the development of the metropolis in the eighteenth century enabled the intermixture of social classes, 'so that even the labouring classes began to adopt some of the habits of sociability, like promenades in parks, which were formerly the exclusive province of the elite' (Sennett 1978: 17). Yet, Sennett argues, the modern city has seen a retrenchment of class division. Starting with Haussmann's rebuilding of Paris in the nineteenth century, modern urbanism has been a process by which 'the intermixing of classes within districts was reduced by design' (Sennett 1978: 134). Leaving aside the objections to Sennett's highly problematic view of the fluidity of class in the eighteenth-century city, this is a suggestive hypothesis about the tendencies of modern urban planning, and it is supported by Levy's depiction of the estate in *Never Far from Nowhere*.

Such perceptions about the divided character of the modern city inform Levy's work as a whole, and *Never Far from Nowhere* in particular raises questions about a certain trend in contemporary depictions of London to frame the *flâneur* or street-wanderer as heroic. A notable

contemporary of Levy's, Will Self, is one of several London writers who
has appropriated the idea of the *flâneur* from the nineteenth-century
Parisian street poetry of Baudelaire, via its subsequent theorization
in the work of Walter Benjamin, then its adaptation in the Situationist
model of *dérive* and in the writings of Michel de Certeau. For Self, walking the streets has become a profoundly political act:

> [W]e understand that to walk the city and its environs is, in a very power-
> ful sense, to use it. The contemporary flâneur is by nature and inclination a
> democratising force who seeks equality of access, freedom of movement and
> the dissolution of corporate and state control. (Self 2012)

Self accords walking a special power, a power to transcend class and
to allow the walker to reclaim the streets from corporate ownership. A
similar motive can be found in Iain Sinclair's work, notably in *London
Orbital* (2002) where he sets out to reclaim the M25 motorway – offi-
cially opened by Thatcher in 1986, and a symbol of her preference for
the private vehicle over public transport – for the pedestrian by walking
around it. Self's and Sinclair's are politically charged pedestrianisms
characterized by bold self-confidence, as the writer lays claim to 'equality of access' and 'freedom of movement', thereby asserting his mastery
of the terrain.

*Never Far from Nowhere* exposes some of the limitations of thinking
about urban pedestrianism in this way, and this points to a key difference between a writer like Levy and contemporaries such as Self
or Sinclair. Where the latter are usually cast in the role of the intellec-
tual or highbrow (sometimes with the scorn that often attaches to these
terms in Britain), Levy is a bestseller, associated with the recent resur-
gence of the historical novel, and a book group favourite – all hallmarks
of the middlebrow. She is an avowed realist who recently boasted 'I
don't have a magic realist bone in my body' (Levy and Morrison 2009:
328). As a result, she may be less likely than either Self or Sinclair to
refer to situationism or psychogeography, but writes in the vener-
able tradition of the 'condition-of-England' novel, which underwent a
revival in Thatcher's Britain, notably in the work of Margaret Drabble
(Brooker 2010: 149). *Never Far from Nowhere* is a kind of 'condition-of-
London' novel that is interested in the way that the urban environment
is divided up along class lines. The council estate appears as an important element of that division and a real threat to the mobility on which
the *flâneur* thrives. Olive's walks around the city are fraught with evi-
dence of her exclusion from it: as Maria Helena Lima writes, '[w]hen
Olive aimlessly walks around the city [. . .] she does not individually
reinscribe it, as Michel de Certeau would want her to, for London does
not feel like her city' (Lima 2005: 67). For Lima race is again the central
issue, but the analysis holds just as well if we consider Olive first and
foremost as a council tenant.

Vivien, by contrast, seems to be able to move more freely, beyond the boundaries of the estate, as she grows older. It is not that the barrier between the estate and the rest of the city has disappeared, however, but that she starts to experience it from the other side. She befriends a middle-class girl called Georgina and starts spending a lot of time with her and her mother in their comfortable Islington home. She starts to feel alienated from her own home: 'I began to hate going back to my house – to my flat – to my council flat' (Levy 1996: 148). Later, when she has moved away and become an art student, Vivien's first return to the estate where she grew up is described in the following terms:

> The first time I went home after college, back to the flats where my mum lived, there was a mattress lying across the road. It had a hole burnt in the middle. Blue flowers trampled grey, fraying, with stuffing and springs poking through the charred-edged gash. The flats looked like some opposing army had finally seized them, plundering them of any value and then leaving. I wondered if they had always looked so raw and desolate, or whether I was looking at them with new eyes. With the eyes of a would-be artist who was getting used to looking for beauty in everything. My footsteps echoed against the walls and sounded like someone was following me. I kept looking around. I was nervous. Jumpy. Like a lost tourist. (Levy 1996: 274)

Far from the self-confident *flânerie* celebrated in Self's essay, Levy's novel uses Vivien's walk in the council estate to show how spatially and architecturally enforced class barriers work both ways, hampering mobility and creating a sense of alienation from the urban environment. Just as Vivien and Carol had felt profoundly shut out from the happy scene in the pub, for Vivien – who has crossed to the other side of a class divide – the estate is now something to be feared.

The hostility of the terrain of the estate itself to streetwalking is due partly to certain typical features of its architecture, and partly to the associations that were later attributed to that architectural style. If the *flâneur* requires the street, then the architecture of council estates like the one in Levy's novel – following the great modernist Le Corbusier's insistence that 'streets are an obsolete notion' (Corbusier 1967: 121) – worked to eliminate the street by replacing it with decks, galleries, walkways and corridors. Alison and Peter Smithson, the architects most strongly associated with the marrying of the ideals of architectural modernism with those of the British welfare state, adapted Corbusier's slogans, arguing that houses, streets, squares and greens no longer represented social reality. Instead they advocated a 'New Brutalism' that aimed for a 'multi-level city with residential streets in the air' (Smithson and Smithson 1967: 26). When Vivien remarks that '[a]t night the well-lit streets of Finsbury Park seemed like a safe haven compared to the flats' (Levy 1996: 226), she draws attention to the architectural contrasts between the 'well-lit streets' (where the *flâneur* might roam) and the estate itself, with

its threatening associations. Lynsey Hanley writes insightfully about
the way in which brutalist architecture – as well-intentioned as it may
have been, and despite some notable successes – came to act as a visual
signifier of poverty, addiction and crime:

> From the mid-1960s onwards you could tell council estates from a mile off,
> giving you the chance to avoid them, to duck out and treat them with the
> suspicion their reputations seemed to warrant. (Hanley 2007: 65)

The experiences of Levy's protagonists throw into question the idea that
such spaces can simply be reclaimed by the heroic pedestrianism of the
*flâneur*.

## Environmental Determinism

*Never Far from Nowhere* is also concerned with a classic question of the
nineteenth-century realist novel: how far does the environment – here,
the estate – determine character? In trying to answer this question for
her own historical moment, Levy makes use of the device of having
two narrators who share the same family and background but have different fates. Vivien believes that coming from a council estate had little bearing on her destiny: 'We had the same chances, we started from
the same place [. . .] and you chose to lead your life and I chose to lead
mine' (Levy 1996: 278). Olive, by contrast, emphasizes the paralysing
stigma that attaches to council estate dwellers, perhaps especially black
ones: 'I didn't have a choice, I never had any choices' (Levy 1996: 278).
The disagreement here centres around the key Thatcherite idea of personal responsibility, which Levy's novel links to questions of narrative
causality.

As Vivien starts to mingle with some of the more middle-class girls
in her grammar school, she finds herself in the Kings Head on Upper
Street in the company of Laurence and Nick, some boys from board-
ing school. Nick represents the new conservatism, arguing that 'if you
give people money it encourages them not to work' (Levy 1996: 203),
and expressing a familiar prejudice: '[m]ost people living on council
estates don't work at all [. . .] They just scrounge off the state' (Levy
1996: 204). This attitude represents an argument that was gathering
momentum at the time about the supposedly feckless, welfare-de-
pendent poor. As Brooker writes, the view represented by Thatcher's
party, and increasingly a part of public discourse, was that 'unemployment benefit and welfare payments could [. . .] actively do harm, dis-
couraging individual endeavour and encouraging Britons to rely on
handouts' (Brooker 2010: 10).

Levy seems keen to insist that such views were not held solely
by the upper classes, as she also ciphers them through the character

of Rose – Olive and Vivien's mother – a Jamaican immigrant of the Windrush generation (like Hortense and Gilbert in *Small Island*) with aspirations to middle-class respectability. The economic historian Frank Trentmann has argued that 'the rise and fall of economic precepts need to be placed in the broad environment of beliefs and values that sustain them' (Trentmann 2008: 317), and any attempt to understand Thatcherism must take account not only of the arguments of a few renegade economists, but also of its popular appeal. This was well analysed by Stuart Hall, one of Thatcherism's perceptive critics on the left, in 1979:

> in the doctrines and discourses of 'social market values' – the restoration of competition and personal responsibility for effort and reward, the image of the over-taxed individual, enervated by welfare coddling, his initiative sapped by handouts by the state — 'Thatcherism' has found a powerful means of popularizing the principles of a Monetarist philosophy: and in the image of the welfare 'scavenger' a well designed folk-devil. (Hall 1979: 17)

Literature can often give us an insight into the 'beliefs and values that sustain' prevalent economic theories, and Levy's novel portrays Rose as someone who has absorbed these populist elements of Thatcherism as outlined by Hall. Indeed, Thatcher had many supporters in the working- and lower-middle classes, channelling a popular moral backlash against the 'libertarianism of the Sixties' and 'the progressive intelligentsia that dominated public affairs in these years' (Judt 2010: 540). And arguments that would later be labelled Thatcherite had even gained ground in the Labour Party in the 1970s. The critique of council housing in particular was not the preserve of the right: Frank Field had proposed in 1975 that the wholesale transfer of council houses to their tenants should become Labour policy, in a bid to 'free the council serfs' (Timmins 1995: 366). John Callaghan's Labour government of the late 1970s broke with postwar Keynesian orthodoxy when it 'acknowledged the inevitability of a certain level of unemployment' and proceeded with 'deep cuts in public spending' at a time of economic downturn (Judt 2010: 539).

Nevertheless, Thatcherite ideas – for all that they crossed boundaries of class, race and (to some extent) party – were far from a matter of consensus, and the period is defined by deep divisions and confrontations that were played out on the nation's sofas as much as in the Houses of Parliament. The counterpart to Rose's Thatcherism – the socialism of the old, collectivist left – is represented in the novel by Olive's boyfriend (and later husband) Peter, a postman and trade unionist with far left leanings who 'talked about how black people were exploited and how we should get together with the workers to overthrow all oppression' (Levy 1996: 39). A series of arguments break out in which Rose would 'rant on about people looking after themselves and how people didn't want to work because "they're bone idle, Peter, bone idle." And Peter would talk about the workers working together to overthrow bosses in factories and idleness would end because workers would control the means of production' (Levy 1996: 48). Rose's Thatcherism is cold and hard, heaping blame on a supposedly undeserving poor, and even working against her own interests. But Peter's anger – directed against villainous 'bosses in factories' – seems to miss the target, and in fact his politics merge into the self-serving dishonesty that infects other aspects of his personality. However noble his aspiration for a revolutionary alliance between black people and workers may be, here it appears in a context where many of the white working classes, who live in close quarters with black people on the estate, are skinheads and racists. The novel presents both sides of the argument, and offers no easy way out.

When Peter leaves Olive, she has no job or qualifications, still lives with her hostile mother and has a baby to support. Levy positions her entirely at the mercy of the state. Her struggle to establish herself independently from her mother and with the basic human requirements of food, warmth and shelter becomes a bitter war with the representatives of Islington council. In three analogous scenes, Olive pleads with various representatives of the welfare state and never finds the understanding or sympathy she craves. First, she is interrogated by a doctor who seems friendly enough at first, but ignores her real problems in his overzealous attempts to foist contraceptives on her, despite her repeated insistence that she is not having sex: 'I never wanted to have sex again' (Levy 1996: 159), the reluctant mother affirms, but the doctor will not listen. Even the intimate details of her sex life seem to be coming under the shadow of state control. And when she cries in frustration the doctor relents and pushes a prescription for sleeping pills into her hand: the National Health Service (NHS) here seems incapable of empathy and instead wants to tranquillize its miserable patients. Olive's frustration is evident: 'I threw his hanky at him, took his prescription and left. I screwed it up and put it in the bin when I got outside. Fuck him' (Levy 1996: 159).

Secondly, in the social security office, Olive is subjected to a series of humiliating and intrusive questions, and complains that they want to 'know the ins and outs of a cat's arse. Everything about me' (Levy 1996: 193). Olive's reporting of the response of the woman behind the glass highlights some intractable problems with the way welfare is administered:

> Four to six weeks, she said, before I would get any money from them. I could starve by then, I told her, and she said that was how long it would take to process me and that it was the same for everyone. (Levy 1996: 194)

Fairness and equality are basic tenets of the welfare state, and they carry positive, progressive connotations. But here, the claim that 'it was the same for everyone', while trivially true (each citizen has the same legal entitlement to benefits), is also obviously false: only the poor have to go through the humiliating experience of trying to extract what little they are entitled to from the intransigent representatives of the state.

Thirdly, when Olive decides finally to leave her mother's flat after a row, she is reduced to a state of utter desperation, sitting on the floor of the housing department, sobbing, with her daughter Amy in her arms:

> People kept coming up to me, wanting me to sit on a chair, wanting me to move, wanting me to be sensible, wanting me to be patient, wanting me to listen to them. Then a woman knelt down beside me and told me with a sympathetic whispered voice and tilted nodding head that if I stayed where I was, that if I didn't return home, then she would have no option but to take Amy away from me. She would have to put Amy into care. (Levy 1996: 211)

The institutions of the welfare state are there to care for citizens when families fail. Here, the fact that the state now takes ultimate responsibility for childcare is used against Olive: 'care' is not a safety net but a threat used against disadvantaged mothers. If we want the state's help we have to sit in line quietly and wait our turn – when Olive finally does get her flat, she has to insist that 'I worked hard for this. No one has ever handed me anything on a plate' (Levy 1996: 232). Through Olive's three encounters with social security, the NHS and the housing department of Islington council, Levy draws attention to the problematic sense in which she has become dependent – a loaded term in this debate – on an unfeeling bureaucracy.

## Feminist Fiction and the Welfare State

Levy's concern with the difficulties faced by the poor in their interactions with the institutions of the welfare state may have been prompted by engagements with similar issues by a number of women writers of the previous generation. In an interview, Levy stated that it was 'feminist publishing [. . .] Virago, The Women's Press' that had influenced her to start writing fiction in the 1980s, when she was in her mid-thirties (Fischer 2005: 361). She cited as an example of the kind of material that had influenced her a now little-read novel called *Benefits*, by Zoë Fairbairns, in which an impassioned if occasionally confused debate about the relationship of women to the welfare state is staged in a weirdly dystopian near future (Fischer 2005: 362). The novel centres around a group of feminists who come to feel that 'social workers are agents of state repression and control' (Fairbairns 1979: 26), and turn a high-rise block of council flats into an autonomous commune. This operates as a kind of anarchist critique of the paternalistic state-collectivism of council housing, and as in Levy's *Never Far from Nowhere*, the estate is used as a setting in order to interrogate the relationship between individual, household and state.

In *Benefits*, a new political party called simply FAMILY rises to power – headed by a sinister former social worker – and uses the apparatus of the welfare state to enforce conservative family values, using benefits as 'a real incentive to women to behave themselves' (Fairbairns 1979: 177). Lynn, one of the novel's protagonists, describes it as 'Benefit. The final solution. Pay women at home and keep 'em there', but then goes on to defend, in what seems like a contradiction, 'the principle that people whose life's work is raising kids should be rewarded in the same way as people whose life's work is anything else' (Fairbairns 1979: 204).

Doris Lessing's fiction – better known and more likely to be found on university curricula – often articulates similar concerns, notably in her short story collection *London Observed* (1992). In 'The Mother of the Child in Question', an interrogation of the politics of the welfare state is again set in a desolate council estate, complete with '[c]ement, everywhere he looked', 'puddles, soft drink cans and bits of damp paper', 'urine-smelling stairs' and a lift that someone has been sick in (Lessing 1993b: 36). A social worker visits Mrs Khan, a Pakistani woman with a very limited grasp of English whose daughter Shireen has special needs. The social worker's task is to get Shireen enrolled in a 'special school', but he fails: the meeting is plagued by communication problems and his presence is perceived as an unwanted intrusion of the state into the family's affairs. The social worker reflects that Mrs Khan has simply refused to acknowledge her daughter's special needs, and – although it constitutes a professional failure on his part – he is impressed by this woman's surly resolve. His human sympathies, we infer, are at odds with the paper-pushing prerogatives of his job as a state bureaucrat. In a similar vein, 'DHSS' gives the reader a snapshot of a life lived, like Olive's, at the mercy of the state. The staff at the DHSS (Department of Health and Social Services, the forerunner of today's Department of Work and Pensions, with a slightly different remit) have gone on strike and the young mother at the centre of the story is reduced to begging, which is even worse than 'hanging around Social Security day after day to try and get my money out of them' (Lessing 1993a: 67). She is rude to the well-meaning former D.H.S.S. employee who gives her food and money, and treats him with suspicion and hostility: 'No I *don't* trust anyone', she says. 'And I never will again' (Lessing 1993a: 70). Olive, a victim of similar circumstances, is just as bitter. Levy has said that *Never Far from Nowhere* is her 'angriest' book (Levy and Morrison 2009: 332), and as such it is the novel that best fits into the tradition of women's writing represented by Lessing and Fairbairns. In the context of this tradition, we can see that the questioning of the welfare state did not belong only to the right. In Fairbairns and Lessing we find a significant precedent for a kind of realist fiction that is deeply ambivalent about the workings of the welfare state, from feminist and socialist perspectives.

Such themes are also present in Levy's depiction of Vivien, who is no stranger to the alienating effects of the state's attempts to support and care for its children and its citizens. As a young teenager, she spends much of her time in the local youth centre – the state's standard response to the problem of juvenile delinquency. Indeed the welfare state (in Britain and abroad) has produced reams of sociological data to suggest that, in the words of one such study, teenagers participating in 'youth activities [. . .] foster social competencies, learn to work with others and develop leadership skills' (Hansen et al. 2003: 28). The youth club could be thought of as an example of a space where some of the traditional functions of the home are transferred into commonly held facilities – a key ambition for modernist architects such as Karel Tiege (Teige 2002), and therefore an element of the architectural logic of the council estate – but in *Never Far from Nowhere*, the youth club is a frightening place. When Vivien and Carol first go to the club there is a bloody fight, and 'the air was thick with screaming and swearing' (Levy 1996: 16). The aims of the youth club are summed up by the figure of Ted, the man in charge, who breaks up the fights and ineffectively tries to stop the teenagers from swearing. 'You lot can kill each other outside, not in here, not on my time – in here you play table tennis' (Levy 1996: 17). Even this limited ambition is mocked by the kids:

> Everyone thought the club was getting boring.
> 'That Ted gets on my bollocks,' Johnny said. 'Him and his fucking table tennis.'
> Tony imitated Ted saying, 'If Hitler had played table tennis we'd never have had a war.' They started hanging round down a pub called the Swinging Sporran instead. (Levy 1996: 88)

The state's ambition to eliminate delinquency, criminality and even the gas chambers by drilling its young people in ping pong seems absurd. Levy is poking fun at the idea that a municipal institution such as a youth club can effectively manage such deep-rooted social and psychological problems. So far, Vivien's experiences of the interventionist state seem to accord with Olive's. It appears as cripplingly paternalistic, and more likely to hold her back than help her along.

Elsewhere, however, Vivien is able to develop a less confrontational relationship with the state and its institutions. Take the issue of school uniform for example – an area where services provided by the state (in this case the universal free schooling ushered in by the 1944 Education Act, another major plank of the British welfare state (Timmins 1995: 92)) come bound up with rules and an effort to standardize experience and behaviour. Olive's attitude to the uniform is characteristically rebellious – she sees it as a 'strait-jacket' and complains that '[y]ou had to wear this hat home – all the way. You were not allowed to take it off until you got home. That was good of them: I didn't have to sit watching Crossroads in my bloody hat' (Levy 1996: 25). She sees the uniform as an imposition and an intrusion and hates it as much as she hates the intrusions of the doctor and the other representatives of the welfare state she encounters. Vivien, by contrast, is happy enough to conform, while paying lip service to rebellion:

> I thought school was great, although I snarled and rolled my eyes with everyone else when they talked about it. The uniform – what crap. The school dinners – disgusting. The rules – bloody stupid. (Levy 1996: 33)

If – beneath this thin veneer of defiance – Vivien is happier to wear the uniform, she is also luckier with her experiences of those in authority. Her ambitions are nurtured rather than crushed when she articulates them to a teacher:

> I wanted to be a film director. And when I told Miss O'Keefe, my English teacher, my favourite teacher, she didn't laugh. She looked at me seriously and asked me what exams I was taking. Then she talked to me about film school and said she could see no reason why I shouldn't try. (Levy 1996: 35)

It is clear that in Vivien's case the welfare state helps her to escape the estate. She benefits from universal free education and even a grant for living expenses when she enrolls at college: 'I thought I'd won the pools' (Levy 1996: 248), she states, in clear contrast to Olive's assertion that '[n]o one has ever handed me anything on a plate' (Levy 1996: 232). In Vivien's case – and again we are left to wonder whether this is as a result of her lighter skin – welfare has been instrumental in providing opportunities to thrive, rather than holding her back in a frustrating struggle with bureaucracy. There is a suggestion that this will happen to Olive when the council provide her with housing benefit and a new flat, though the main cause for celebration is that '[i]t wasn't on an estate, it was on a street' (Levy 1996: 231). Olive's optimism about the British state is short-lived, however, as she is arrested by two racist policemen who say that 'you niggers usually have a bit of ganja on you' (Levy 1996: 258), before planting the drug on her. She finally resolves to move to Jamaica, '[w]here being black means you belong' (Levy 1996: 273).

Levy's novel seems delicately poised, then, asking powerful questions about where the responsibilities of the individual and the family end, and those of the state begin. The Thatcherite argument is set out in the novel, but its championing of 'personal responsibility' (Hall 1979: 17) rings hollow, just as it does when Rose admonishes Olive 'to stand on your own two feet' (Levy 1996: 173). These may be worthy aspirations, but Levy's novel resists the implication that they can be achieved simply by reducing state (or parental) support. The state has a role to play in allowing people to develop the independence that they themselves desire, and this novel suggests that for people like Olive there is nowhere else to turn. Implicitly, though, the novel acknowledges that the 'cradle to grave' provision imagined in the Beveridge report and which Attlee and Bevan attempted to put into practice in 1945–51 had already eroded by the 1970s. Rather than a universal system, the welfare state appears in Levy's novel as a safety net for the very poor. In the context of the council estate, this leads to an ever-increasing social marginalization, a spatial division of London between the owner-occupying majority and enclaves of council tenants on estates that are represented as miserable or even dangerous places to be.

# Existing in More than One Plane of Time: Memory and Narrative Form in *Every Light in the House Burnin'*

## MICHAEL PERFECT

**Chapter Summary:** While *Every Light in the House Burnin'* has often been treated as a relatively minor text in Levy's body of work, this chapter re-situates it as a major text in her oeuvre, analysing the ways in which it introduces issues that are to become key to her later, better-known works. Through a close analysis of its narrative form, I argue that *Every Light* interrogates the ways in which, and the degree to which, the past might equip us to deal with the present, and with traumatic experiences in particular. I argue that *Every Light*'s primary significance is not sociological – that is, that it gives an 'accurate' account of a particular kind of experience – but that it explores the ways in which the past and the present give meaning to each other, and that it is in this sense that it should be seen as providing the foundation for texts such as *Fruit of the Lemon*, *Small Island* and *The Long Song*.

When asked in interview about how she began writing, Andrea Levy replied as follows: 'My Dad dying was the impetus. [. . .] I think I just wanted to make him visible, record something of his life, and also the experience that we'd gone through with it' (Levy quoted in Fischer 2005: 362). There can be little doubt that Levy's debut novel, *Every Light in the House Burnin'* (1994), was the result of her desire to 'record' something of her father. A coming-of-age story, the novel is narrated by Angela Jacobs, who – much like her creator – is a British-born girl of Jamaican descent who grows up in a working-class household in North London in the 1960s. At the very heart of the novel is the figure of Angela's father, Winston. Winston's lengthy struggle with illness, his increasing infirmity and his eventual death – all of which take place when Angela is an adult – are juxtaposed in the novel with Angela's recollections of much earlier scenes from her childhood.

*Every Light in the House Burnin'* does little to hide the fact that it is a work which is very much drawn from its author's experiences. The name of the novel's narrator clearly echoes that of its author, seemingly suggesting that there is little distance between the two; while 'Angela' is, of course, very similar to 'Andrea', 'Jacobs' is, as Susan Alice Fischer notes, 'a name which sounds Jewish, as does the author's' (Fischer 2004: 203). Moreover, it is noteworthy that the name of Angela's father is, like Andrea's father, Winston. Quite clearly, *Every Light in the House Burnin'* is not only a novel that is largely autobiographical, but one which sees no reason to shy away from its status as such.

It is too often the case in literary studies that to acknowledge that a work of fiction is based largely on the experiences of its author is to enter rather risky territory; indeed, it might be said that the risks involved are particularly acute – and the stakes particularly high – when that author happens to be a member of an ethnic minority. For some, to recognize that Levy's first novel is a largely autobiographical work is immediately to identify its primary significance as sociological. To say that its true importance lies in its supposedly 'accurate', 'authentic' account of growing up as a working-class, black British girl in 1960s London. This chapter certainly will not deny that Levy's work has sociological importance. However, it will take issue with the assumption that her earliest fiction is of sociological rather than literary importance. While *Every Light in the House Burnin'* should certainly be considered a foundational text in Levy's oeuvre and as one which prefigured her later work, it is *not* the case that it did so simply in the sense that it saw Levy begin to turn her own experiences into literary works. Rather, it is a novel that, through a complex and nuanced structure, subtly interrogates the ways in which the past and the present give meaning to each other. It is in this way, I want to suggest, that *Every Light in the House Burnin'* prefigures novels such as *Fruit of the Lemon* (1999), *Small Island* (2004) and *The Long Song* (2010), and it is in this way that it should be (re)situated within her oeuvre.

I have argued elsewhere that silences and the unspoken are ubiquitous in Levy's fiction and that her work attempts to confront historical silences, insisting on the importance of engaging with the past (Perfect 2010: 31–41). Indeed, over the course of her last few novels, Levy's work has become increasingly historical in scope and has become increasingly concerned with drawing attention to the contemporary significance of historical moments and historical narratives which it sees as too often overlooked, misrepresented or simply forgotten. Somewhat paradoxically, while *Fruit of the Lemon* is Levy's most 'contemporary' novel in the sense that, of her five to date, it has the most recent temporal setting, it is also the novel which marked the beginning of a more historical bent in her writing. A *bildungsroman*, *Fruit of the Lemon* identifies an individual crisis of identity as symptomatic of a family's silence about their past and, more broadly, situates that crisis of identity (which takes place during the 1980s) within a wider cultural amnesia surrounding the complex historical relationship between Britain and its colonies in the Caribbean. Set primarily during the 1940s, *Small Island* draws attention to the all-too-often forgotten role played by Britain's colonial subjects in the Second World War, and to the racism experienced by those who migrated from British colonies to the 'motherland' after the War had ended. As such, while *Small Island* examines events in recent British history that are not only familiar but also widely celebrated, in doing so it seeks to stress aspects of key historical moments which have often tended to be pretermitted. Levy's most recent novel, *The Long Song*, is her first to have a temporal setting that is unequivocally beyond living memory, and can, as such, perhaps be considered her first real work of 'historical fiction'. Set on a plantation in Jamaica during the nineteenth century, the novel examines a historical moment which Britain has too often shied away from, and it is careful to debunk the myth that colonial oppression and brutality in the Caribbean ended with the abolition of the slave trade within the British Empire or, indeed, with the abolition of slavery itself. A twist that occurs in the final stages of the novel emphasizes that understanding contemporary, multicultural Britain depends on a willing, robust and unflinching engagement with the horrors and the complexities of Britain's colonial past.

While Levy's early fiction does not deal directly with *historical* silences, silences of a more intimate, familial nature feature heavily. In *Every Light in the House Burnin'*, Angela grows up in a household that, while unquestionably intimate and loving, is full of secrecy. The six members of the Jacobs family, who share a fairly small, three-bedroom flat – while Angela shares a bedroom with her brother John, her two sisters, Patricia and Yvonne, also share a room – are certainly close-knit, and yet there is also the sense that they willingly remain largely unknown to each other. Indeed, the very lack of private space in the house seems to encourage the various members of the family to be as mysterious to each other as possible, and – much to her frustration – Angela finds both her siblings and her parents to be enigmatic and evasive.

The form of *Every Light in the House Burnin'* is rather at odds with the silences and secrecies that it recalls, and nowhere more so than in the novel's opening chapter. One of the few things that Angela's dad, mum, brother and sisters all have in common is that they want to remain mysterious to, and do not particularly want to be talked about by, each other. It is ironic, then, that Angela introduces them in sections titled, respectively, 'MY DAD', 'MY MUM', 'MY BROTHER' and 'MY SISTERS'. Two subsequent sections in the novel's opening chapter – and we can only presume that the order employed is one that reflects descending importance – are titled 'THE CAT' and 'THE TELLY'. While this technique may reflect Angela's youth – a childish desire to itemize everything around her – it also serves as a comic but determined refusal to allow the members of her family to remain as mysterious as they would seemingly like.

Introducing her father in the opening pages of the novel, Angela recalls that he did not like to talk about his work (Levy 2004a: 3), did not like anyone knowing his name, and refused to tell people his age (Levy 2004a: 3–4). Moreover, Angela recalls that Winston refused to speak about his own past:

> My dad was from Jamaica – born and bred. He came to this country in 1948 on the *Empire Windrush* ship. My mum joined him six months later in his one room in Earl's Court. He never talked about his family or his life in Jamaica. He seemed only to exist in one plane of time – the present. There is an old photo of him – grainy black and white that shows him dressed in an immaculate tailored suit with wide baggy trousers, wearing a shirt with a collar held by a pin, and a proper tie. His hair is short and well groomed. He is standing by a chair in the grounds of what looks to be a beautiful house. The photo looks like my dad as a 'Great Gatsby'-type millionaire. When I asked my dad about the photo that fascinated me, he would grudgingly admit that it was where he lived. But when I pressed him to tell me more he would shrug and tell me not to bother him. Or he'd suck his teeth and ask me why I was interested. He would ask this in the manner of somebody who does not want an answer – of somebody who would like you to leave them alone. (Levy 2004a: 3, italics original)

The disparity between Winston's lifestyle in Jamaica and his lifestyle in Britain – highlighted in this passage by the contrast between the image of him looking like a '"Great Gatsby"-type millionaire' and subsequently occupying, with his wife, just one room in Earl's Court – seems to be key to his reticence about the past. After travelling to London to find 'better opportunity' (Levy 2004a: 6), Angela's parents quickly discovered that the opportunities available to Jamaican immigrants to Britain were, in fact, severely limited. Understandably, then, Winston finds it painful to acknowledge that, despite his best efforts, he is bringing his children up in a background that is (in a relative sense, at least) far less affluent and privileged than the one into which he was born. Moreover, as Charlotte Beyer notes, the fact that Winston doesn't even tell his children that he has an identical twin called Louis until he (Louis) has died suggests that it is highly likely that Winston has 'experienced fractured familial relationships and painful or shameful secrets' (Beyer 2012: 108) even if neither we nor Angela are ever able to find out much about their nature. Accordingly, Winston is inclined towards attempting to simply forget about his own past, meaning that – to his daughter – he 'seemed only to exist in one plane of time – the present' (Levy 2004a: 4).

Much like their father, Angela's brother and her sisters all seem determined to remain enigmas. Of her brother John, Angela says:

My brother was born with red hair – a red, fuzzy head of hair that people would stare at in the street. 'It's the Scottish in you', my mum would say to him but she never explained where the Scottish came from. My brother lived in a secret world. He went out and nobody knew where he went or who he was going with. 'Just going to see a man about a dog', he would say if you asked him where he was going, and if you asked him where he had been he'd shrug and say, 'Been to see a man about a dog.' (Levy 2004a: 15)

While Angela's mother never tries to explain her children's complex ethnic background to them – making them, it could be argued, something of a mystery to themselves – her brother will never tell anyone where he has been or where he is going. In the subsequent section ('MY SISTERS'), the first thing Angela says is 'My sisters were a bit of a mystery to me' (Levy 2004a: 20).

As a child, Angela is often admonished for, or causes conflict by, speaking in situations in which she is expected to remain silent; indeed, this happens twice just in the novel's opening chapter. In church with her mother, Angela fails to understand that she is supposed to remain silent during prayers:

At last the vicar stopped talking and my mum slid off the pew and knelt on the cushion in front of her. I heard her knees crack as she went down. Then I heard knees cracking all over the congregation and a faint 'Ooohh' coming from all around. I knelt down but I found myself in a horrible dark space at the back of the pew. I couldn't see anything and I had nothing to hold on to. I stood up again and I was the same height as my mum. I could look her straight in the eyes.

'Look, Mum, I'm the same height as you.' I put my hand to my head and then to my mum's to show her what I meant.

'Okay, child – now kneel down', my mum whispered to me.

'It's dark down there, Mum', I said.

'Well, just stand there and be quiet nuh.' My mum spoke quickly in a whisper.

'What's happening now, Mum?' I said. I heard someone in the congregation laugh. As I looked round I noticed everyone was staring at me. Some were smiling, some not. 'Everyone's looking at me, Mum.'

'Sschh', my mum said and hit me gently on the knee with her hand. (Levy 2004a: 13–14)

The scene concludes with Angela's mother angrily dragging her out of the church and telling her 'You show me up, [. . .] I'm not taking you again, you hear – I'm not taking you again!' While she clearly intends to reprimand her daughter here, given the account that Angela gives of the experience of going to church – where she was forced to endure a vicar who 'went on and on and on and on' and to sit on a seat that was 'so hard that [her] backside couldn't bear to be pressed against it any more' (Levy 2004a: 12) – it seems likely that what her mother intends to be an admonishment represents, to Angela, something of a triumph.

In the scene that immediately follows (the one in which she introduces her brother), Angela again finds herself at the centre of consternation and conflict because she speaks when she is expected to remain silent. After John tells her the facts of life – informing her that 'The man puts his willie [sic] in the woman's hole – then the woman gets pregnant' (Levy 2004a: 17) – she is rather sceptical about (and, indeed, rather horrified by) what she has been told. In order to seek clarification about the process of human reproduction (and to remove any lingering doubts that what her brother has told her may not, in fact, be entirely erroneous), she passes the information on to her parents. While they neither confirm nor categorically deny the accuracy of what Angela's brother has told her (her mother simply tells her to disregard it – to 'Take no notice of what he said'), they are clearly aghast. Moreover, they are furious with their son and, when he returns to the house (presumably from having been to see a man about a dog), give him a fairly severe chiding. Angela can't hear exactly what is said but she is certainly aware of how angry her parents are (if not, exactly, for what reason): 'I knew I'd got my brother into big trouble. Bigger than the time he forgot me and left me at the shops. Bigger even than the time he persuaded me to show my unusual protruding belly button to all his friends' (Levy 2004a: 19–20). Again, Angela's decision to speak rather than remain silent brings about conflict, and she expresses concern about what further fallout there may be from the episode: 'I was scared what my brother would do to me. Maybe he wouldn't talk to me any more' (Levy 2004a: 20). It is notable that the repercussion that Angela fears most is neither physical nor verbal retribution but, rather, a kind of silencing.

While these two scenes are obviously comic and serve to endear us to the young, wide-eyed, ingenuous Angela, they also introduce one of the novel's major themes: refusing to remain silent. As a young child, Angela doesn't understand the complex nuances of social protocols, and it is only unwittingly that she talks loudly during church prayers and informs her parents that her brother has told her all about sexual reproduction. However, the older, mature Angela who narrates the novel has made a conscious decision to refuse to be silent. She has determined – indeed, she *is* determined – to narrate. Over the course of the novel, Angela's recollections of her father as a strong, indomitable presence contrast with her account of his increasing frailty later in life, and this contrast serves to emphasize her feelings of grief and disbelief at just how much he has changed. Paradoxically, however, while Angela's determined recollection of her childhood makes later events all the more dissonant and shocking to her, it also helps her to make sense of them.

Much as in Levy's later fiction, *Every Light in the House Burnin'* suggests that a frank, unflinching engagement with the past – one that refuses to slip into a sentimentality which might allow one's own memories to be falsified, even while making allowances for nostalgia – is key to an understanding of the present. Although her father 'seemed only to exist in one plane of time – the present', Angela's narrative is one that insists on the importance of remembering one's own past, particularly when faced with traumatic situations such as the death of a loved one. In this sense, *Every Light in the House Burnin'* enacts a struggle to exist in more than one 'plane of time'.

In an early narrative shift that establishes the shape of the entire novel, the second chapter of *Every Light in the House Burnin'* moves forwards a number of years to the time of Winston's retirement. The contrast between Winston as a middle-aged man in the first chapter and as an older man in the second is immediately made clear. While the first ends with him grumpily fighting with his children over control of the television, complaining vocally that he doesn't get to watch as much of it as they do, in the second Angela recalls noting, with an appropriate sense of alarm, that he seemed to adopt a new listlessness around the time of his retirement: 'When he had a cold he would lie in bed moaning and whimpering like a feeble dog. My mum would fetch and carry and roll her eyes when we asked how he was. But he was behaving differently with his new complaints. He became stoical. He said it was "nothing"' (Levy 2004a: 35–6). Significantly, silence is an extremely ominous sign here, and Winston is soon told that he has had a stroke; he is later diagnosed with both brain and lung cancer and suffers from a number of secondary conditions as well. As the novel progresses, its chapters continue to focus alternately on scenes from Angela's childhood (recalled in oddly numbered chapters) and on her father's deterioration years later (recalled in evenly numbered chapters). While the chapters that recount Winston's worsening condition are chronological in arrangement, those that recall scenes from Angela's childhood are not. In many of the latter, Angela's exact age at the time is not explicitly given, and yet there are moments at which it is clear that chronology has been disregarded; in the thirteenth chapter, for example, Angela recalls events that occurred when she was four years old (Levy 2004a: 155), despite the fact that earlier chapters have already recounted events that occurred much later, when she was seven or older. Crucially, after the first few chapters have established the novel's narrative shape, Angela's childhood recollections are frequently arranged in accordance with their relevance to her father's deterioration; that is, scenes from Angela's childhood are recalled in response to, and in order to attempt to make sense of, the traumatic experience of watching her father move slowly but inexorably towards death.

When Angela decides that her father is not receiving a satisfactory level of care or support from the National Health Service (NHS) – or, rather, from the bewildering array of different services and subdivisions that she discovers actually constitute it – she goes to see a General Practitioner (GP) to find out what more can be done, having ascertained that 'the gateway to all services was through a willing GP' (Levy 2004a: 88). The doctor that she sees is not only unhelpful but also inconsiderate, patronizing and dismissive; far from helping her to navigate her way through the many layers of bureaucracy before her, he actively contributes to them. While Angela's concern and her desperate desire to care for her father have been evident from early on in the novel, it is at this point that her feelings of helplessness and her sense of frustration with the NHS really begin to crystallize. Significantly, the chapter that immediately follows begins with an episode titled 'THE DOCTOR'; in it, Angela recalls having tonsillitis and being visited by a GP on a day when only she and her father were at home. Winston is keen both to look after his daughter and to make the house as presentable as possible. However, when the doctor arrives she is brusque and condescending; apparently repulsed by the domestic environment that she finds herself in, she is openly disparaging of his efforts to look after his daughter. While she does not say anything explicitly racist, that she asks Winston what food he gives her and speaks to him loudly (Levy 2004: 96–7) suggests that she may harbour preconceptions about the family on account of their being black as much as on account of their being working-class. Whatever the nature of her prejudices, she is quick to assume that Winston is a negligent parent; while this is certainly not the case, he doesn't attempt to correct her, and holds his tongue until she has left the house.

It is no coincidence that this scene from Angela's childhood directly follows her encounter as an adult with a dismissive, arrogant, unhelpful GP; indeed, the later experience appears to have reminded her of the childhood experience. That the two are juxtaposed in the novel in this way may constitute a criticism of the NHS or of the medical profession more broadly, suggesting that it is sometimes the case that the people to whom we look to make the act of caring for a loved one less burdensome can, unfortunately, sometimes make it more so. More significant, however, is what this narrative juxtaposition suggests about memory and intimacy. Even as Angela struggles desperately to be able to care for her father and is frustrated in her attempts to do so, she is brought closer to him through an act of remembering. As a child suffering from tonsillitis and being cared for by her dad, Angela does not fully understand the supercilious attitude of the doctor that attends her, or indeed Winston's anger after she (the doctor) has left their house. However, when faced with another dismissive and disdainful doctor later in life, when her and her father's roles as patient and carer have been reversed, drawing on this particular memory seems to allow her to better understand (albeit belatedly) the anger and frustration that he must have experienced when she was young and in his care. That is, at the same time as

Angela is becoming increasingly conscious of the fact that she is losing her father, she is also coming to better understand who he is; somewhat paradoxically, then, at this point in the novel there is a sense in which she is getting closer to him just as he is becoming more distant to her.

Chapters that recount events from Angela's childhood continue to be arranged in relation to those that describe her father's steady decline, although – in what, it might be said, is a fairly accurate reflection of the nature of memory – the relationship between the two often seems fairly arbitrary. When Winston's leg swells up and he can no longer cope with stairs, he takes to his bed and is visited by a nurse who he repeatedly addresses as 'sister' (Levy 2004a: 110–11). This seems to prompt Angela to recall, in the subsequent chapter, the occasion on which she first met her aunt; that is, Winston's actual, familial sister. When Winston is admitted to casualty (which Beryl mistakenly refers to as 'casuality' (Levy 2004a: 130), thereby giving an unwitting clue as to the rather casual attitude which the NHS seems to adopt towards Winston and his family), Angela finds that her mother seems oddly prepared for her husband's death; when Angela asks her how she feels, she replies 'Oh, a bit funny, a bit funny, [. . .] but that's life. What the Lord giveth, the Lord taketh away' (Levy 2004a: 131). It is on these words that the chapter ends. The subsequent chapter then recounts two key events from Angela's childhood: one titled 'THE NEIGHBOURS' and one titled 'THE SUNDAY SCHOOL'. In the former, Angela recalls the day that she found out that her family's next door neighbours, the Simpsons – a couple who seemed to her so pleasant, accommodating and good-natured that, she confesses, she sometimes wished they were her parents (Levy 2004a: 135) – were, behind closed doors, a deeply unhappy and troubled couple. Unaware that Angela can hear them, the couple scream abuse at each other; Mrs Simpson threatens to leave her husband and, in response, he even threatens to kill her (Levy 2004a: 137). The young Angela pretends not to have overheard anything and does not tell anyone what she has witnessed, but she is clearly shocked by the fierce hostility that she finds concealed underneath the idyllic-looking surface of the Simpsons' marriage. In the next section, Angela recalls being the victim of racist abuse at her local church's Sunday school; a boy who, Angela notes, was himself the victim of bullying insists that she and Ada, another black girl, are both 'dirty'; that 'all darkies are dirty' (Levy 2004a: 144). When the vicar subsequently finds out what has happened, he interrupts his service to deal with the problem but, instead of admonishing the boy responsible, humiliates the victims, forcing Angela and Ada to stand at the front of the church while hymns are sung; as such, he punishes the victims, rather than the perpetrator, of racist abuse.

Significantly, both these episodes seem to be recalled in direct response to the final moments of the preceding chapter. Angela reacts with confusion and disbelief to the calm, collected preparedness with which Beryl awaits Winston's inevitable death, and it is this that seems to prompt her to recall discovering, for the first time, that marriages are often not what they appear (while there is no suggestion in the novel that Winston and Beryl are ever abusive towards each other, the implication is that their marriage is far more complex than Angela had ever realized). In turn, Beryl telling her daughter that 'What the Lord giveth, the Lord taketh away' – a declaration which rings rather hollow – seems to prompt a recollection from Angela's childhood that serves as a reflection on whether religion offers a legitimate source of either meaning or support in traumatic times. It is, of course, one that finds religion and religious institutions lamentably lacking; indeed, they do not seem any more likely to provide help, guidance or enlightenment to Angela's family during Winston's death than they did to the young Angela when she was the victim of racism.

The subsequent chapter describes a visit that Angela pays to her father in hospital. While Winston initially seems to be more cheerful than he has for some time, the hospital's poor conditions – and the negligence and disregard of its staff – soon become apparent. Angela describes the trauma of his being forced to 'shit on the floor like a baby' (Levy 2004a: 150) because of a lack of available nurses, and the nurse who eventually tends to him is thoroughly unmoved by the degradation of the experience. In the following chapter, Angela describes being admitted to hospital herself with scarlet and rheumatic fever at the age of four. She recalls how a doctor tried to examine her and how, after she – absolutely terrified – resisted, he shouted at her aggressively. She then recounts an episode which is titled 'THE POTTY', and which clearly relates to her father's experience; despite young Angela's repeated pleas for help, an irritable nurse refuses to assist her with a bedpan, and she finds herself wedged into it. The ill-tempered nurse then returns to attempt to free her from it:

> She screwed up her face as she tugged. Suddenly I heard a loud sucking noise. The potty flew off my bum and into the air with force. The nurse screamed as the potty spun into the air and emptied its contents all over the bed and her. I laughed. It had turned funny.
>
> 'You should have come sooner', I told her.
>
> 'Oh, shut up', she said, picking at the lumps of shit and putting them back into the potty. (Levy 2004a: 161)

While this scene obviously reflects Winston's experience one chapter earlier and many years later, there is a clear contrast in that he was demeaned by his experience while Angela was rather amused by hers. Significantly, though, the narration of this particular scene at this particular moment seems to afford a kind of retrospective triumph; having watched helplessly as her father underwent such a humiliating experience because of a negligent, uncaring nurse, it seems to be with some pleasure that Angela then recalls subjecting another negligent, uncaring nurse to a similarly humiliating experience. Paradoxically, the narrative structure of the novel here creates a fleeting sense of victory even as it emphasizes Angela's ultimate sense of helplessness. Moreover, the juxtaposition of the two episodes offers a perceptive, poignant account of the paradox of the elderly and infirm becoming childlike; Winston's experience is both similar to and yet tragically dissimilar to that of his four-year-old daughter.

Winston's final progression towards death is narrated alongside, and in counterpoint to, Angela's coming to maturity. She recalls his attempt to commit suicide – that is, his loss of any kind of hope whatsoever about the future (Levy 2004a: 178) – directly before she recalls developing distinct aspirations and hopes about her own future (Levy 2004a: 179–92). A scene showing Winston at his very weakest, barely able to sip from a cup of tea (Levy 2004a: 203), is juxtaposed with one showing him at his most tyrannical; having found his daughter kissing a boy in the doorway of the family home, he bellows furiously at her until she weeps and tells him that she hates him (Levy 2004a: 207–9). While much of the novel is devoted to Angela's happy memories of her father, here she engages with her least pleasant memories of him, and the striking contrast between Winston as a tyrant and as frail and incapacitated movingly emphasizes Angela's sense of his decline and his impending death as being somehow inconceivable. When Winston's condition worsens still further, Beryl and Angela decide that he needs to be moved to a hospice. In between this decision being made and Angela actually trying to make the necessary arrangements, though, an episode from her late teens is recalled. Titled 'THE MOVE' (217), it recounts Winston proudly announcing that he, Beryl and Angela – who, by this point, is the only one of their children to still be living with them – are going to be moving to a new house. To his disappointment, Angela informs him that she is looking into getting a flat with her college friends, and both her parents are rather hurt that she is planning to leave them. The narrative then shifts back to Angela making arrangements for her father to move to a hospice:

> I felt a sudden panic. My dad would have to know that I wanted to put him in a hospice. He'd think I'd given up on him, that I now wanted him to die. He said he didn't want to go, not yet. Would he want to be somewhere where all that was expected of him was that he leave this life? I saw him looking at me, as he realized he was being sent to die. A final betrayal. (Levy 2004a: 227)

While Angela moving out of her parents' house may seem to have little connection with her father moving into a hospice, both episodes find her wrestling with feelings of guilt even though she is convinced that she is doing the right thing. Moreover, in both cases she worries that her father either feels or will feel abandoned by her, and this implicitly gestures towards the sense of abandonment that she is going to experience herself when he finally passes away.

Owing to the absurdities of NHS bureaucracy, Angela and Beryl discover that Winston cannot go directly from hospital to hospice and must first return to the family home; upon bringing him home, however, they quickly find that they simply cannot care for him adequately there. A scene titled 'THE VISITOR' then follows in which Winston has, again, returned to the family home, albeit in rather different circumstances: it transpires that he has been to the Midlands to see his identical twin Louis. It is in this scene that Angela, at the age of 25 (Levy 2004a: 236), learns for the first time that her father even has a twin. Understandably, she reacts with some surprise:

> 'I never knew you were an identical twin, Dad. I never knew that – you never told me.'
>
> 'Oh, I never told you?' he said. 'Well, now you know.' He smiled.
>
> 'How was he then? God, I can't believe this', I said. 'And he lives in this
>
> country, but we've never seen him?'
>
> 'We lost touch, but, you see, he was ill so that's why they contact me. He wanted to see me, so I went', he said.
>
> 'He's ill – what's wrong with him?'
>
> My dad curled his mouth up and said, 'Lung cancer', quietly. He looked away from me and stubbed out his cigarette. He stood up and went to the sink.
>
> 'Do you want a cup of tea, Anne?'
>
> 'Is he in hospital?'
>
> 'He was', he said.
>
> 'What, is he out now then?' I asked.
>
> 'No, Anne – he died.'
>
> I sat back in my chair. This conversation was brief, but condensed. First, I find out that I have an uncle in this country. Second, that he's my dad's identical twin and lastly, that he is dead. I had learnt more about my dad in those few minutes than in most of the years that got me to that point. (Levy 2004a: 236–7)

While this episode pre-dates Winston becoming ill, this seems to be the moment at which Angela consciously acknowledges for the first time in her life that her father will himself one day die, with the image of his identical twin dying of cancer foreshadowing Winston's own death (perhaps particularly so given that the presence of a cigarette is noted). While Angela excitedly reports that she learnt more about her dad from this single conversation than she did during whole years of living with him, one of the things that she seems to learn about him here is that he is not going to live forever. Here, the joy of getting to know one's parent as a fellow adult is subtly linked to the pain of recognizing their mortality.

In the penultimate chapter of the novel, Levy touchingly describes the last time Angela saw her father before his death. As he cries out in pain and raves frantically to people who are not present, she is ashamed to discover that she is angry with him for refusing to die 'gracefully, with dignity'; for dying 'kicking and screaming, being pulled from life, being robbed' (Levy 2004a: 243). After he has passed away, she and her mother go to see his corpse, and a particularly poignant moment captures the seeming impossibility of Winston's trajectory from, in Angela's view, all-powerful protector to lifeless corpse: 'I sat on the other side of his bed and laid my hand on top of his. His hand that I always held to cross the road' (Levy 2004a: 248).

While it is in this penultimate chapter that Winston's death occurs, it is the following, final chapter which is titled 'THE DEATH'. Here, the novel returns for the final time to the narrative of Angela's youth, and while (as above) this narrative has not been arranged chronologically, this does seem to be one of the latest episodes (if not the latest) recalled as part of that narrative. There is the sense that the final chapter of the novel brings this narrative to a moment that occurs not very much before Winston's retirement nor, hence, very much before the beginning of the chronologically later narrative that began in the second chapter of the novel. As such, in its final stages *Every Light in the House Burnin'* comes to assume a somewhat cyclic narrative form that is satisfying even while it is devastating.

The final chapter describes Beryl's concern for the missing family cat for which Winston has a particular fondness. She worries that it 'went somewhere to die' (Levy 2004a: 250), and the parallel with the previous chapter and with Winston's going somewhere to die is obvious. The singularity of 'THE DEATH' suggests that this is Angela's only experience of death before her father's, and the juxtaposition of these two chapters serves to question the degree to which one death has prepared her for the other. While there is certainly an emphasis on the inability of her earlier experience to prepare her for her bereavement, there is also, nonetheless, an emphasis on the importance of drawing on one's memories in order to better make sense of traumatic experiences. Beryl tells Angela that, with great surprise, she saw Winston cry for the first time ever when he realized that the cat might have died. He is also, Beryl reports, anxious to give the cat a dignified burial: 'He's taken the day off work just to look for her. He says even if he can just find her body, at least he can give her a decent burial. Says he can't stand the thought of her being eaten or chased or something nasty happening to her' (Levy 2004a: 250). Paradoxically, Winston's anxiety that the cat should have a peaceful, dignified death both recalls and foreshadows Angela's anxiety (later in life but earlier in the novel) over the manner of *his* death. While it is clear that the death of a family cat can certainly never prepare Angela for the death of her father, crucially, the revelation of her father's grieving – surprising even to Beryl after decades of marriage to Winston – *does* seem both to help prepare Angela for her own grieving and to bring her closer to her father even as she finally loses him.

In its final moments, then, *Every Light in the House Burnin'* asserts that even though our personal memories cannot always adequately prepare us for traumatic experiences, those memories *do* help us to give meaning to traumatic experiences, and vice versa. This is, I suggest, by far the most important sense in which Levy's first novel prefigures her later work, in which the significance of engaging with the past is increasingly emphasized. It might be noted that the narrative structure of Levy's first novel prefigures that of her second, *Never Far from Nowhere* (1996), in which chapters are alternately narrated by two sisters. Indeed, much as the later novel takes two sisters who often refuse to see eye-to-eye and places them in dialogue with each other, the narrative form of Levy's debut novel takes two sets of memories which are not only distant from each other but also, at times, discordant, and places them into dialogue with each other. While the novel has at its centre a struggle to come to terms with a death – that is, with someone coming to exist only in the past – it is a work which itself enacts a struggle to exist in more than one 'plane of time'.

# CHAPTER FOUR

# The Immediacy of *Small Island*

## DAVID JAMES

**Chapter Summary:** *Small Island* has often been hailed as a virtuosic example of historical realism, as a novel that submerges the reader in past experiences through striking period details and the authentically rendered attitudes and voices of its narrators. Reading against the grain of Levy's own strong identification with realist writing, this chapter pursues instead a series of close readings of *Small Island* that reveal how inventive Levy can be at the level of syntax, diction and rhythm. Here the reading experience itself plays a key role in interpretation, as Levy creates a sense of immediacy that leads to our intense involvement in events, a sense of involvement that is at the same time often qualified when our full sympathetic identification with characters is forestalled. The chapter explores the extent to which Levy has it both ways: involving us in the experience of events without necessarily provoking our empathy. By developing this closer appreciation of just how emotive Levy's syntax can be – even as she gives us pause in our desire to empathize with narrators who so intimately address us – we can begin to understand how involvement and distantiation, immersion and impartiality coexist in crucial ways that highlight how *Small Island* cultivates ethical forms of response.

Shower time. What could be more mundane, more utterly routine, more unworthy of serious historical treatment and imaginative investment? Not so, for Andrea Levy. A writer who has often, and rightly, garnered praise for her treatment of some of the most profound and enduring legacies of empire, Levy nonetheless refuses to overlook the incidental. To re-illuminate unexceptional emotions and events is for her not to turn away from historical gravities, but to immerse us with greater intensity in the lived texture of the past. Hence, shower time. An event that could easily have been side-lined in the portrait of Hortense's first days at teacher training college, but which in the early stages of *Small Island* offers a set-piece exemplifying the linguistic dynamism Levy achieves across this novel, a dynamism that arguably distinguishes it from her earlier fiction. 'I don't have a magic realist bone in my body', attests Levy (2009: 328). But the scene in question nonetheless pushes the envelope of realism as such, exhibiting a rhetorical magic of its own as it moves from the oneiric to the everyday:

> Michael was holding his closed hand out to me. This fully grown man with stubble hair piercing the skin of his chin was grinning on me as a schoolboy would. Opening his hand he revealed, resting in his palm, an ink-black scorpion, its tail erect and curled. I wanted to warn him of the danger of its murderous sting, but no words would come. I moved to strike the insect from his palm but my arm was being pulled away. Someone had my wrist clasped in their hand as tight as vine round a tree.
>
> I had never had such a rude awakening. The cover on my bed was pulled back. I could not for a moment remember where I had laid my head to sleep. I was revealed half naked on the mattress – my nightdress rolled and twisted at my waist with the movement of my dreams. I was being pulled so hard I could do nothing but follow. My feet fumbled for solid floor as I tugged at my nightdress to hide my shame. And before I was entirely convinced I was no longer dreaming I found myself running for my life. (Levy 2004: 54)

The first sentence – which is itself the start of a new section, meaning that we're plunged without context into the image described – involves us directly in Hortense's dream, with Michael's presence and actions tracked with a verbal frankness that makes them seem all the more present, actual, suspenseful. We're given a vividly intimate depiction of his physiognomy, the observation of which blends trepidation and flirtation – a blend of moods into cautious excitement that's reciprocated phonetically by the cheekily nimble rhymes of 'skin', 'chin' and 'grin' that bounce the sentence towards its endearing simile. This playful idiom shifts – tonality is always prone to do so in dreams, of course – with the revelation of the scorpion, a creature at once ordinary and unavoidably archetypal. Upping the tempo, the subsequent two subject- and verb-led sentences reflect the urgency and mounting exasperation of Hortense's mute immobility in this dreamworld: their galloping qualifying clauses ('but no words would come', 'but my arm was being pulled away') carry an iambic pulse that creates a level of phrasal acceleration, embodying metrically Hortense's consternation. What is only the second simile of the paragraph is then reserved for the sentence that bridges her dream and harsh actuality: the juxtaposition of trochee and iamb invite us to pause momentarily over that image of a 'vine round a tree', an image that's not only suitably visceral but appropriately non-human, thereby anticipating Hortense's impression of her 'rude awakening' as something impersonal, involuntary, inhumane. Percussively composed almost exclusively from single clauses, the ensuing paragraph unfolds through a succession of subject-led sentences with proliferating negatives – 'never', 'not', 'nothing', 'no longer' – which together amplify Hortense's account of helpless bewilderment. The action itself is as visceral again as the dream, though now devoid of any embellishing simile. For this time, it's the alliterative combination of fricative verb and noun that effectively conveys the thump and tumble of Hortense's exertion, as her 'feet fumbled for solid floor'.

All of which makes this scene sound more solemn than it is. And that's the risk with close reading: you end up sucking the animating life from the very tonal and rhetorical intricacies you're trying to do justice to. In observing the way it's constructed, that is, we're in danger of missing how this account of Hortense's unceremonious trip to the washroom is comic in its commotion, traumatic though she recalls it to be. Which is of course the point: Levy re-conjures in all its immediacy the fear and confusion of Hortense's younger self, preserving the vividness of the emotions conveyed from mediation and potential censorship by adult recollection.

Why might this quality of immediacy be important and what scale of analysis should we adopt to appreciate how it matters for Levy? Furthermore, how do we as readers relate to this immediacy? Is it simply a matter of involvement and sympathetic connection? Or does Levy try to have it both ways, by involving us in the experience of events in all their sensory and social detail without necessarily provoking the reader's empathy? In other words, might involvement and distantiation, immersion and impartiality coexist in this novel for significant ends? I pose these questions because, first, such issues to do with the phenomenology of style and our reactions to it haven't been addressed as explicitly as they deserve to be in critical work on Levy so far, and secondly, because the nature of our relationship with this novel's language points to a complexity of readerly response that allows us to complicate *Small Island*'s generic affinity with historical realism. Part of this essay will be given over to elucidating why an attention to the rhetorical textures of Levy's work doesn't usually take centre-stage. Punctuating this discussion with textual readings, I'll take some initial steps towards redressing what I perceive to be something of an imbalance in criticism on Levy that has resulted in the thematics of memory and perspective taking precedence over more localized elements of composition. This counterbalancing approach could fruitfully be pursued for earlier novels too; but it has particular implications for engaging with *Small Island*, a text that marks a considerable stylistic shift in gear for Levy's writing. Very much the product of her own willingness to be more audacious with form after serving on the judging panels for the Orange Prize in 1997 and Orange Prize Futures in 2001, *Small Island* showcases a greater sense of daring, a more explicit risk-taking, not only at the level of image and voice but also at the level of syntax and rhythm – components, I suggest, that are crucial to the novel's success at realizing the arresting immediacy of the historical events it delineates.

Indeed, it's this immediacy, as already hinted, that allows Levy to press beyond the conventions of straightforward historical fiction, inhabiting voices rather than recording facts. Where choice of mode is concerned, this has proved decisive: 'To have something in the first person', Levy asserts, 'where you are seeing something entirely from somebody else's point of view, I just think is more dynamic' (2009: 334). That dynamism hasn't gone unnoticed by reviewers. Mike Phillips partly construed it as a measure of authenticity in his original piece for *The Guardian*, arguing that 'If ever there was a novel which offered a historically faithful account of how its characters thought and behaved, this is it' (Phillips 2004: n.p.). But he qualified this estimation, indicating that *Small Island*'s success had to do with something other than historical accuracy alone. To Phillips, it wasn't just Levy's research but 'her imagination' that 'illuminates old stories in a way that almost persuades you she was there at the time' (Phillips 2004: n.p.). This qualification highlights why it might be important for us to recognize the difference between a writer's fidelity to the facts and her skill at imaginative amplification, offering us a fruitful premise for thinking about what's at stake for Levy in 'creat[ing] a style which reproduces the rhythm and content of her characters' speech' (Phillips, 2004: n.p.). It's from this premise that I want to work, in order to suggest – in contrast to a good deal of criticism on *Small Island* praising its manipulation of viewpoint and its intimate, period-specific details of an emerging post-imperial consciousness – that we entertain how the novel renders the immediacy of characters' emotions and situations at a more micro-level, by considering syntax instead of structure, focusing on phrase over form, listening to acoustic resonance rather than tracing architectural design.

While in Sukhdev Sandhu's view (and his praise is representative), Levy maintains 'a plain, homely style, one that is keen for us to attend to the subtle shifts and twists that its characters undergo' (Sandhu 2004: n.p.), *Small Island* invites us to dig a little deeper and ask whether Levy's language really is as 'homely' as it seems – or as is critically assumed. One pay-off of my localized analyses of style will hopefully be to paint an alternative portrait of Levy as a self-professed realist – one that suggests how we might refine a modified notion of that very category – whose inventiveness as a historical novelist is paradoxically due to the way she makes culturally distinct and racially particularized experiences feel so immediate and emotionally tangible for contemporary readers.

Getting in touch with *Small Island* at this linguistic and affective level need not be incompatible with the convincing cases that critics have made for recognizing Levy's handling of larger narrative elements, namely perspective and episodic structure. Indeed, any judicious reading of the novel needs to acknowledge its moving account – facilitated and refracted by Levy's multi-perspectival narration – of the disappointments and deprivations that befall Caribbean immigrants who at mid-century were encountering a hostile Britain. How readers relate to

Levy's multiplication of viewpoints has become a key area of interest. In moving across her *oeuvre*, Michael Perfect, for instance, draws attention to her novels' 'increasing engagement with the legacy of imperialism and their increasing narrative polyvocality' (Perfect 2010: 32). Alert to the interpretive ramifications of *Small Island*'s manifold organization, Perfect astutely observes that: 'In the privileged position of having the four protagonists' different accounts alongside each other – of having them presented contrapuntally by the novel – the reader is able to discern connections between them of which they remain ignorant' (Perfect 2010: 39). A consequence of this hermeneutic 'privilege' is that we move beyond straightforward sympathy, as Levy compels us to at least negotiate, even if we don't firmly adopt, a series of evaluative and impartial standpoints towards characters' decisions and actions. As such, Perfect reminds us of the novel's 'rather unsettling ending' (a climax that's certainly more ambivalent than the flash-forward drawing the BBC adaptation to its nostalgic close), and he argues that 'if the child born at the end of the novel is ultimately representative of a new, post-war, post-*Windrush* generation, the implication is that this generation will never fully recognise the complexity of its own history – and so never understand its own, subsequent contemporary moment – because of a failure of conflicting voices to become dialogic voices' (Perfect 2010: 40).

Aspects of this disquieting failure of dialogue and reciprocity are dramatized in the scene of arrival and immediate alienation recounted by Gilbert, where he and his fellow servicemen struggle to reconcile the idea and projected image of the 'mother country' from the socially and environmentally austere realm that greets them. However, the gesture of dialogic sympathy is there nonetheless. Or at the very least, it is attempted rhetorically, as Gilbert turns to his implied audience. His mode of address, angled straight at the reader, somewhat counteracts the prevailing tenor of mutual misrecognition and incompatibility that Perfect sees as a symptom of the novel's polyphony. In the face of that kind of failure of empathic connection, we hear from Gilbert: 'Let me ask you to imagine this. Living far from you is a beloved relation whom you have never met. Yet this relation is so dear a kin she is known as Mother' (Levy 2004: 116). With this thought-experiment in place, we're then asked to picture the following scene of demoralization:

Some of the boys shook their heads, sucking their teeth with their first long look at England. Not disappointment – it was the squalid shambles that made them frown so. There was a pained gasp at every broken-down scene they encountered. The wreckage of this bombed and ruined place stumbled along streets like a devil's windfall. Other boys looking to the gloomy, sunless sky, their teeth chattering uncontrolled, gooseflesh rising on their naked arms, questioned if this was the only warmth to be felt from an English summer. Small islanders gaped like simpletons at white women who worked hard on the railway swinging their hammers and picks like the strongest man. Women who sent as much cheek back to those whistling boys as they received themselves. (Levy 2004: 116–17)

While the affective function of this episode is to convey alienation and – despite what Gilbert says – inevitable 'disappointment', its affective immediacy has less to do with what Anouk Lang calls 'the novel's focus on the culturally contingent limitations of perspective' (Lang 2009: 129), than on the invitation for us to 'imagine this' perspective as our own, almost as though we're a shadowing witness. Almost, but not quite. The catalogue of responses – the 'pained gasp', the 'gloomy' sky reflecting pathetically the men's gathering despondency – is relayed not through our direct alignment with observations of others' perspectives but through our bearing witness to the reactions Gilbert recalls. Levy thus strategically denies full identification. Here, as elsewhere, she advances a distinctly implicating, if not collaborative, form of realism that none-theless alerts us to our distance from the situations described. The mode of address (aided, in this passage, by the second-person 'you') summons readers to hypothesize the scenario for themselves while making appar-ent the limits of empathy. A degree of immediacy in such a scene is thus sustained without depending at the same time upon a degree of empathic identification that bridges the historical distance between characters' reactions and the reader's own.

At the heart of this collaborative realism lies Levy's facility with lan-guage. Where much critical attention, as I've noted, has been drawn to the novel's perspectival construction, the vitality of *Small Island*'s expres-sive articulation, at the level of the sentence, has been somewhat down-played. As for Gilbert's dispirited troops, so in the case of Queenie's dispossessed Londoners, we're given a first-hand account that isn't sim-ply a recollection but rather a reanimation of a shared spectacle:

> Sometimes they were still smouldering like a burnt pie pulled from an oven. The pungent stench of smoke, the dust from rubble steaming off them. Shuffling in or being carried. Some wrapped in blankets, their clothes having gone flying off with the blast. Blackened, sooty faces, red-rimmed, sunken eyes with whites that suddenly flashed, startled, to look around them agog like they'd stumbled on to another planet. And shivering, there was so much shivering.
>
> Population, we called them at the rest centre. The bombed-out who'd had the cheek to live through the calamity of a world blown to bits. (Levy 2004: 230)

The 'burnt pie' simile might seem bathetic or somehow – inappropri-ately – comic in the circumstances. But the bluntness of the comparative image, posed straight from the shoulder, befits Queenie's uncompromis-ing way of announcing what she sees and her unpretentious allegiance to imparting how unusual, how unimaginable, in short, just how *beyond* description were the events she's retrospectively depicting. Yet that simile itself takes second place to the vibrancy of Levy's phonics, as sounds within clauses contribute to the sense – and indeed sensation – of the scene as it unfolds. Nowhere in the novel are there so many sibilant phrases that rasp in alliterative constellations of adjectives and verbs, engaging the senses on both visual and olfactory levels – from the 'stench of smoke', to the 'sooty faces' and unnerving glances that 'suddenly flashed, startled'. Interspersing this sibilance, however, is the more deadening labial ricochet of associated adjectives – 'burn', 'blackened' – which resonate, of course, with the very governing cause of this pitiable spectacle: 'the blast'. The final sentence offers a reprise of these plosive acoustics in summarizing the prospect of the homeless as a 'population' who've acquired a new collective noun, 'The bombed-out' – not 'blown to bits', but uprooted and domestically dismembered nonetheless.

As in the case of Gibert's evocative picture of bewilderment in encountering England's austerity, here we're again invited to participate fully in the episode's pathos without presuming to identify empathically with such a 'population', one whose 'desperation made them seem like the feckless', the tragic sight of whom confirms for Queenie that she 'would never forgive Hitler for turning human beings into that' (Levy 2004: 231). Description – at both semantic and acoustic levels – vivifies this scene of displacement. But our position is one of an onlooker, for whom the process of witnessing entails an acknowledgement of necessary detachment. In this respect, perhaps the stance of her reader complements Levy's own, as her 'reliance on historical fact', as Mike Phillips puts it, affords her 'a distance' which at the same time still 'allows her to be both passionate and compassionate' (Phillips 2004: n.p.).

Structurally focused readings of *Small Island* are likely to miss this doubleness, this combination of compassion and distance. A curious blend of immediacy and qualified involvement, it's a manner of engagement that seems distributed between narrator and audience, linking in timbre the novel's description and its reception. That's not to say Levy has necessarily suffered from a critical preoccupation with broader characterological and organizational aspects of *Small Island*'s reconstruction of memories. Far from it: these features have become the substance of consistent praise. But it does tend to re-inscribe the view that Levy's alternations in temporality and perspective are the most innovative things she attempts in a novel that's otherwise 'largely realist', in Lang's phrase, 'and without much formal inventiveness' (Lang 2009: 139). Lang may be right to conclude that '*Small Island* is likely to be of less interest to literary critics than denser and more overtly stylized texts' (Lang 2009: 139). Yet that depends on our criteria for what counts as admirable stylization, and it depends too on how readerly 'interest' is attributed. Still, Lang is not alone in being underwhelmed by Levy's outlook where form's concerned. John Mullan for one suggests that *Small Island*'s apparent flair has been naturalized, made palatable by contemporary readers' familiarity with televisual conventions. Once upon a time, argues Mullan, 'this elaborate structure – both multiple narrators and a back-and-forth movement in time – might have seemed disconcerting, but the huge popularity of *Small Island* suggests that readers have found it no special challenge' (Mullan 2011: n.p.). What we can draw from this, according to Mullan, is that 'the narrative tricks of film and TV have made us more receptive to such formal complexities' (Mullan 2011: n.p.).

But this hunch about Levy's approachability relies upon an assumption that readers' principal challenges, pleasurable or otherwise, in confronting her fiction typically have to do with structure. It also relies upon the conviction that the most innovative aspect of *Small Island* is its temporal oscillations and episodic arrangement, over and above more discreet components of grammar or diction of the kind I've been considering here. In contrast, Lang's valuable research drawn from the *Small Island* Read 2007 initiative pursues a less speculative and generalizing account of Levy's transparency – including the features that complicate presumptions about the novel offering 'no special challenge'. For Lang, in fact, Levy gives us a far-from-comfortable ride, as the 'complexity of characters on both sides of the race divide prevents readers from settling into an easy identification with either' (Lang 2009: 134). Lang rightly implies that the novel is more about the 'limitations of perspective' than about our unquestioning acceptance of any one point of view as providing a historically authentic lens on racial conflict. 'While shifts in narrative perspective', notes Lang, 'appeared to offer readers a decodable pleasure, they also served as an impediment for others' (Lang 2009: 136).

Yet if Levy doesn't encourage us to identify in any stable way with the social and personal situations evoked, then we certainly are involved with *how* those situations are emotively relayed. Immediacy in evocation is substituted for empathy, as we've seen, as though Levy solicits our immersion, our participation ('let me ask you to imagine this'), without presuming our compassion for a particular character's position is either inevitable or sustainable. This facet of solicitation becomes all the more problematic, of course, when we encounter Bernard. Someone who, as Blake Morrison notes, receives 'a kind of sympathetic or certainly understanding portrait', Bernard proved to be among the most difficult voices for Levy to ventriloquize (Levy, 2009: 331). As she admits, 'I think in order to write a character like him, I truly did have empathy', for Bernard is 'somebody who has grown up in a society where they have been told they are the greatest creature on the planet – a white Englishman' (Levy 2009: 331). In creating such a character, Levy had to put herself in a position where she could 'really see how [serving in a foreign country] would be incredibly disturbing and how one way of dealing with it is to find the Other and hate them. That's how racism works' (Levy 2009: 331). Inviting our 'understanding' towards Bernard – deeply unsettling though that sense of potential pity remains in light of his irascibility, intolerance and racial ignorance – turns out to be part of Levy's ethically purposive strategy of instruction: 'You can't get rid of something unless you truly look at it in the face and try and understand it. That's not to say that I'm sympathetic – there's absolutely no sympathy there – but I do see how it can come about. And I think it's important to see how it can come about' (Levy: 2009: 331).

Interestingly, Levy makes a pointed distinction here between empathy and sympathy. She implies that you can empathize with an attitude you abhor without excusing it, whereas to sympathize with such a mind-set is to grant it a measure of reprieve. What she seems to want us to cultivate, then, is a self-interrogative strain of empathy, one that's alert to the risks of misplaced compassion, a variety of empathy Levy particularly encourages in episodes featuring Bernard. In these scenes, his frustration and desensitization is vividly rendered; but this immediacy prompts a sort of critical involvement from readers that carries its own affective sanctions. For we know the perspective to which we're privy belongs to bigotry, however pitiable the physical situation turns out to be, especially when Bernard conveys the circumstances of his subservience in the face of his senior officers' ineptitude. This helpless situation of compliance with the farce of military disorganization provokes a momentarily charitable reading of someone who we know is unforgiving towards cultural and racial otherness:

> The army CO turned out to be useless. His idea of pinpointing was to wave his arms about in the general direction of the hills. 'Have you got a more precise bearing, sir?' Maxi (diplomat) asked cautiously.
>
> One indecisive finger flicked instead. 'You'll need a mule', he told us.
>
> 'Have you got one we could use, sir?'
>
> 'No.'
>
> Maxi threw me a look I quickly caught. Sometimes it was hard to understand we were fighting a war together, side by side with these khaki chaps. He left us with a curt warning, 'Watch out up there. Jap patrol was spotted earlier', before waving us off.
>
> Looks like curly cabbage from afar, the forest on the hills. Harmless. Playful. Think you could fall and bounce on it. Soon change your mind. Slashing through dark, wet, stinking undergrowth. Painfully slowly. Ticks dropping bloody inside my shirt. Flies sipping on the moisture in my eyes. Mosquitoes massing thick as cloth. The relief at seeing the track the fallen plane had made had Maxi and me hugging like goal scorers. Not too far away, we both agreed. Still took us hours, though. Tunnelling through the undergrowth – each step as hard won as a miner with his coal. Would Queenie have recognised her husband now? (Levy 2004: 290–1)

Exhaustion, frustration, the boredom borne by pointless exertion under the pretence of strategic military advancement – these are among the emotive inflections captured here by Levy's curt, paratactic syntax. Pronouns drop away from leading clauses, such that sentences begin instead either with active, directly visual verbs ('slashing', 'tunnelling'), or by giving primacy to the grim fauna Bernard endures ('Ticks', 'Flies', 'Mosquitoes'). Listing such elements, Levy could have in another scene blunted their effect; but here the catalogue of life on the forest floor enhances, as a grammatical vehicle, the sensory content it conveys. Similarly, the unfolding accumulation of adjectives ('dark', 'wet', 'stinking') offers in its dull thud a rhythmic analogue for how 'painfully slowly' these men progress. 'Would Queenie have recognised her husband now?' is a question obliquely suggested to Levy's readers as well. That is, do we still recognize Bernard for what he is, xenophobic and discriminatory? Or does our partaking in his experiences – thanks to what I've been calling Levy's collaborative realism – solicit our 'understanding', in Blake Morrison's words, fully aware though we are that his habitual prejudice and austerity are inexcusable?

Such are the questions Levy poses to the sort of reader who suspects that *Small Island* isn't merely an easily digestible historical novel, and who's willing to countenance that some of the less conspicuous ingredients of its discourse might actually belie a degree of inventiveness, of expressivity, that's quite free of the realist proviso to convey facts with transparency and mimetic fidelity. Levy's realism, I've suggested, is far from transparent: not because it somehow fabricates or embellishes the historical realities it reconstructs, but because its manner of articulation dramatically contributes to the affective force with which *Small Island*'s personal histories are re-lived for us from the perspectives of its narrators. Each of these figures, in his or her own way, comes across as an absorbing and persuasive stylist of personal testimony – none is a slave to reportage or a mere impartial mouthpiece for social documentary. As such, their voices contribute to the novel becoming 'an event', as Derek Attridge has conceptualized it, 'an event that occurs in a medium' (Attridge 2011: 333). By attending closely to the constitution of this aesthetic medium – in Levy's case, the rhetorical warp and weft of her narration – 'the pleasure we experience as participants in the event is a pleasure in the medium itself as it reveals some of its powers and possibilities' (Attridge 2011: 333). This participatory experience is equivalent to, indeed a component of, Levy's collaborative realism: she invites readers to negotiate complex gradations of pity and distance, compassion and critique, amusement and discomfiture – all of which are components informing, rather than detracting from, the way we admire how scenes are visually and tactilely realized.

Were we to look for an episode that appears not only to encapsulate these dynamics of attention and detachment but to stage them diegetically, unfurling them within the very fabric of events, then we would do worse than to turn to the morning after Queenie's night of lovemaking with Michael. Arthur discovers Michael's wallet. Hiding her guilt,

Queenie zeros in on its contents. Her patient notation of the wallet's aura is itself an enticement for close reading, dramatizing a lingering attentiveness to resonant elements, a gradual perception of the object's facets from various angles that Levy's own prose has been inviting and deserving:

> He'd found a battered leather wallet that Sergeant Michael Roberts must have mislaid or forgotten in his rush to get away. There were photographs in its tattered inside. One of an old negro man standing formally in front of a house. Looking to all the world like a chimpanzee in clothes, this lord of the manor stood behind a seated black woman with white hair and a face as grumpy as Monday morning. Another was of a little darkie girl with fuzzy-wuzzy hair tied in ribbons as big as bandages. They were like any airman's photos, dog eared and fading with sentiment. The wallet must have fallen from his jacket when he was rummaging for his war-time weapons of seduction – his tin of ham, his orange. But there was something about its tattiness that let you know this wallet had been places. Stuffed into a pocket, jammed into a kit-bag, sheltered in a hat. It was so beloved its preciousness warmed my fingers as I held it. It might even have been his good-luck charm. I was told that most flyers had them – that they weren't safe flying without them. This was Michael Robert's fortune and it had no place lying in my hand. So I dressed quickly with the idea of catching him at the station, handing it to him before it was too late. (Levy 2004: 249–50)

The blend of offensive similes ('a chimpanzee in clothes', 'a face as grumpy as Monday morning') is counterpointed with the sincerity of Queenie's tenderness towards this most irreplaceable of possessions. This sets the tone for what is an uncomfortable juxtaposition in this scene of latent prejudice and plaintive endearment. Our mind's eye is immediately drawn to an object bearing the impress of nostalgia. Both 'battered' and 'tattered', it attracts a loving attention from Queenie, yet her respect for the wallet's gravity as a 'good-luck charm' sits discordantly alongside her ethnic stereotypes. This braid of attitudes, whereby respectfulness weaves with unquestioned racial clichés, invites our cautious involvement. For Queenie's detailed reconstruction of a kind of biography for the wallet – imagining it 'stuffed into a pocket, jammed into a kit-bag, sheltered in a hat' – is undeniably moving, not least because her affection toward something just found emblematizes the 'preciousness' of the person she's effectively lost. The pathos of this loss is compounded further by a chain of associations, linking the bygone moments captured in the photos to her raw and more proximate memories of Michael. Thus despite her reduction of race to alterity, the sentimentality Queenie identifies in the 'dog-eared' pictures becomes movingly applicable to her too as she resolves to follow Michael, for 'the idea of catching him' seems as contingent upon that same sense of 'fortune' that the wallet itself serves – a wishful prospect of reunion whose likelihood is already 'fading'.

What we have, then, surfacing from amid the bric-a-brac of everyday things, is another sequence of the kind that I've been tracing in *Small Island* where Levy solicits simultaneously sympathetic and qualified reactions. Queenie's affecting response to this seemingly mundane object – just like Hortense's recollection of the humdrum affair of bathing with which we began – is portrayed with as much emotive immediacy and linguistic verve as any of the novel's more obviously dramatic, pathetic, or erotic scenes. Apparently incidental details catalyse insights, as we've seen elsewhere; but here, the episode contains the germ of a larger metacritical invitation. That is to say, might the sort of attention Queenie confers on the wallet, on all that it encapsulates and memorializes for the life of another, be itself a model of critical intentness? Is there – in a scene where our full and unequivocal identification with the narrator is once again unsettled, where Queenie both deciphers (in effect, close-reads) an object that she knows she can never fully possess – is there a simulation of the very combination of involvement, humility and necessary detachment that could be crucial to approaching this novel in its entirety?

Sukhdev Sandhu prophetically concluded in his *Telegraph* review of *Small Island* that 'One can easily see it being turned into a popular drama.' His implication here is that Levy had written a novel already ripe for adaptation, if the opportunity came, precisely because 'It's neither splashy nor experimental' (Sandhu 2004: n.p.). In questioning this impression of the novel – one that confuses its candour and directness with its author's supposed will-to-accessibility – the case I've tried to make is certainly not for revisiting *Small Island* as somehow covertly experimental, as if it's productive to read Levy counter-intuitively against the grain of her own ostensibly realist sensibility. Rather, there *is* a case to be made for re-examining a novel that on closer inspection – by adopting a smaller ambit of analysis, by moving beyond matters of structure and historical verisimilitude alone, by appreciating the buoyancy of her syntax and subtle radiance of diction – is more inventive than it might otherwise appear to be. That way, in turn, we have a good chance of seeing how Levy can usefully belie and challenge a greater array of preconceptions about contemporary realism than we might well have expected.

# CHAPTER FIVE

# *Small Island*, Small Screen:
# Adapting Black British Fiction

## RACHEL CARROLL

**Chapter Summary:** This chapter will situate the 2009 BBC television adaptation of Andrea Levy's *Small Island* within two critical contexts: the first concerns the production of cultural value within contemporary literary culture and the second concerns the representation of black British identity and history in television drama. It will suggest that the novel's adoption by the *Small Island* Read in 2007 is a key reference point when analysing this adaptation; a mass public reading event designed to commemorate the abolition of the slave trade, this project enlisted the novel in specific 'cultural work' (Fuller and Procter 2009: 26). The introduction of a contemporary narrative framework to the adaptation of Levy's novel can be considered in this context; more specifically, this chapter will explore the ways in which this strategy serves to orient a historical fiction towards the future and to construct the birth of a mixed-race child as the origin of a multicultural present.

In her 2012 study *The Adaptation Industry: The Cultural Economy of Contemporary Literary Adaptation*, Simone Murray suggests that 'the processes by which contemporary literary fiction is created, published, marketed, evaluated for literary prizes and adapted for the screen have lacked sustained academic attention' (Murray 2012: 11). Murray is not alone in arguing for the study of contemporary literary culture to be extended beyond the purely textual; James F. English's analysis of the cultural economy of the literary prize (2005), Claire Squires's study of the marketing of contemporary writing (2009) and Jim Collins's examination of shifting categories of literary and popular taste (2010) all provide new frameworks for the analysis of twenty-first century fiction which foreground questions of cultural value extrinsic to the text itself.[1] In this context, this chapter seeks to combine an appreciation of the significance of extra-textual contexts with close interpretative analysis of a

literary adaptation; more specifically, it aims to explore how such contexts can inform the reception of black British fiction through a focus on
the 2009 BBC television adaptation of Andrea Levy's 2004 novel *Small
Island*.

In 2007, Levy's prize-winning novel was selected for a mass reading
event designed to engage the British public in the historical commemo-
ration of the abolition of the slave trade; half a million copies of the novel
were distributed to book clubs hosted in major port cities whose histories are widely recognized to be implicated in the Atlantic slave trade
(namely Liverpool, Bristol, Glasgow and Hull). In their analysis of the
*Small Island* Read project Danielle Fuller and James Procter ask 'what
*cultural work* [. . .] the novel [was] assumed to perform by the organisers,
sponsors, and institutions associated with this event [emphasis added]'
(Fuller and Procter 2009: 26). This chapter seeks to extend this question
to the BBC television adaptation of Levy's novel, first broadcast on BBC
One in 2009.[2] The 2009 adaptation is distinctive in bringing the classic adaptation treatment to bear on a contemporary novel focusing on
black British history, in foregrounding black British perspectives, and
in casting black British actors in leading roles in a period drama. This
chapter will begin by situating the 2009 BBC adaptation of *Small Island*
within two critical contexts: the first concerns the production of cultural
value within contemporary literary culture and the second concerns the
representation of black British identity and history in television drama,
including the literary adaptation. It will then go on to examine how the
introduction of a contemporary narrative framework to the adaptation
of Levy's novel serves to orient this historical fiction towards the future
and to construct the birth of a mixed-race child as the origin of a multicultural present; in this way, the 2009 BBC adaptation can be seen to be
extending the 'cultural work' (Fuller and Procter 2009: 26) of the *Small
Island* Read project by providing a dramatic 'hinge' (Fuller and Procter
2009: 30) between past and present.

## Constructing Cultural Value: The *Small Island* Read

Since its publication in 2004 Andrea Levy's novel has been awarded
major literary prizes, adopted by a national mass reading project and
adapted for a mainstream, prime-time, television audience. The literary prize, the book club and the adaptation are all distinctive features
of contemporary literary culture and, moreover, significant agents in
the complex production of cultural value. In *Marketing Literature: The
Making of Contemporary Writing in Britain*, Claire Squires argues that literary prizes 'play a crucial role in the interaction between genre and the
marketplace, and are one of the forces that come to influence notions of
cultural value and literariness' (Squires 2009: 97). Indeed, in *The Economy
of Prestige: Prizes, Awards and the Circulation of Cultural Value*, James F.

English examines the ways in which the prize serves to authorize 'the distribution of esteem and reward on a particular cultural field' (English 2005: 51). In the context of contemporary British and Commonwealth fiction the Man Booker Prize most exemplifies this function and its success has arguably contributed to the proliferation of literary prizes in recent decades – prizes whose relationship to 'genre and the market place' (Squires 2009: 97) is increasingly nuanced. Where the award of a prestigious literary prize once functioned to strictly demarcate 'literary' fiction from 'mass market' and 'genre' fiction, a new generation of awards have arguably contributed to a new genre within the marketplace, one which combines the literary with the popular; in other words, a genre which aims to reconcile the cultural capital more commonly associated with elite taste (and confirmed by the award of the literary prize) with the economic capital ensured by market success (and evidenced by popular sales).[3]

Where the Man Booker prize (launched in 1969) is awarded to the 'best, eligible full-length novel in the opinion of the judges',[4] the Costa Book Award (formerly the Whitbread Book Award, first launched as the Whitbread Literary Award in 1971) recognizes 'well-written, enjoyable books that [the judges] would *strongly recommend anyone to read* [emphasis added]'[5] and more recently the Orange Prize for fiction (first launched in 1996, and now the Women's Prize for Fiction) celebrates 'excellence, originality and *accessibility* [emphasis added].'[6] Levy's *Small Island* was awarded both the Orange and Whitbread Prizes in the year of its publication and was thus identified as a leading title in the field of what we might call popular literary fiction. The adoption of Levy's novel by an Arts Council funded mass reading project can in part be attributed to this public endorsement not only of its literary merit but also its readability (both 'accessible' and 'enjoyable').[7] Murray has written that 'literary prizes constitute a crucial but commonly overlooked node of the adaptation network' (Murray 2012: 104); the sponsored book club, whether publicly funded or commercially endorsed, can be added to this network.[8] In turn, the increased market visibility and extended readership which follow both literary prize and nationwide book club nominations promise a readymade audience for a prospective screen adaptation, especially one commissioned by a public service broadcaster with a mission to 'inform, educate and entertain'.[9] It can be argued that in the years following its publication *Small Island* became the object of a unique confluence of legitimating forces – the popular literary prize, the book club endorsement and the BBC adaptation – which together served to canonize this novel by a black British writer in specific ways. I would argue that the *Small Island* Read project is a key reference point when considering the cultural significance of the adaptation with which this chapter is principally concerned.

In her article 'Africa in Europe: Narrating Black British History in Contemporary Fiction', Sofía Muñoz-Valdivieso observes that there have been 'two momentous occasions in Britain in the last decade when the presence of the African diaspora in the country has come to the fore in media representations and cultural productions' (Muñoz-Valdivieso 2010: 160): the first being the fiftieth anniversary of the docking of the SS Empire Windrush at Tilbury in 1948, and the second being the bicentenary of the abolition of the slave trade in the British Empire in 1807. Had its publication not post-dated the 1998 commemorations, Levy's novel might have provided the perfect fictional counterpart to the former. Matthew Mead has argued that 'the memorializing of the Windrush moves in contradictory directions, on the one hand ambivalently challenging and on the other unconsciously reaffirming the borders of the nation and the historical conception of Britain as centre of a global empire' (Mead 2009: 137). In other words, while it serves to mark a significant period in post-war immigration from the British colonies in the Caribbean it may also serve to obscure the presence of black British people in the British Isles prior to 1948. In this context, it is significant that Levy's novel not only reconstructs the experiences of first-generation immigrants from the British West Indies, but also contests the myth of the Windrush as a formative first encounter through its focus on the experiences of enlisted Jamaican airman, Gilbert, stationed in North Yorkshire during the war. However, the public reading event for which Levy's novel was selected was not designed to commemorate the landing of the Windrush but rather the abolition of the slave trade. The oddity of this choice is worth some reflection. The experience and legacy of British involvement in the Atlantic slave trade is one which leading Caribbean and British writers had explored in some depth in novels published before 1998, including Kittian-British writer Caryl Phillips's *Crossing the River* (1993) and *Cambridge* (1991) and British-Guyanese writer Fred D'Aguiar's *The Longest Memory* (1994) and *Feeding the Ghosts* (1997). Levy's *Small Island* can readily be situated within the context of postcolonial literary and cultural studies in its exploration of the historical legacy of the British Empire; however, in terms of popular narrative modes – that is, those on which a mass public reading event is likely to depend – it is not a novel which explicitly requires its readers to confront the realities of slavery. In this context the 'cultural work' (2009: 26) to which Fuller and Procter refer becomes quite complex and extends beyond the immediate narrative concerns of the novel. Fuller and Procter suggest that the novel is 'asked to operate as a hinge between "the past" (slavery and its abolition; post-war immigration) and the present (contemporary multicultural diversity)' (2009: 30). In this act of 'state-sanctioned multiculturalism' (Fuller and Procter 2009: 31) *Small Island* is somehow required to stand for slavery and its history without directly addressing it, and to speak for contemporary Britain without explicitly representing it. The black British text is put to work in service to an agenda which seems to obscure its nominal object – the history of slavery – even as it offers to remember it. This paradox is inherent in the anniversary itself, which, in its focus on the abolition rather than the institution of slavery, celebrates the British state as a liberating force even as it acknowledges its role as an agent of oppression. In this context it is not simply the novel's accessibility which makes it so amenable to the *Small Island* Read project but also its narrative design; Levy not only creates four distinct characters with compelling storylines but also integrates British and Jamaican perspectives in her narrative structure. In doing so the novel gives equal space to white and black perspectives on post-war immigration from the Caribbean. In other words, while its subject matter might seem to have 'minority' appeal in the eyes of the mainstream publishing industry, its narrative approach serves to ensure that white British voices remain central to this black British story. Anouk Lang suggests that:

> [The novel's] achievement is that it lays out the complex interrelations of race and class in two locations – the Caribbean and Britain – in such a way as to demonstrate the prejudices and flaws of the black characters while not for a moment exempting its white British and American characters from complicity with wider currents of racism circulating in the 1940s. (Lang 2009: 133)

Indeed, the racial prejudices of white British characters are given frank and unapologetic expression in Levy's novel where they are unmediated by the intervention of an omniscient narrator. In this context it is significant that the BBC 2009 adaptation not only omits the narrative perspective of its most explicitly racist white British narrator, Bernard, but also introduces a voiceover which assumes the authority of an omniscient narrator. It could be argued that the former intervention serves to diminish the complicity of its white British narrators in the racism of the period, and as such testifies to the compromises exacted from the black British text in the name of assuring a crossover (that is, white, mainstream) audience. However, the latter intervention arguably serves a more complex populist intent and in some ways ensures that the adaptation fulfils its function as 'as a hinge between "the past" [. . .] and the present' (Fuller and Procter 2009: 30) in ways which the source text was unable to do. Before turning to a closer comparative analysis of these interventions I wish first to place this literary adaptation within the broader context of representations of black British identity and history on television.

## Adapting Black Britain: The Classic Adaptation and Multicultural Television

In an article published on *The Guardian*'s website in November 2011, British actor Paterson Joseph welcomed the casting of black British actors Solomon Glave and James Howson in the roles of the younger and older Heathcliff in Andrea Arnold's acclaimed film adaptation of

Emily Brontë's classic 1847 novel *Wuthering Heights*: 'Black actors belong in British costume drama. After all, we've been around for a lot longer than 1948.' The sense that Black British actors have been – and continue to be – 'locked out of a whole tradition of "quality", high-budget, often heritage-based drama' (Malik 2002: 142) is one confirmed in Sarita Malik's *Representing Black Britain: Black and Asian Images on Television*. In this historical study of British television, Malik suggests that 'The lengthy and pre-meditative process involved in drama production (deliberate decisions about scripting, casting, directing and scheduling), has positioned it at the heart of talks around multicultural content, integrated casting, narrative diversity and minority access' (Malik 2002: 135). Malik argues that the situation comedy was the key vehicle through which British multiculturalism became visible in the 1970s, through popular series such as *Till Death Us Do Part* (BBC1, 1966–8, 1972, 1974–5), *Curry and Chips* (LWT, 1969), *It Ain't Half Hot Mum* (BBC, 1974–81), *Rising Damp* (Yorkshire TV / ITV, 1974–8) and *Mind Your Language* (LWT / ITV, 1977–9). While some of these comedies provided opportunities for black British actors to pursue an acting career in television, others perpetuated the theatrical tradition of 'blackface' performance, with white British actors 'blacking up' for comic effect. Moreover, Malik observes that 'many of the comedies "about race", were actually comedies about Blacks signifying *trouble*; *trouble* with the neighbours, *trouble* with language, *trouble* with fitting in [emphasis in original]' (Malik 2002: 97). Malik notes that from the early 1980s, the increasing popularity of long-running drama series/serials set in contemporary Britain established a new small-screen stage for black British actors; however, by deploying black British actors to denote the modernity of contemporary urban contexts, these dramas did nothing to remedy their exclusion from the more prestigious genres of period drama, of which the classic adaptation is a prominent example.

Literary adaptation continues to be a central feature of the '"quality", high-budget, often heritage-based drama' (Malik 2002: 142), with adaptations of 'classic' novels by nineteenth-century authors such as Jane Austen and Charles Dickens proving a recurring staple in broadcast schedules, occupying sought-after prime-time slots and taking pride of place in Sunday evening and public holiday programming. Such adaptations can be relied upon to attract significant viewing audiences and to feature prominently both in the quality press review pages and in the shortlists for national and international television awards; granted economic value by the market and cultural value by institutionalized arbiters of mainstream taste, the genre's capacity to combine both critical and commercial success goes some way to explain the repeated commission of new adaptations of the same set of source texts. Moreover, the extension of the aesthetic idiom of the historical period drama – with its privileging of notions of 'authenticity', especially in relation to the material cultures of costume, artefacts and interiors – to the classic adaptation arguably serves to gloss over the extent to which the historical period in question is itself mediated by the prevailing narrative conventions and dominant ideologies of the time. The prominence of adaptations of a very historically and culturally specific set of source texts within the version of national cultural heritage propagated by the mass medium of television both at home and abroad (the classic adaptation being a prime cultural export) has ideological implications which have proved the focus of key interventions in adaptations studies. Sarah Cardwell cites Paul Kerr as playing a key role in bringing critical attention to the 'institutional, social and ideological' (Cardwell 2002: 78) contexts within which the classic adaptation on television is produced and consumed. In this way, 'classic-novel adaptations' have been seen as 'operat[ing] as part of an ideological project to elevate and perpetuate an elite liter-ary culture [. . .] and to build reactionary nostalgia for a mythologized "ideal" era in Britain's colonial past' (Cardwell 2002: 78).[10] Indeed, these adaptations tend to focus on an era when the power and wealth of the British Empire was at its height but on texts which give little represen-tation to the inequities of colonial rule; they offer contemporary audi-ences a vision of national identity as rooted in an imperial past and of a Britishness implicitly equated with whiteness. In terms of cultural representation, the experience of non-white colonial subjects beyond the British Isles and the historical presence of black British people within them are rendered invisible; in terms of cultural industry, black British actors are largely precluded from the creative and professional oppor-tunities which such productions present. Classic adaptations have often played a formative role in establishing actors within the national con-sciousness and can offer a prestigious platform for the launch or revival of careers in television drama. However, the striking absence of inte-grated casting strategies in classic adaptations has meant that talented black British actors are denied the opportunities extended to their white peers. [11] Indeed, in recent years leading black British actors have turned to the United States for opportunities which the British television indus-try seems unable to match, including Marianne Jean-Baptiste (*Without a Trace*, 2002–9), Idris Elba (*The Wire*, 2002–4) and David Harewood (*Homeland* 2011–12).[12]

The extension of the 'classic adaptation' treatment – defined by an aesthetics of fidelity to the source text, an attitude of deference to its author, and narrative strategies of historical realism – to a contemporary novel can become instrumental in the popular 'canonisation' of that text as a contemporary classic. Tracey L. Walters has written that:

> black writers in Britain have been rendered invisible mainly because most of the literature they produce is ushered into a separate white canon distinct from the larger body of work produced by white writers [. . .] Every few years, though, the literary establishment recognises a Black writer as British. (Walters 2005: 314)

In this context, the commission of an adaptation of *Small Island* by a national broadcasting organization with a public service mandate, and the production of this adaptation within the conventions of a genre associated with high cultural value and prestige, might seem to mark a gesture of 'recognition' on the part of the cultural establishment. While the 2009 BBC adaptation of Levy's novel is largely faithful in tone and content, two significant changes are made to its narrative structure: the first concerns the omission of one of the four narrative voices which make up the multiple narrative structure of the novel and the second concerns the introduction of a prominent voiceover whose function is equivalent to that of an omniscient narrator. I will argue that these interventions have important implications for the representation of the history and future of British multiculturalism in this adaptation of Levy's source text.

## Framing the Black British Family: Narrative Voices in the 2009 BBC *Small Island*

Andrea Levy's novel opens with an arresting and provocative account of a white child's encounter with an adult man during a family visit to the 1924 British Empire Exhibition at Wembley:

> But then suddenly there was a man. An African man. A black man who looked like he had been carved from melting chocolate [. . .] A monkey man sweating a smell of mothballs. Blacker than when you smudge your face with a sooty cork. The droplets of sweat on his forehead glistened and shone like jewels. His lips were brown, not pink like they should be, and they bulged with air like bicycle tyres. His hair was woolly as a black shorn sheep. His nose, squashed flat, had two nostrils big as train tunnels. And he was looking at me. (Levy 2004: 6)

In the context of the novel the offensive nature of this language is mitigated by its attribution to the perspective of a child and by the parodic subtext which underlines this litany of racial stereotypes. The adaptation of this particular first-person narrative perspective represents specific challenges if the audience is not to be alienated; the way in which this scene is adapted in the 2009 BBC television adaptation tells us much about its dramatic priorities.

In the adaptation this scene is not directly depicted but retrospectively recalled by the adult Queenie (Ruth Wilson); moreover, the memory is triggered during a moment of domestic intimacy with her Jamaican lover, Michael (Ashley Walters). As they talk by the kitchen range, Queenie lapses into a kind of reverie; the camera lingers on her entranced expression and the viewer's identification with her rapture is uninterrupted by reaction shots which might otherwise prompt us to consider Michael's perspective on this objectifying episode. In the novel Queenie's first encounter with a man of African origin is slyly sexualized when one of her father's farmhands presses her to kiss him; however, her confusion and embarrassment is defused when the 'big nigger man' (Levy 2004: 6) civilly offers her his hand to shake instead. The possibility that this memory might be the source of a racialized sexual desire is evidently not precluded in the television adaptation, but it is dignified by being incorporated into a heterosexual romance narrative. Moreover, Michael is enlisted to play a willing role in the white woman's fantasy; in a gesture that echoes that of the African man in the novel, he takes her hand but this time kisses it. I would suggest that the translation of this scene in the 2009 adaptation is significant in two ways: it is indicative of the ways in which white British racism is contained and defused in the adaptation and of the way in which the conception, birth and adoption of a mixed-race child is foregrounded.

The use of multiple narrative perspectives is a common device within literary fiction and this novel assists the reader in navigating between linguistically marked voices by indicating the identity of the speaker in each chapter heading. Levy's narration alternates between four first-person narrators, two male and two female, two white British and two Jamaican: Queenie, Hortense, Gilbert and Bernard. The narrative point of view of three of these narrators – Queenie, Hortense and Gilbert – is retained in the television adaptation which depicts unfolding events from their respective perspectives. However, while Bernard (Benedict Cumberbatch) remains a key character within Queenie's story – and a passing character in Hortense and Gilbert's – his own narrative, and crucially his experience as a British soldier in colonial India, is omitted. Of the four narrators in Levy's novel, three give voice to opinions or perspectives informed by colonial discourses of race (Gilbert perhaps the only exception); yet it is Bernard who gives voice to the most unmitigated racial prejudice with his repeated and contemptuous references to 'chocolate-drop troops from West Africa' (Levy 2004: 366), 'bloody coolies' (Levy 2004: 369) and 'wretched, simpering little wog[s]' (Levy 2004: 393). His language is depicted as motivated rather than casual and is directly allied to his conviction both in the legitimacy of the British Empire and the illegitimacy of its subjects' right to live and work in the Mother Country. Moreover, his encounters with non-white British subjects serve not to broaden but to narrow his understanding of Britishness; he returns from a war fought against fascism convinced of the necessity for racial segregation:

> The war was fought so people might live amongst their own kind. Quite simple. Everyone had a place. England for the English and the West Indies for these coloured people [. . .] I've nothing against them in their place. But their place isn't here [. . .] These brown gadabouts were nothing but trouble. (Levy 2004: 469)

The omission of Bernard's narrative perspective from the 2009 BBC adaptation has the effect not only of removing a wider colonial context but also of diminishing the extent to which racist attitudes are given expression by its white British protagonists.

A further effect of the exclusion of Bernard's point of view from the television adaptation is to upset the gendered symmetry of the novel's narrative structure. As a result, a triangular heterosexual romance plot is emphasized, whose object is not the remaining male narrator, Gilbert (David Oyelowo), but Michael, whose function in the narrative is characterized by his absence (leaving his family home to enlist, returning to war, being assumed lost in combat, emigrating to Canada). In the 2009 adaptation Michael's absence is figured by his photograph, an object cherished both by Hortense (Naomie Harris), who harbours a lifelong unrequited love for her adoptive brother, and Queenie, his wartime lover and future mother of his son. Tucked into Queenie's mirror and Hortense's wallet, the private longing and wistful gazes which this photograph attracts is a recurring motif in the adaptation. Chance intervenes on more than one occasion to ensure that the two women remain in ignorance of their shared passion for Michael; indeed, their dual ownership of Michael's image serves less to construct Hortense and Queenie as romantic and sexual rivals than to underline the shared nature of their experience. Both women are depicted as alienated from their family home, undertaking marriages for pragmatic rather than romantic ends and motivated by a desire for social mobility. Indeed, property plays a key role in their pursuit of the latter; Queenie rents out rooms in the house she has inherited from her husband (who is missing, presumed dead) and Hortense's skills in domestic management, depicted as comically wanting in the cramped space of the rented room she and Gilbert first share, come into their ascendancy when Gilbert enters the property market by purchasing a dilapidated property for renovation. These parallels prepare the way for the maternal substitution with which the novel concludes and which prefaces the 2009 adaptation's most innovative departure from Levy's narrative structure.

The adaptation closes with Gilbert and Hortense moving into their own home with their newly acquired adopted baby; as she gently loosens his swaddling blankets, Hortense discovers an envelope containing a photograph of his birth mother. An unexpected flash forward – the first employed in a drama which has otherwise been firmly located in the past – follows a black woman as she enters the same property, but now in the present day, where her two children are discovered poring over a family album with their grandfather, an activity evidently instigated by the older man who admits to doing 'the genealogy thing'. It is only in these closing scenes of the second and final feature film length episode of the adaptation that the voice of the narrator is revealed as belonging to a character in the drama, rather than as a disembodied narrative device. Moreover, it belongs to a character who does not feature in

Levy's source text: namely, Queenie and Michael's unnamed adult son, now a grandfather and our contemporary. The viewer's ability to identify the voiceover with the actor playing this new character is significantly assisted by the casting of one of the most widely recognized and distinguished black British actors of his generation: Hugh Quarshie. The casting of the classically trained Quarshie brings with it a set of extratextual meanings which place the adaptation within the broader context of the history of black British actors, given that Quarshie became a figurehead for the Royal Shakespeare Company's adoption of the practice of integrated casting in the 1980s.[13]

A close-up of the photograph album identifies 'great grandma' as Hortense pictured in a graduation gown, an image which anticipates an event beyond the action of the main drama and which assures the reader that her professional ambitions where not thwarted by British colonial double standards. However, it also reveals an image with which the viewer is familiar but which provokes the grandchildren to exchange glances of consternation – that is, an image of Queenie, immediately recognizable from the preceding action and now identified as the white paternal great-grandmother of the children. The birth of a child, as represented in fiction, is routinely figured as signifying an alternative futurity; in the context of postcolonial fiction, the mixed-race child is burdened with a particular kind of generational legacy.[14] However, Queenie's decision to give up her child in some way contradicts the reading of his arrival as a symbol of the 'birth of multicultural Britain' (Grmelová 2010: 83); her conviction in the impossibility of being a white mother to a mixed-race child, actually confirms the racial segregation which Bernard and his neighbours advocate and which Queenie has previously seemed to challenge. Moreover, the novel's depiction of Hortense and Gilbert's willingness to assume the parenting of their landlady's child evokes a racial politics of reproduction which is troubling. While the BBC adaptation infers a thwarted desire for motherhood on the part of Queenie prior to her pregnancy, Hortense does not exhibit or express any maternal ambitions; when she is commandeered to assist Queenie in her delivery her reaction is one of distaste. In this scene her failure to demonstrate an innate capacity for midwifery cannot help but echo the famous scene in David O. Selznick's 1939 film *Gone with the Wind* where the inadequacy of Scarlett O'Hara's young maid (played by Butterfly McQueen) is the object of racialized comedy. In this context Hortense's willingness to adopt Queenie's child, and to implicitly postpone her professional ambitions and forego her own experience of maternity, seems hard to explain; in ways which are historically familiar a black woman is placed in service to white women's reproductive sexuality, and her willingness to nurse and rear another woman's child attributed to altruism rather than to economic or political hierarchy.

However, the introduction of the adult version of this infant serves in some way to recuperate this problematic narrative climax; his status as a respected, trusted and *present* father to his own child and her children retrospectively affirms his own family roots. The image of the doting domesticated grandfather, baby-sitting his daughter's children and gently instructing them in their maternal legacy in some ways restores the image of black paternity, which has otherwise been depicted as punishing or absent. The family home is a key location for British television drama; the location of this scene within a property purchased by first-generation Caribbean immigrants confirms their place within the British property owning tradition, situates their present within a historical continuity with the past and presents a scene in which British and Black identity are identical.[15] Most significantly, in dramatic terms, it identifies the voice of the narrator as Queenie and Michael's son; his interventions in the storytelling process now take on a political dimension as they can be seen retrospectively to serve as the 'hinge' between past and present to which Fuller and Procter refer (2009: 30). I would argue that this orientation towards the future has important effects in terms of the 'cultural work' of the 2009 BBC adaptation; it perhaps confirms that it is less concerned with confronting historic white British racism than with legitimizing contemporary black British identity through the mobilization of heritage motifs.

In conclusion, then, we can note that the 2009 BBC television adaptation of *Small Island* deploys traditional narrative and dramatic techniques in its efforts to engage a mass audience in identification with its key characters, both black and white. In so doing, it arguably underplays the representation of racist sentiment by ordinary British subjects which is given such frank and provocative expression in Levy's novel. However, the deployment of a contemporary narrative framework serves to suggest the continuity and integration of mixed-race British heritage through a focus on the family as a key-holding frame for national identity. While the adaptation does not situate itself within a tradition of critical anti-racist social realist drama, it employs the conventions of populist period drama to subtly reconfigure assumptions about what constitutes a British family history.

## Notes

1 Work within the field of postcolonial literature and theory has played a significant role in the emergence of this new body of knowledge, with the role of the Man Booker Prize in popularizing certain modes of postcolonial fiction receiving particular attention; see especially Huggan (2001).

2 Directed by John Alexander, screenplay Paula Milne and Sarah Williams, and featuring Benedict Cumberbatch (Bernard), Naomie Harris (Hortense), David Oyelowo (Gilbert) and Ruth Wilson (Queenie).

3 As Murray notes, prevailing frameworks for the analysis of constructions of cultural taste (as informed by Pierre Bourdieu) would suggest that 'elevation of a cultural property's stock in the economic sphere serves [. . .] to reduce its symbolic capital in inverse proportion' (2012: 117).

4  Man Booker Prize website, www.themanbookerprize.com/entering-the-awards [accessed 31 December 2012].

5  Costa Book Award website, www.costabookawards.com/faqs.aspx [accessed 31 December 2012].

6  Orange Prize for Fiction website, www.orangeprize.co.uk/ [accessed 31 December 2012].

7  Lang links the 'very accessibility of Levy's text' to its 'enthusiastic acceptance by a large number of readers in Britain' noting that it is 'largely realist . . . [and] without much formal inventiveness' (2009: 134, 138). Fuller and Procter suggest that the 'centrality of character in *Small Island*' may be 'one reason for the novel's popularity with book groups and other non-academic readers' (2009: 32).

8  For example, the Richard and Judy Book Club in the United Kingdom, televised by Channel 4 from 2004–9 and now sponsored by retailer W. H. Smith, and the Oprah Winfrey Book Club, broadcast between 1996–2011. In May 2010 *O, The Oprah Magazine* published a Reading Guide to Levy's *The Longest Song* and in January 2011 the Richard and Judy Book Club listed Levy's *Small Island* as one of the 100 Books of the Decade. The relationship between the televised book club and hierarchies of literary taste is not without its controversies; see Kathleen Rooney (ed.) (2008), 'Jonathan Frantzen Versus Oprah Winfrey: Disses, Disinvitation, and Disingenuousness', in *Reading with Oprah: The Book Club That Changed the America*. University of Arkansas Press, 33–66.

9  BBC (British Broadcasting Corporation) website www.bbc.co.uk/aboutthebbc/insidethebbc/whoweare/mission_and_values/ [accessed 31 December 2012].

10 For an analysis of how the heritage film engages in 'the artful and spectacular projection of an elite, conservative vision of the national past' see Andrew Higson (ed.) (1996), 'The Heritage Film and British Cinema', in *Dissolving Views: Key Writings on British Cinema*. London: Continuum, 232–48.

11 Ayanna Thompson describes the ethos of 'integrated', or 'colorblind,' casting as follows: 'neither the race nor the ethnicity of an actor should prevent her or him from playing a role as long as she or he was the best actor available' (2006: 6).

12 Marianne Jean-Baptiste was the first black British actor to be nominated for an Academy Award for her performance in Mike Leigh's *Secrets & Lies* in 1996; the following year she was omitted from a showcase of (exclusively white) young British acting talent hosted by British Screen for the Fiftieth Anniversary of the Cannes Film Festival. Jean-Baptiste was reported as commenting 'What more do they want? Maybe I should have done a soap. It is a shame on Britain. I see myself as British and I want to be celebrated by Britain.' *The Guardian*, 15 May 1997, www.guardian.co.uk/film/1997/may/15/news.danglaister [accessed 1 January 2013].

13 Quarshie made RSC history when he was cast as *Hotspur* in Henry IV (1982) and as Tybalt in *Romeo and Juliet* and Banquo in *Macbeth* (1986); see Celia R. Daileader (2000), 'Casting Black Actors: Beyond Othellophilia', in Catherine M. S. Alexander and Stanley Wells (eds), *Shakespeare and Race*, Cambridge: Cambridge University Press, 177–202. It was not until 2000 that the RSC cast a black British actor in the role of an English king; the actor was David Oyelowo, who plays Gilbert in *Small Island*. Integrated, or 'colorblind', casting, first pioneered by Joseph Papp's New York Shakespeare Festival in the 1950s, is a practice which has been extended to film and television adaptations of Shakespeare's plays but not to adaptations of classic novels; it is the absence of integrated casting in UK television drama productions which makes the prominence of period drama so problematic for black British actors.

14 Levy is not alone in deploying this motif and, in her analysis of Zadie Smith's 2000 novel *White Teeth*, Fowler argues that 'The child she [Irie] conceives near the end of the novel, with Magid or Millat, acts further to disrupt notions of binaries and point to the prevalence of racial and cultural multiplicity in the future in Britain' (2008: 13).

15 James Procter has argued that the 'dwelling place was [. . .] the site at which the regulation, policing and deferral of black settlement were most effectively played out' (2003: 22).

# CHAPTER SIX

# Exquisite Corpse: Un/dressing History in *Fruit of the Lemon/The Long Song*

## JEANNETTE BAXTER

**Chapter Summary:** This chapter opens up the possibility of reading *Fruit of the Lemon/The Long Song* as exquisite corpses of sorts. Employing a methodology of un/folding, a technique integral to the Surrealist ludic practice of exquisite corpse, I focus on the complex relations between verbal/written historical accounts and individual/collective acts of historical storytelling as they manifest themselves across the two novels. By reading and interpreting *Fruit of the Lemon/The Long Song* in relation to one another, I seek to exploit the non-synthesizing energies of the un/fold in order to tease out neglected textual crossings, and foreground overlooked historical and political associations within and across both novels.

As I got older Mum began to throw me little scraps of her past – 'I met your dad at a bus stop' – which I would piece together like a game of Consequences I used to play as a child – fold the paper and pass it on – until I had a story that seemed to make sense. (Levy 1999: 4–5)

It is no coincidence that *Fruit of the Lemon* foregrounds a form of storytelling that is also a game of chance. 'Consequences' is another name for *cadavre exquis* or exquisite corpse, a ludic practice first invented by the French Surrealist group in the 1920s. Two versions of exquisite corpse are most commonly played today: the pictorial version in which a number of players take it in turns to draw a person, with each player drawing a bodily part before folding the paper over (and thus concealing the bodily part) and passing it on; and the written version, a collaborative act of storytelling, in which each player composes a sentence that is subsequently concealed by folding the paper over and passing it on to the next narrator. In both versions, exquisite corpse initiates ways of upsetting established modes of representation. While the hybrid, illustrated corpse challenges the 'containment and closure of the classical body' (Adamowicz 1998: 160), the verbal corpse disturbs all notion of the linear composition of narrative by generating 'fresh chains of associations' (Kern 2009: 10). Not to be dismissed as a mere act of meaningless play, exquisite corpse is better understood as a creative and critical practice that intervenes in the smooth telling of stories by opening narrative composition up to the play of juxtaposition and the power of contingency.

In this chapter, I want to open up the possibility of reading *Fruit of the Lemon/The Long Song* as exquisite corpses of sorts. Specifically, I want to focus on the complex relations between verbal/written historical accounts and individual/collective acts of historical storytelling as they manifest themselves across the two texts. Within the contexts of my discussion, the use of the splice (/) is deliberate. Graphically, it represents the mechanism of the fold, which is so integral to any practice of exquisite corpse: 'edges and new figures are created by a fold [. . .] This edge allows for the processing of information in endless varieties of undulations' (Miller 2009: xxiii). The fold not only juxtaposes disparate words and images, bringing random elements together in order to forge new visual and verbal relations, but it is also a site upon which individual/collective voices meet and exist in a dynamic relation with one other. At the same time, however, the concomitant act of unfolding is crucial for the ways in which, in the acts of reading and interpreting, it refuses to flatten the verbal or visual narrative in order to render meaning fully accessible and available. This is because there is no final or complete sense of the paper being unfolded. Instead, in the interventionist practice of exquisite corpse, the relation between the fold and the unfold is one of inter-animation: the act of folding leads to unfolding which leads to further acts of folding, and so on. Hence my neologism: un/fold.

Clearly, my use of the un/fold methodology is metaphorical, and it takes two distinct but related forms. First, the un/fold works at the level of narrative as a metaphor for storytelling. At the beginning of *Fruit of the Lemon*, for example, Faith Jackson's official familial history manifests itself visually and verbally in the form of a conspicuously sparse family tree, consisting of her father, mother, brother and herself. Yet, with each individual story that Faith narrates, the family tree gradually un/folds to reveal branching structures of alternative histories and experiences. *The Long Song* similarly foregrounds tensions between individual/collective voices and visual/verbal forms of historical narrative in the contest between the fixed, printed word favoured by Thomas and the shifting, unstable storytelling upon which his mother, July, insists. Turning ('turn' comes etymologically from 'fold') away from bounded historical accounts of slavery and its legacies, July constructs a narrative of endless twists and detours – 'Let me unfold to you' (2011: 25) – as she gives voice to multiple and contradictory stories of her life and the lives of others. Secondly, the un/fold works as a metaphor for the act of critical reading and interpretation. By reading and interpreting *Fruit of the Lemon/The Long Song* in relation to one another, I hope to exploit the non-synthesizing energies of the un/fold in order to tease out neglected textual crossings, and foreground overlooked historical and political associations within and across both novels.

In relation to this, I suggest that Faith and July's strategies of narrative un/folding reveal themselves to be identifiably counter-historical in impulse. On the one hand, the black female narrators seek to expose the limits of traditional historiographical practices, with their closed and totalizing versions of the past, in order to initiate a form of witnessing that insists on history as alive, open and in process. On the other hand, Faith's and July's un/foldings of theirs and other people's stories are replete with various and complex tensions involved in the telling of black history. Although *Fruit of the Lemon/The Long Song* issue challenges to modes of knowledge, authority, subjectivity and memory produced and regulated by the historical archive, both novels also, and inevitably, recognize their debt to a range of historical, cultural and social histories that un/fold within and across them (see the novels' respective 'Acknowledgements' pages). This is because stories do not simply un/fold in *Fruit of the Lemon/The Long Song* in order to disentangle individual histories from dominant historical accounts of empire and its legacies. Rather, stories un/fold in order to entangle still further, and to force unexpected and disquieting connections.

A particularly unnerving set of connections emerges out of a conspicuous narrative motif that repeats, with difference, across the texts; namely, the motif of dressing. If we recall, Faith Jackson, much to her family's bewilderment, strives to fulfil an early career ambition to be a 'dresser' at the BBC, the home of British historical costume drama. July, meanwhile, is snatched from her mother and enslaved as a 'dresser' (or 'lady's maid') at the plantation house on Amity. When read in isolation, these models of dressing are certainly far from straightforward. Faith's promotion gestures to a certain upward mobility at the same time that it is caught up in wider discourses of racial in/equality and reverse discrimination in 1980s Britain. July's abduction and traumatic re-location to the plantation house is born out of deeply unpalatable moments of exoticism (Levy 2011: 39–45), yet her newly acquired duty also accelerates her within a hierarchy of slavery: 'But in the great house she will at last feel to be a white man's child. Miss July at the great house! Come, she will get shoe!' (Levy 2011: 48). What happens to these already highly ambivalent models of dressing, then, when we un/fold them in relation to one another? What kind of relationship exists between Faith's desire to un/dress the white actors of history, and July's enforced role in un/dressing her colonial mistress? And how are we expected to reconcile these two conspicuous models of dressing, bound up as they are in questions of racial identity, prejudice, resistance, complicity and inheritance? As I go on to discuss below, the exquisite corpse narratives of *Fruit of the Lemon/The Long Song* set in train lines of associative enquiry such as these, thus forcing into being difficult and urgent questions about the un/folding of the colonial past within and across the postcolonial present.

## *Fruit of the Lemon* and the Politics of Dressing

It has not gone unnoticed by readers that *Fruit of the Lemon*'s attempts to engage with the 'long' history of slavery sets it somewhat apart from Levy's earlier writings. Although intricate relationships between contemporary black British identity and the history of empire haunt *Every Light in the House Burnin'* and *Never Far from Nowhere*, they do so predominantly through the conspicuous presence, and persistence, of historical silences (see Perfect 2010: 31–41). Certainly, silences resurface at various points, and to varying degrees, throughout all of Levy's novels, and only two pages into *Fruit of the Lemon*, Faith Jackson concedes: 'My mum and dad never talked about their lives [. . .] There was no "oral tradition" in our family' (Levy 2004: 4). This admission is tellingly situated, however, coming as it does immediately after Faith's account of a school history lesson on the 'facts' of the slave trade and immediately before she likens her own form of storytelling to a game of exquisite corpse. From the very outset, then, *Fruit of the Lemon* marks itself out as a 'novel of transition', as it emphasizes the 'relations and tensions between historiography and vernacular story-telling traditions' (Knepper 2012: 5), and as it moves towards an alternative accounting of the complexities of contemporary black British experience.

Take the Jackson family tree, the text's first official verbal/visual account of history, as a telling illustration of what Faith's exquisite corpse narrative sets out to challenge. Striking for what it does *not* reveal – Mildred Campbell, Wade Jackson, Carl Jackson and Faith Jackson are the only listed family members – this conspicuously truncated genealogical structure makes manifest a familial history marked by erasure. Bearing no trace (beyond the immediate nuclear family) of intergenerational relationships (sisters/aunties; brothers/uncles; nephews/nieces/cousins), let alone trans-generational relationships (grandparents, great-grandparents, great, great-grandparents), the Jackson family tree is rooted firmly in a present fostered on forgetting. Where, precisely, are the Jackson family's various histories of dislocation, exile and migration? Where are the lines denoting the family's slave heritage? And what has happened to those lines connecting the Jacksons with their white, colonial ancestors? Memories, stories and experiences have been systematically excluded from the family tree, so that all that remains is an 'innocuous pattern', one which, like the 'black pattern of tiny people laid in rows as convenient and space-saving as possible . . . Slaves in a slave ship' (Levy 2004: 4), is not innocuous at all. Disavowing the very stories and histories that have produced it, the Jackson family tree signifies a limited and bounded present, one cut-off unequivocally from the past and the future.

Even though Faith's narrative strategy of un/folding multiple and contesting familial voices seeks to interfere with the severely edited accounts of her familial history, it should not be understood as existing in simple opposition to repressive historiographical practices. Indeed, Faith's exquisite corpse narrative only really comes into full effect in the second part of the novel when, following a crisis of identity and a nervous breakdown, Faith's parents send her 'home' to Jamaica and into the loquaciousness of her extended family. One of the more problematic aspects of *Fruit of the Lemon* in general, and the first part of the novel in particular, therefore, is the way in which it asks us to negotiate Faith's complicity in the suppression of her own black identity from her contemporary experience. Lodging with white, middle-class friends, for instance, Faith observes how her brother's sudden entrance into the living room rendered him 'out of context' (Levy 2004: 53). Her father's impromptu visit to the house is also a source of much discomfort, and not least because of his final line of enquiry: 'Faith – your friends, any of them your own kind?' (Levy 2004: 28). That Faith responds to her father with a question of her own – 'No. Why?' (Levy 2004: 29) – is doubly revealing. While it gestures to Faith's sense of socialization within a multicultural, multiracial Britain (these are recurrent and tension-ridden issues for Levy's young black British protagonists), it also belies a reluctance on Faith's part to even consider herself in terms of racial difference: 'I didn't ask him to explain. I didn't ask him to finish what he was saying. I didn't want him to' (Levy 2004: 29).

A less obvious aspect of Faith's everyday life that further implicates her in a narrative of racial denial concerns her work in the costume department at the BBC. As Rachel Carroll observes in her essay in this volume (see Chapter Five, 65–77), the BBC may be popularly regarded as the quintessential home of British costume drama, yet the institution's long history of erasing black British experience from its heritage-based vision of national identity renders its reproductions of history deeply problematic. Indeed, television period dramas or adaptations of literary 'classics' by novelists such as Jane Austen (whose work is a conspicuous feature of the heritage film industry) are intimately bound up with questions of historical authority, national politics and identity. More specifically, historical dramas typically broadcast by the BBC 'tend to focus on an era when the power and wealth of the British Empire was at its height' (Carroll 2014: 71). Giving 'little representation to the inequities of colonial rule; they offer contemporary audiences a vision of national identity as rooted in an imperial past and of a Britishness implicitly equated with whiteness' (Carroll 2014: 71).

Levy's novel taps into these complex issues in a number of ways. We might recall the scene in which Faith, newly employed as a costume assistant, finds herself queuing up for 'my pork chop and two veg behind Queen Victoria and in front of Gandhi' (Levy 2004: 68) in the BBC canteen. The suggestion that history can be variously dressed-up for mass consumption manifests itself tellingly here, as does Faith's decision to eat 'meat and two veg', a cliché that arguably positions her closer to the Queen of Empire than the vegetarian Indian nationalist. It is in Faith's subsequent remark, however – 'It was in the canteen that I really knew I worked somewhere glamorous' (Levy 2004: 68) – that her lack of awareness of her own role in the recreation of the historical imaginary comes through. Just as the violent material and political realities of colonial rule in India are glossed over in a bizarre historical performance in the lunch queue, so other historical events are evacuated of all substance and reduced to a set of costumes and props. We learn, for example, that one of Faith's jobs involved typing up 'a full and complete description of World War One army uniforms' (Levy 2004: 135). Something of an archivist working under the pressure of authenticity and the illusion of totality, Faith checks, describes, labels and catalogues the clothes that will dress the actors of world history (Levy 2004: 37). And in so doing, Faith is not only complicit in the preservation of a heritage industry that offers escape routes from the present into mythologized constructions of the past, but she is also complicit in the production of palatable historical narratives that deny her.

As Carroll observes, a significant feature of the BBC's more popular and 'prestigious' interpretations of British history is the conspicuous absence of black actors (Carroll 2014: 71). *Fruit of the Lemon* engages with this issue of discrimination when Faith's colleague in the costumes department, Lorraine, encourages her to apply for the newly advertised post of dresser: 'because some of them are now on television, aren't they?' (Levy 2004: 71). The implication, of course, is that with the small but increasing number of black actors on television, there will be an increasing need for black dressers, a flawed and reductive logic that bears the hallmark of segregationist prejudice. Even more perturbing, perhaps, is Lorraine's suggestion that the BBC's institutionalized racism is so pervasive that it extends to all kinds of behind-the-scenes activities: 'But they don't have black dressers [. . .] I don't mean to be horrible but it's just what happens here. Haven't you noticed there aren't any coloured people dressing?' (Levy 2004: 70–1). Although Lorraine employs the euphemism 'coloured' to soften any offence, it comes far too late in a gossipy flurry replete with hypocrisy and ignorance. Furthermore, Lorraine is utterly oblivious to the racism inherent in her own language choices, be it her use of cliché to dismiss embedded forms of prejudice ('it's just what happens'), or her euphemistic use of the epithet 'horrible' when she really means 'racist'.

Whether Faith is eventually offered the position as the 'first black dresser' at the BBC on merit, or, as the text infers, as a result of positive discrimination is never resolved (Levy 2004: 108, 148). Neither are the tensions surrounding the stalling of Faith's career as she is forced to wait for weeks in the dressers' 'pool'. Too inexperienced to work in production, Faith is required to be on hand, just in case 'Richard Briers might have trouble getting out of his tights or twenty German extras might get the zip caught in their lederhosen (Levy 2004: 147–8). Notably, the opportunity to dress a 'prestigious' history by Shakespeare or a World War Two drama never materializes for the black employee, and Faith starts to become haunted by memories of her job interview: 'Let me reassure you now, Faith, that there is absolutely no question of racial or any other prejudice going on here' (Levy 2004: 148). While the voice of company policy is meant to alleviate her anxieties, any gesture of equal opportunity is undermined by the news that Faith's first dressing role will be for a children's television programme, and that her 'actors' will be a huge teddy bear and a gangly rag doll. Reminiscent of Playschool, the hugely popular BBC series that launched the careers of two black presenters, Floella Benjamin and Derek Griffiths, and which featured 'Big Ted' and 'Jemima' the rag doll, the unnamed programme will allow Faith the opportunity to dress history after all, albeit a highly consumable, child-friendly account of medieval chivalry featuring a rag doll in distress and a valiant teddy in 'cardboard armour' (Levy 2004: 149).

Of course, Faith's work as a dresser is much more historically significant than she realizes, and this is something her brother, Carl, unwittingly touches upon in his blunt response to her promotion: 'She wants to put clothes on people's backs for a living [. . .] A bit like a servant. I couldn't do that' (Levy 2004: 139). Carl's reaction is proleptic, gesturing as it does to the extensive and complex history of servitude in his family that the second half of *Fruit of the Lemon* will give voice to. It is also somewhat ignorant, revealing an overly simplistic understanding (one that Faith also shares) of work as an activity purely linked to agency when it can also, as his family history so painfully bears out, be linked to dispossession. Indeed, a distinguishing feature of the many and various stories told to Faith by her Jamaican relatives is the emphasis that they place on work as a necessary form of survival: fixing, mending and sewing clothes (for people and toys); working in 'service' for rich American and European families; digging the Panama Canal; serving the Empire during the World Wars; working as lowly paid housemaids, gardeners and servants across the post-abolitionist Americas; and labouring as slaves on colonial plantations.

The history of labour that emerges out of *Fruit of the Lemon* identifies the novel as a contemporary extension of what Mary Lou Emery has termed 'plantation modernism'; namely, narratives which explore the links between 'the labor performed in the plantation system with that of early twentieth-century Europe, England and the United States' (Emery

2013: 421–2).[1] Re-reading the work of early modernist writers such as Jean Rhys (an important literary reference point for Levy), Emery suggests how, in works of plantation modernism, 'the subjectivities of working women engage the twinned dynamics of freedom and dispossession, agency and commodification, which have their beginnings in the plantation' (Emery 2013: 422). We encounter this 'interplay of dispossession and agency' (Emery 2013: 427) repeatedly in *Fruit of the Lemon*, and not only in the working histories of women. From the fallacious 'new deal for black ex-service men' (Levy 2004: 216) promised to, but denied, the likes of Earl; to the racial restrictions placed on Eunice's teaching career in pre-Civil Rights America; to Amy's mother, an unnamed slave, who was born into a life of service; and to Faith, the first black dresser at the BBC whose career is curtailed by racial discrimination, *Fruit of the Lemon* gives voice to an ambivalent politics of labour, one that embeds the Jackson family in the long and difficult history of slavery. It is surely not coincidental, for example, that William and Grace tender a small holding that they christen 'Amity' (Levy 2004: 231).

As Faith collects and re-tells the stories told to her by her Jamaican relatives, the visual model of the Jackson family tree extends, and gradually re-establishes a range of trans-generational, trans-cultural and trans-national familial connections that had formerly been erased. That is not to say, however, that this genealogical model reveals itself to be a definitive version of events. For one of the legacies of Faith's slave ancestry, as indicated by dotted lines between relatives and question marks where names should be, is a certain crisis of identity and, specifically, an uncertainty surrounding issues of inheritance and origin. Stories of Mr Livingstone's infidelities at 'home' and across the plantations, for instance, are just one expression of colonialism's sexually exploitative and oppressive forces: 'Rumour had it that this English plantation owner – "Mr Livingstone I presume," – fathered several hundred children by the slave women on his estate' (Levy 2004: 259). What this, and many other stories like it (we might recall the alliteratively patronizing tale of 'randy Reverend Bunyan' (Levy 2004: 131)) suggest is that the slave body is also something of an exquisite corpse, a composite and ambiguous body that is not simply black or white, but a complex juxtaposition of black *and* white.

Indeed, as the family's multiple and contesting stories un/fold, the question of racial purity, and its attendant issues of prejudice and discrimination, reveals itself in a number of ways. Faith learns how her relatives are invariably denied work out of fear of racial contamination, how they are socially shunned and racially abused in the street, and how some are simply beaten, or worked to death, because of the colour of their skin. An equally disquieting feature of the stories that we hear, however, is the presence – and persistence – of racism within and across familial relations. Without exception, every story foregrounds either the racial composition of the teller, or the objects, of the tale. In the following case, the black bodies, or exquisite corpses, under intense 'investigation' are Faith's parents: 'She [Margaret] wanted to know was Mildred a quadroon, an octoroon, a half-breed or just black [. . .] Margaret eventually told Wade that Mildred had too much African in her blood' (Levy 2004: 288).[2] This tale, like the many others that echo it, is disquieting for the revelation that racial discrimination is not an exclusively outside force or, indeed, the preserve of white colonial thinking. It is also deeply embedded within formations of black identity and experience, manifesting itself, in the discriminators, in forms of physical and psychological abuse (Wade's father beat him to the point of him developing a stutter), and residing, in the discriminated, in feelings of humiliation, resentment and self-loathing. It is hardly surprising, then, that Wade and Mildred should choose not to speak of familial histories that so brutally treated and, ultimately, denied them.

Faith's exquisite corpse narrative is significant for the ways in which it ruptures a family history marked by silence, disavowal and repression. With each story that un/folds across the narrative, Faith comes a little closer to understanding her own, individual history as it exists in an intricate, and often difficult, relation to a rich ancestral collective:

> Let those bully boys walk behind me in the playground. Let them tell me, 'You're a darkie. Faith's a darkie.' I am the granddaughter of Grace and William Campbell. I am the great-grandchild of Cecilia Hilton. I am descended from Katherine whose mother was a slave. I am the cousin of Afria. I am the niece of Coral Thompson and the daughter of Wade and Mildred Jackson. Let them say what they like. Because I am the bastard child of Empire and I will have my day. (Levy 2004: 326–7)

With a renewed acceptance of her black inheritance, and all of its complexities and ambivalences, Faith is 'coming home to tell everyone' (Levy 2004: 339). The game of exquisite corpse – of 'folding the paper and passing it on' – will, and, indeed must, continue. This is not only because, as the incomplete family tree shows, and Auntie Coral observes, stories and histories are never quite closed: 'Well, now you know a little, Faith. But there is more. There is always more' (Levy 2004: 325). It is also because there will always be a need for intervention. Faith may be returning 'home' to England, but this is not a utopian homecoming that foresees a future without prejudice and discrimination (be that across or within racial groups). Indeed, the future directions of black British experience remain uncertain and unnerving. Nevertheless, Faith's exquisite corpse narrative will always provide her with a form of resistance, as its juxtaposing energies counter the smooth telling of dominant historical narratives, and as it insists on alternative and sometimes unexpected un/foldings of history and experience.

## Contest and Collaboration in *The Long Song*

> THE BOOK YOU ARE now holding within your hand was born of a craving.
> My mama had a story – a story that lay so fat within her breast that she felt
> impelled, by some force which was mightier than her own will, to relay this
> tale to me, her son. Her intention was that, once knowing the tale, I would
> then, at some other date, convey its narrative to my own daughters. And so it
> would go on. The fable would never be lost and, in its several recitals, might
> gain a majesty to rival the legends told whilst pointing at the portraits or
> busts in any fancy great house upon this island of Jamaica. (Levy 2011: 1)

*The Long Song* announces itself self-consciously as a form of exquisite
corpse. Thomas's 'foreword' to his mother's narrative immediately gives
voice to the counter-historical energies of what will follow: a story, or
collection of stories, of intervention, resilience and resistance that will
rupture flat, official versions of imperialist history, and generate, in turn,
forms of witnessing that insist on history as alive, open and in process. That Thomas's editorial 'foreword' is itself a form of intervention
designed to contextualize and contain July's storytelling is not insignificant. Thomas's trade as a printer means that he deals in the stabilization
of language, and this move to fix words on the page places his historiographical practices in direct tension with the oral forms of storytelling
on which his mother insists. From the very outset, then, *The Long Song*
also enacts a contest of narrative forms, one that pitches written and
bounded historical accounts against an unfinished, shifting body of stories – 'And so on it would go'.

July's stories of her life and the lives of others are constantly on the
move, and this is nowhere more evident than in the multiple tales that
she tells about her own origins. The bastard child of the overseer Tam
Dewar, July constructs a 'tall tale' of beginnings that starts over and
over again: 'July was born on a cane piece [. . .] With some tellings it was
not the rain that beat down [. . .] but the hot sun [. . .] Other times it was
a wind [. . .] While a further version had a tiger' (Levy 2011: 13). Turning
away from the temporal restrictions of linear narrative, July composes
an exquisite corpse – 'Let me unfold to you (Levy 2011: 25) – that travels
across time and space, in turn flaunting its instability and its unreliabil-
ity. For a slave conceived in the act of rape, this particular form of storytelling is significant for the ways in which it opens up opportunities
for historical revisionism. Speaking herself repeatedly into being, July
is able to fashion some sense of ownership over her body, identity and
history as she creates a story – or body of stories – that she can at least
survive by. Whether July's versions of events are at all close to being
accurate, or even believable, is really of little consequence to her. This is
because, as far as July and Levy are concerned, there is no substantive
difference between historical writing and storytelling; both are mere
forms of narration full of limitations and possibilities. What matters

is how these forms of narrative are put to use in the articulation and recording of lived experience.

Although *The Long Song* is replete with tensions between historiographical and storytelling traditions, it is perhaps in Levy's elliptical re-imaginings of the Baptist Wars that the contest of narrative forms reaches its fullest expression. While July spends time recounting a domestic rebellion (engineered by Godfrey) in which she lays a 'soiled bed sheet' in place of a fine linen table cloth on Miss Caroline's Christmas table, Thomas commands his mother to discipline her stories to the service of historical writing: 'But this is the Baptist War, Mama [. . .] the time of the Christmas rebellion' (Levy 2011: 101). For the printer-cum-historian, the urgent historical imperatives that should be driving July's narrative are clear: to establish the exact geographical location of the rebellion's origins ('Salt Spring' or 'Kensington Pen, up near Maroon Town'); to pen a full biography of the rebellion's leader, Sam Sharp; to speak with authority, and on behalf of all negroes, on the issue of Abolition; and to bear witness to the militia's defeat at 'Old Montpellier' and Shuttlewood Pen' (Levy 2011: 101–2). Clearly Levy has researched her historical subject matter meticulously, and the extensive list of source documents in the 'Acknowledgements' section at the end of the novel bears witness to her work in the archive. Tellingly, however, July feels under no such pressure to recreate any form of realist, historical narrative and, rather cheekily, she refers the reader to additional (fictional) reading matter should they feel the need for 'a fuller account of what happened during this time': George Dovaston's pamphlet, *Facts and documents connected with the Great Slave Rebellion of Jamaica (1832)*, and John Hoskin's *Conflict and change. A view from the great house of slaves, slavery and the British Empire* are selected, although the latter is to be avoided, in July's opinion, for its narrow ideological perspective (Levy 201: 103).

At stake in this contest of narrative forms is an enduring tension between, what Jean-François Lyotard has termed, metanarratives (or historical 'grand narratives') and micronarratives (or 'little narratives') (Lyotard 1984: xxiv). According to Lyotard, there emerged in the second half of the twentieth century a profound disbelief in grand explanatory theories that made absolute claims to knowledge and truth. He cites, as an example, the belief in human progress towards perfection characteristic of Enlightenment philosophy, a defining European philosophical perspective which, as Levy (quoting Emmanuel Kant) observes, reserved 'perfection' for 'the white race' (Levy 2011b: 406). Traditionally, Lyotard argues, 'grand narratives' function to regulate and restrain individual subjects by validating certain political and philosophical positions, and forms of historical knowledge, over others. They also, crucially, exercise their homogenizing and unifying perspectives at the exclusion of 'little narratives', forms of imaginative resistance that seek to challenge and dismantle 'grand narrative' accounts of legitimate knowledge and truth. In their conversations about how to best represent the Baptist Wars, we see how Thomas and July exercise these conflicting narrative strategies: for Thomas, authenticity lies in fixing historical experience in a definable and *named* historical event; yet, for July, authenticity lies in admitting to what she simply does not, and cannot, know: 'If there was such an invention at the time of this Baptist War (as my son does name it), then I am sure I would have known what was going on everywhere at one time. But there was not' (Levy 2011: 103).

One of the conspicuous features of Levy's novel about the 'long' history of slavery and its legacies is the conspicuous absence of named historical events. The text even refuses to make any grand announcement about Abolition; instead, the larger story of racial emancipation un/folds across the text in the form of little stories:

> The negro woman [. . .] bent slyly to the cook to murmur what she had heard from the preacher-man about them all soon to be free. Whispered close, yet spoken fast, Hannah did not hear every word [. . .] but she nodded with feigned understanding [. . .] The mulatto woman [. . .] she had heard that it was the King who said there were to be no more slaves [. . .] The fisherman [. . .] had heard nothing [. . .] that free coloured woman with brown skin [. . .] said all this chat-chat was nonsense – that the white massa were correct, the King-man had said nothing about them being free. (Levy 2011: 81)

Stories of Abolition, and its denial, are either passed on partially or with embellishment, taking detours along the way, and allowing, in turn, new plot lines to develop. That these tales of emaciation have the potential to travel in any direction gestures simultaneously to the limitations and possibilities of narrative. This is a tension Levy admits to knowing all too well when she speaks of the 'excellent body of scholarship, both in Britain and in the Caribbean, on the history of slavery' that, despite its rigour, has inevitable gaps: 'I wanted to put back in the voices of everyday life for black Jamaicans that are so silent from the record' (Levy 2011b: 414). The impulse behind Levy's act of historical recovery does not limit itself, therefore, to ensuring that an alternative black narrative body, an exquisite corpse of multiple stories and histories in this case, is allowed to speak 'of and for' itself (Levy 2011b: 409). There is a further impulse to turn the historical gaze, one which has been so well trained to scrutinize grand events, towards an examination of the quotidian: for a whole host of alternative histories and stories are to be found in the seeming innocuousness of the everyday.

Let's return, briefly, to another version of the scene above:

> The mulatto woman who had bought her own freedom and a cart upon the same day and sold cedar boxes full of sugar cakes frosted in pink, white and yellow – the one who was saving for a donkey so it was no longer she that had to pull the produce – she had heard that it was the King who said there were to be no more slaves. (Levy 2011: 81)

This quotidian scene of labour is striking for the way in which it folds into *Fruit of the Lemon* and subsequently un/folds a series of neglected connections across *Fruit of the Lemon/The Long Song*. Faith, we recall, has something of a sweet tooth, but her very favourite sweet treats are 'Fondant fancies' (Levy 2011: 40, 41, 45), small pink, white and yellow cakes that boast a particularly high sugar content. What this conspicuous moment of un/folding reveals is a complex set of historical connections linking an imperial past, fuelled by the slave and sugar cane trades, and a postcolonial present.

Yet, as so often with Levy's writings, the relationship between the colonial past and the postcolonial present is not simply one of opposition. As Bill Ashcroft notes, the 'process of imperial power and its resistance never operates in this binary way' (Ashcroft 1999: 119). Instead, colonial and postcolonial identities are shown to emerge out of an intricate and simultaneous process of resistance *and* accommodation. There is every chance, for instance, that Faith may have inherited her sweet tooth from July, the slave 'born upon a cane piece' who eventually becomes the free woman writing with a cup of sweetened tea beside her: '(although not quite sweet enough for my taste, but sweetness comes at a dear price here upon this sugar island)' (Levy 2011: 9).[3] Faith's and July's daily sugar intake may be something to watch for health reasons. But it is also something to keep an eye on for what it might just reveal about how we are to understand the contemporary moment in relation to the past. Ashcroft observes how globalization, an inescapable feature of the modern, everyday 'has a long history embedded in the history of imperialism, in the structure of the world system of international capitalism, and in the origins of a global economy within the ideology of imperial rhetoric' (Ashcroft 1999: 123). The fact that Faith cannot really afford Fondant Fancies – she helps herself to the boxes in her mother's cupboard – suggests much more than her earning capacity at the BBC. Embedded in this quotidian act of consumption is a complex history of consumer-capitalism and exploitation from which no-one is exempt: just as the mulatto woman profiteers from selling versions of a commodity that once enslaved her, so July and Faith take pleasure in consuming a commodity with a long and incredibly bitter-sweet history.

Another significant narrative of resistance and accommodation un/folds across *Fruit of the Lemon/The Long Song* in the form of July's work as a dresser or 'lady's maid' to Miss Caroline. As I have discussed at some length, Faith's 'promotion' to dresser at the BBC is caught up in a long history of racial inequality, both in terms of the Corporation's employment opportunities and its white historiographic adaptations of British experience. Although it is clearly inappropriate to speak of July's transition from Amity field slave to 'the missus's favoured lady's maid' (Levy 2011: 58) as some form of promotion, this individual story of slave labour is notable for at least two reasons. First, it points to a hierarchy of slave labour within and across the plantations – July is rather put out to be cleaning the hall floor, for instance (Levy 2011: 79); secondly, it gives voice to a slave experience that alongside hideous accounts of 'hardship, cruelty and humiliation [. . .] runs a constant thread of small but courageous acts of defiance' (Levy 2011b: 415–16). We witness small acts of resistance, for instance, in an amusing scene in which Florence, Lucy (the washerwomen) and July strip Miss Caroline's best dress of its ornamentation (lace collar, pearl buttons, securing hooks, black wire bars), and flatten its 'many frills, flounces and furbelows' until the garment – its 'rigid arms stuck out in front as if the dress were pleading for someone to embrace it' (Levy 2011: 61) – is transformed into a wicked parody of the mistress's unloved body.

As Steeve Buckridge observes in his cultural history of dress and slavery: 'African slaves in the Caribbean participated in resistance and accommodation activities that were vital to their survival in a society that sought to dehumanize them' (Buckridge 2004: 7). Often subtle and complex in their expressions of defiance, the slaves were also creative, as was frequently the case in their 'use of dress for cultural expression and to make a political statement' (Buckridge 2004: 7). *The Long Song* picks up on the various tensions and significances of dress for the slave body. In one of her many conflicting encounters with Clara, for example, July's clothing (she is wearing 'her missus' discards') belies her social standing, or rather that of her colonial master, by whose worth she is judged:

> July was wearing her best – a new blue kerchief upon her head, her pale-blue cotton blouse stitched with lace and two pearl buttons, recently fallen from her missus's garment – yet within the shade of Clara's distinction, she felt as ragged as a half-plucked turkey [. . .] 'Your massa have no money for white muslin for you.' 'Me massa have plenty money', July replied. (Levy 2011: 93)

We would be hasty to reduce July's and Clara's daily bickering about their dress to mere outbursts of idle pettiness. For slave society 'was divided according to class, ethnicity and even occupation, and the divisions were reflected in slave dress' (Buckridge 2004: 27). While July's gesture of transcultural resistance is lost among Clara's show of sartorial superiority, what is really at stake here is the implication that July is not just sartorially inferior, but racially inferior among the slave communities. The Friday dances run by Miss Clara do have a very strict dress code, but admittance is only gained once a particular set of physical requirements have been met: 'you know me dances be just for coloured women' (Levy 2011: 241). Despite her mulatto inheritance, July fails the humiliating physical examination because she is not as white as her heritage would imply: 'your skin be just too dark [. . .] You is too full of negro' (Levy 2011: 243). With this articulation of racism embedded within racial communities (the novel is replete with such moments of racial prejudice), *The Long Song/Fruit of the Lemon* un/fold once more to force disquieting historical connections.

And it is on this issue of internalized racism and its potentially dev-astating consequences that *The Long Song* ends, although, of course, in a novel self-consciously replete with endings and beginnings, *The Long Song* does not end at all. Thomas's closing words to the reader are the ver-bal equivalent to 'folding the paper and passing it on'. But we, the read-ers, are not only in receipt of an exquisite corpse of histories and stories, some of which largely remain untold. We are also in receipt of a weighty responsibility: 'In England the finding of negro blood within a family is not always met with rejoicing. So please, do not think to approach upon Emily Goodwin too hastily with the details of this story, for its load may prove to be unsettling' (Levy 2011: 398). *Fruit of the Lemon/ The Long Song* unfold once more, then, as Thomas's speculations about Emily invoke Faith's lived experiences: 'Perhaps she is in England, unaware of the strong family connection she has to this island of Jamaica' (Levy 2011: 398). In this speculative utterance, the past, an imagined future and the present are juxtaposed to reveal a highly complex black contemporary moment. Perhaps another neologism is required to discuss the complex-ities of black experience in Levy's texts: post/colonial. What this allows for is an un/folding of times that disrupts 'unif[ied] temporal orders' so embedded in the 'colonial project' (Luckhurst and Marks 1999: 4–5), and that offers, instead, 'alternative articulations of historical pasts, presents and futures' (Osborne 1999: 45) that will un/fold in all sorts of unex-pected and disquieting ways.

In this chapter, I have restricted myself to un/folding *Fruit of the Lemon/The Long Song* in order to tease out neglected textual and histori-cal connections within and across both novels. However, my un/folding methodology holds perfectly well for reading Levy's other writings in relation to one another. Indeed, replete with dynamic critical and crea-tive tensions, the interventionist practice of exquisite corpse provides us with a useful way of thinking about, and testing, Levy's own formal and contextual interventions in black British writing. Across and within Levy's work – the novels, short stories, non-fictional writings and inter-views – multiple and contesting histories, stories and experiences strive to give voice to 'our shared past' (Levy 2004: 326). But this is not a past to be understood as closed or complete. Rather, Levy's writings of 'our' history are intensely alive, open and in process; and the various pleas-ures and challenges of encountering this exquisite body of work is that it might just un/fold in any direction.

## Notes

1  I am following Emery's use of the term here, although it should be noted that Emery gives full credit to Amy Clukey for the term 'plantation modernism'. See Amy Clukey (2009), 'Plantation Modernism: Irish, Caribbean, and American Fiction, 1890–1950', PhD Thesis, Pennsylvania State University.

2 'Miscegenation in Jamaica gave rise to gradations of coloureds: a *sambo* was the child of a mulatto and Negro; a *mulatto* was the child of a white person and a Negro; a *quadroon* was the child of a mulatto and a white person; and a *mustee* was the child of a quadroon and a white person. The more common term for this caste was *mulatto*.' See Steve O. Buckridge (2004), *The Language of Dress: Resistance and Accommodation in Jamaica, 1760–1890*. Jamaica, Barbados, Trinidad and Tobago: University of the West Indies Press, 9.

3 Levy's novels are replete with troubling connections between the colonial past, the post-colonial present and processes of globalization. To take just one more perplexing example from *Fruit of the Lemon*: what are we to make of Wade Jackson's accountancy job at Tate and Lyle, that iconic, multinational sugar company whose corporate history intersects so troublingly with the 'long' history of slavery?

# 'I am the narrator of this work': Narrative Authority in Andrea Levy's *The Long Song*

### FIONA TOLAN

---

**Chapter Summary:** Commencing with a consideration of narrative technique in *The Long Song*, this chapter suggests that Levy's novel works to both recall and reframe late twentieth-century feminist critical readings of female narrative voice. In particular, it locates *The Long Song* within the contentious literary critical heritage forged by *Jane Eyre* and *Wide Sargasso Sea*. It suggests that, while *The Long Song* utilizes familiar twentieth-century postcolonial and feminist literary strategies as it works at 'putting back the voices that were left out', in its irrepressible and often comic energy, it also moves to take those strategies in new directions, requiring a critical re-engagement with the points of contact between postcolonial and feminist analysis.

---

'I am the narrator of this work', declares the indomitable voice of July, inscribed in gilded embossed print on the yellow cover of the hardback first edition of Andrea Levy's 2010 novel, *The Long Song*. In a text that consciously foregrounds the materiality of the book in its approximation of the aesthetics of a late nineteenth-century volume, July's declaration perpetuates the conceit of the fictional author, deflating the editor's puff, which would have the narrative proclaimed 'a thrilling journey' through 'the last turbulent years of slavery', with a characteristic 'Cha . . . what fuss-fuss'. 'Come', says July, rejecting the publicist's stratagem: 'let them just read it for themselves' (Levy 2011: flyleaf). Operating, to use Gerard Genette's term, as part of the 'threshold' of the novel – 'an "undefined zone" between the inside and the outside' (Genette 1997: 2) – the external performance of July's voice on the fringe of Levy's text lays claim to the character's narratorial authority over 'her' book. Working against this seemingly irrepressible paratextual incursion of the female narrative voice onto the book's cover, however, is the novel's opening 'Foreword', ostensibly penned by July's son and editor, Thomas Kinsman, whose 'Afterword', occurring nearly 400 pages later, neatly completes the editorial circumscription of the ex-slave's story. As any student of feminist analysis might observe, Levy's narrative structure thus positions July's subversive tale of trauma, rebellion and liberation as mediated and delimitated by an authoritative masculine narrative frame. Like the tripartite narrative of Jean Rhys's *Wide Sargasso Sea* (1966) – the textual precursor that Levy's similarly neo-Victorian novel most readily recalls – *The Long Song* pits male and female subjectivities against one another, thereby readily highlighting a politics of identity and representation.

While Levy's novel certainly invokes such familiarly problematic narrative structures, it equally works to circumvent their repressive potential. July's autobiography recounts her story of growing up in slavery on *Amity*, a Jamaican sugar plantation, and proceeds through emancipation and the subsequent years of 'apprenticeship'. It is told in old age, when July is reunited with the son she abandoned as an infant on the doorstep of a Baptist preacher, and who, after being educated in Britain, has now returned to Jamaica as 'one of the finest printers upon this island' (Levy 2011: 3). It is Thomas's idea that she write her story, as he explains in his introduction: 'My mama had a story – a story that lay so fat within her breast that she felt impelled, by some force which was mightier than her own will, to relay this tale to me, her son' (Levy 2011: 1). In an attempt to divert his mother's compulsive storytelling energies, Thomas suggests that she might better write rather than speak her story, to which she 'thankfully agreed' (Levy 2011: 4). July's narrative, however, cannot so readily be contained and it spills far beyond the limits of the 'chapbook – a small pamphlet' (Levy 2011: 2) that her longsuffering son had originally envisioned. Commencing with a birth myth of magical realist proportions, and proceeding through elements of oral tradition, satire, tragedy and farce, socio-historical treatise, *bildungsroman*, and postcolonial 'con-text' (Thieme 2001), encompassing multiple histories and ventriloquizing a cacophony of voices, July becomes a female trickster-narrator, wily and disruptive.

As Jeanne Rosier Smith explains, tricksters (folkloric West African prankster figures) 'infuse narrative structure with energy, humour, and polyvalence, producing a politically radical subtext in the narrative form itself' (Smith 1997: 2). Clearly familiar with the trickster tales that migrated from Africa to America and the Caribbean with the Middle Passage of the slave trade, July appropriates this storyteller role for herself, concluding her opening sequence with the comment: 'And so ends the story of July's birth – a story that was more thrilling than anything the rascal spider Anancy could conjure' (Levy 2011: 13). Though largely conforming to her beleaguered son's request that she 'speak true' (Levy 2011: 185), July's narrative is nevertheless imbricated within an enduring, global tradition of 'tall-tall telling' (Levy 2011: 168). Consequently, Thomas's well-intentioned attempt to limit and order his mother's memoir is so humorous in its futility that it effectively demonstrates the remove at which Levy's twenty-first-century novel stands from the kind of late twentieth-century feminist readings of narrative structure that it clearly anticipates. *The Long Song* utilizes familiar postcolonial and feminist literary strategies as it works at 'putting back the voices that were left out' (Levy 2011b: 410) but in its irrepressible and often comic energy, it also takes those strategies in new directions, proffering a narrator who both demands and is assured of her own narrative authority.

## You May Take My Word upon It: History and Narrative Authority

*The Long Song* is, in many ways, a departure for Levy, whose previous works have primarily been concerned with the second-generation children of postcolonial migrants to Britain. For the British-born characters of these novels, the recurring trope of Jamaica is a complex and contradictory site of exotic otherness and fantasized belonging: both 'a land of crawly things that bite, sting and kill you' (Levy 2004: 202) and 'somewhere where being black doesn't make you different' (Levy 2004b: 272). The young protagonists in Levy's early works commonly articulate this shifting ambivalence towards what Salman Rushdie evocatively termed an 'imaginary homeland' (Rushdie 1992), which recurs in much recent black British fiction. As Maria Helena Lima notes, 'Readers already familiar with some of the post-colonial rewritings of the conventions of the novel of development feel comfortably "at home" when reading Andrea Levy's coming-of-age novels' (Lima 2005: 56). Indeed Levy's earlier novels have largely conformed to what Mark Stein terms 'novels of transformation': that 'large section of black British literature [that] describes and entails subject formation under the influence of political, social, educational, familial, and other forces and thus resembles the *bildungsroman*' (Stein 2004: xiii). *The Long Song* continues Levy's preoccupation with this now familiar postcolonial incarnation of the *bildungsroman*, evident from her first novel, *Every Light in the House Burnin'* (1994), and extends the burgeoning interest in historical fiction evinced in the 1950s setting of *Small Island* (2004). In its reconstruction of nineteenth-century slavery and colonial society, however, *The Long Song* perhaps most readily lends itself to comparison with a steadily developing canon of neo-Victorian fictions that encompasses such disparate but overlapping texts as Rhys's *Wide Sargasso Sea* (discussed in more detail below), Toni Morrison's *Beloved* (1987), and Peter Carey's *Jack Maggs* (1997). Such texts, which commonly include 'the self-conscious rewriting of historical narratives to highlight the suppressed histories of gender and sexuality, race and empire, as well as challenges to the conventional understandings of the historical itself' (Kaplan 2007: 3), strive to recover and reanimate lost histories.

Discussing the current and apparently inexhaustible preoccupation with what she prefers to broadly categorize as 'Victoriana', Cora Kaplan suggests that the phenomenon may be best understood as intimately bound up with contemporary definitions of 'history' as 'a kind of conceptual nomad, not so much lost as permanently restless and unsettled' (Kaplan 2007: 3). Still reacting to what Jean-Francois Lyotard famously identified as postmodernism's 'incredulity toward metanarratives' (Lyotard 1984: xxiv), much contemporary historical fiction engages in what Linda Hutcheon terms a 'postmodern ironic rethinking of history' (Hutcheon 1988: 5), exposing the limits of authorized historical accounts and self-consciously dismantling the grand narratives of the past. In identifying a similarly postmodern impulse within neo-Victorian fiction, Kate Mitchell nevertheless makes a pertinent distinction between that genre and the more sceptical historiographic metafictions (as categorized by Hutcheon), which more readily collapse the distance between history and fiction. In contrast, 'while demonstrating a vivid awareness of the problematics involved in seeking and achieving historical knowledge,' suggests Mitchell, neo-Victorian novels 'remain nonetheless committed to the possibility and the value of striving for that knowledge' (Mitchell 2010: 3). Accordingly, Levy's *The Long Song*, which is replete with multiple narratives, alternative histories, tall tales and contested accounts, nevertheless retains a palpable moral certainty regarding the necessity and value of its reclamation of the unreported past.

In an essay on 'The Writing of *The Long Song*', Levy describes her novel as a response to a question she once heard raised regarding the difficulty of feeling pride in a Jamaican ancestry that merely signified – so it was argued – a heritage of enslavement and victimization. Contemplating the capacity of storytelling to counteract the formal Eurocentric historical narrative of Britain's exploitation and subsequent liberation of African-Caribbeans, which too commonly posits the slaves as 'simply a mass of wretched voiceless victims' (Levy 2011b: 409), Levy turns instead to an imaginative reconstruction of the complex social systems that inevitably evolved out of nearly 300 years of slave economy. Within the terrible strictures of 'a giant, brutal island factory', muses Levy, 'People were suffering and dying. But clearly people were living and surviving as well' (Levy 2011b: 409). With a combination of ingenuity and cunning, resilience and humour, Levy's characters lay claim to a social sphere and individuality denied them by the dehumanizing processes of slavery. For Levy, the fictional space of the novel provides a means of reconstituting the lost lives of 'people who, from their tiny islands, have made a mark on the world' (Levy 2011b: 416), thereby reconstituting them not as victims but as survivors. It is from this ethical premise – that a lost history that could inspire admiration rather than pity may be salvaged from the margins of 'History' – that Levy commences her novel.

Unimpressed by existing available accounts of plantation domestic life – 'the puff and twaddle of some white lady's mind' (Levy 2011: 8) – July is, she informs her reader, 'a woman possessed of a forthright tongue and little ink' (Levy 2011: 7), and as such she commences her story, without preamble, with the rape of her mother, Kitty, by the plantation overseer, Tam Dewar. The scene provides the first of many editorial disputes between July and Thomas who declares it too 'indelicate a commencement of any tale' (Levy 2011: 7). As an opening, however, it serves multiple functions. The assault is, we are to understand, commonplace; only distinguished in this instance by the crumpled bolt of cloth subsequently thrust into Kitty's hand, leaving her puzzled as to 'whether she should be grateful to this white man for this limp offering or not . . .' (Levy 2011: 7). While Levy was reluctant to create another 'harrowing tale of violence and misery' (Levy 2011: 406), the early scene of Kitty's rape nevertheless determinedly positions the casual brutality of slavery inescapably at the inception of her frequently humorous novel. As a synecdoche of slavery – a heinous abuse of power followed by startlingly insufficient recompense – it condenses centuries of exploitation into a single, terrible moment. Kitty's unprotesting submission to Dewar's assault, rapidly contrasted with her near-mythic figuration as an Amazon, a machete-wielding, bare-breasted 'colossal woman' (Levy 2011: 12), works to epitomize the perversely misaligned power structures wrought by slavery. Whereas the resultant conception of July, instead, points forward to subsequent generations, gestated in the violence and abuses of colonialism, but maturing into new and surprising futures outside of its confines; a multicultural future that Levy, elsewhere, has termed the 'one positive legacy' (Levy 2004c) of the British Empire.

From its contested commencement to its multiple points of attempted conclusion, July's narrative persistently resists attempts to authorize, corroborate or contest its veracity. Her story recounts her infancy in the cane fields, her redeployment as lady's maid to Caroline Mortimer (sister of plantation owner John Howarth), and a subsequent illicit relationship with Robert Goodwin (later Caroline's husband and owner of Amity after Howarth's death). While developing amidst urgent national and international political upheavals, this narrative is determinedly intimate and domestic, charting the political progress of imperial Jamaica only obliquely. Approaching the moment of the Christmas Rebellion of the 'Baptist War (as my son does name it)' (Levy 2011: 102), July's focus is instead oriented around an account of 'Caroline Mortimer's unfinished dinner' (Levy 2011: 101), which is sabotaged by a wily staff long before it is disrupted by the mustering of the local militia. These two narratives – domestic and military – overlap and coexist, and July refuses to cede the former to the latter. Accepting a Baptist pamphlet on the rebellion proffered by her well-meaning son, July sanguinely observes both its uses and limitations, equating its gaps and omissions with those of her own parallel account: 'nothing that appears within this minister's pages was witnessed by my eye, and what my eye did see at the time does not appear in this man's report' (Levy 2011: 103). July rejects the implied superiority of the authoritative tract and posits a relativism that would seem to draw her towards a postmodern democratization of textualities. At the same time, however, an essay penned by Thomas's adoptive mother recounting her meeting with a desperate and pleading postpartum July is charged with a reprehensible misrepresentation of the truth. And although her own story 'purport[s] to be a fiction' (Levy 2011: 397), July's response to discovering the alternative account is to reassert her writerly authority, declaring: 'I must now return to my story with some haste, before another foolish white woman might think to seize it with the purpose of belching out some nonsensical tale on my behalf' (Levy 2011: 195). With this pronouncement of sole narrative ownership, July in effect defines the limits of Levy's postmodern sympathies.

July balks at any form of historiographic or narrative practice that might undermine her ultimate authorial control. Nevertheless, her text contains multiple instances of unresolved, hyperbolic and contradictory narratives that foreground experiential rather than factual accounts and problematize notions of authority and veracity. In one of the most unreliable sequences of the novel, July triumphantly witnesses the procession and burial of the symbolic coffin of slavery, when 'every slave upon this island did shake off the burden of their bondage as one' (Levy 2011: 182). Only when challenged by Thomas does July admit that 'when the chains of bondage were finally ripped from the negro, and slavery declared no more, our July was not skipping joyous within the celebrations', but was instead 'confined within the tedious company of her missus' (Levy 2011: 195–6). As Levy notes in 'The Writing of *The Long Song*', 'Dramatic events happened in Jamaica during this time', but 'July is never really at the centre of the action' (Levy 2011b: 415). Here Levy exemplifies the manner in which the great moments of history rarely coincide with everyday lived experience. The scene also contains the 'theoretical self-awareness of history and fiction as human constructs' that Hutcheon defines as typical of historiographic metafiction (Hutcheon 1988: 5). It locates July on the periphery of the historical record, but in the reluctant recommencement and subsequent refiguring of July's narrative, it also demonstrates the illusory nature of what Hayden White terms the 'formal coherence' of the historical account, whereby events are orchestrated into 'a comprehensible process with a discernible beginning, middle and end' (White 1973: 7). Emancipation, which would seem to conclude the narrative of slavery, and upon which July wishes to neatly close her memoir, is exposed as a single inconclusive moment within a tangled stream of consequences that will continue to be played out without foreseeable end.

Functioning alongside July's thwarted attempt at a carefully emplotted resolution are various contestable narrative reconstructions. Many are self-aggrandizing: after killing a small band of rebel slaves in a stumbling assault, the militia contrive 'quite a heroic tale to tell' (Levy 2011: 146); while Caroline's dramatically embellished account of her brother's 'murder' becomes, with frequent retellings, 'a tale worthy of the most flamboyant writer' (Levy 2011: 199). The most vivid contested narrative in the novel, however, is that of July's rescue from Dewar by Kitty; as July explains, 'What happened next has been told in so many ways by so many people [. . .] that it is hard for your storyteller to know which version to recount' (Levy 2011: 172). Comprised of contradictory fragments, the details debated and contested, the story takes on fantastic proportions. At one point, Kitty is transfigured into the legendary figure of the flying African, who sheds his wings during transportation and forgets the secret of flight, but who, in a moment of great need, 'simply says a word or phrase and putting his arms up, flies away, back to Africa' (Higgins 2001: 7). In the service of her stolen daughter, Kitty reclaims these same mythic powers, as one witness attests: 'Miss Kitty? She fly, oh she fly. Her feet no longer upon God's earth; me see her soar t'rough the air. Give me the book so me can place me hand upon it. Me tell you, she fly!' (Levy 2011: 169). Rumour, gossip, myth and legend all compete in the account of the rebellion and its aftermath, and although these various folk discourses are met with the brutal counter-discourse of the law that would condemn Kitty to death in her absence, the multiplicity of voices nevertheless challenge any attempt at a unified, authoritative truth.

*The Long Song* is swollen with exaggerated accounts, but it is also characterized by certain gaps and silences such as Howarth's refusal to protest at the horrors he witnesses during the rebellion, and his subsequent inability to speak to his sister of what he saw. In a description focalized through Dewar, Howarth's silence is revealed as a consequence of a value system perverted by empire; witnessing brutality and torture, he 'did shake his head in mild reproach' and 'then he rode on' (Levy 2011: 148). For Levy, Howarth is another victim of empire, his humanity fundamentally corroded by its injustices. So invested is he in the myth of British superiority that only the sight of Englishmen dressed as women and beating a preacher is able to finally transgress his corrupted moral code, leaving him, eventually 'sickened, ashamed and disgusted' (Levy 2011: 149). Unable to reconcile his neighbours' actions with a deeply invested concept of Britishness, the episode leaves Howarth devastated as his circumscribed worldview crumbles, and his inability to speak presages his suicide: a symbolic gunshot to the mouth that silences him forever.

Gaps and silences also mark other narratives. Repeatedly and determinedly asserting his gratitude to his loving adoptive parents and their Christian generosity – a gratitude that deeply irritates July – Thomas proves equally incapable of articulating both the casual racism his adoptive family frequently betrayed towards 'Black Tom' (Levy 2011: 376), and the wider prejudice he suffered in England, culminating in his thwarted attempt to run the London printing office he was bequeathed by his former employer. Instead: 'No pleading, nor complaint will start the story again before three silent years have passed and Thomas Kinsman is, once again, back upon the island of Jamaica' (Levy 2011: 389). In an article on Levy's earlier fiction, Michael Perfect relates a similar idea of narrative absences to Edward Said's concept of the 'contrapuntal' (a term taken from musicology): 'to read a text contrapuntally is to pay attention to its silences, with an exploration of what is *not* said allowing us to uncover histories and experiences that are concealed by (and yet in an interdependent relationship with) its dominant voice(s)' (Perfect 2010: 32). Within Levy's work, suggests Perfect, there is a recurring emphasis on engaging contrapuntally with multiple narratives, with attention to, in Said's words, 'the polyphony of many voices playing off against each other' (Said quoted in Perfect 2010: 32), thereby revealing and exploring resonant silences. Accordingly, in *The Long Song*, Thomas's silence gestures towards a colonial tradition of flawed Christian philanthropy and missionary zeal that forms part of a muted but complex web of narratives underpinning and diversifying the particularities of July's story. Thomas's oblique account of his time in England provides a counterpoint to July's memoir, touching upon another, unspoken narrative born of slavery – this time, male, diasporic – that must be decoded by the attentive reader, for whom the gaps and absences mutely articulate the injustices that Thomas's determinedly positive history wilfully elides.

The question of history and its telling continues to trouble July throughout *The Long Song*. At times, she evinces a clear scepticism regarding the function and purpose of historical discourse that brings to mind White's assertion that 'it is possible to view historical consciousness as a specifically Western prejudice by which the presumed superiority of modern, industrial society can be retroactively substantiated' (White 1973: 2). Similarly, describing the manner in which racism became endemic alongside European imperialism, Levy notes that 'making "negroes" into non-people – into sub-human livestock – was an important aspect of justifying slavery' (Levy 2011b: 407). Within the novel, this impetus to sustain economic processes with moral arguments finds particular expression in documents such as '*Conflict and change. A view from the great house of slaves, slavery and the British Empire*'. Written by a planter whose 'eyes would be shut to all but his own consequence', July decries its colonialist perspective and peremptorily dismisses any reader who might find his or her 'head nodding in agreement at this man's bluster' (Levy 2011: 103). History, as July recognizes, both justifies and modifies. Like the artist who paints the Jamaican landscape but omits the slave village – for 'no one wished to find squalid negroes within a rendering of a tropical idyll' (Levy 2011: 296) – the historian can work to erase the voices that threaten to disrupt and destabilize the authorized national narrative. July's response to these exposed omissions and elisions is not to assert the greater reliability of her own text – for it is frequently wilfully unreliable – but rather to provide a story that Mikhail Bakhtin might describe as 'multiform in style and variform in speech and voice' (Bakhtin 1981: 261); one that, in its polyphonic possibilities, enters into disruptive dialogue with the comparatively monologic narrative of European colonial history.

### In the Room under the House: Textual Hauntings

Narrative authority is a recurrent refrain throughout *The Long Song*. When pressed to extend her story beyond its premature and falsely happy conclusion, an indignant July declares: 'This tale is of my making. This story is told for my amusement. What befalls July is for me to devise' (Levy 2011: 185). Gesturing towards the historiographic and metafictional debates discussed above, this proprietary assertion accumulates further resonance when Levy's novel is situated within the tangled literary legacy of Charlotte Brontë's *Jane Eyre* (1847) and its 1960s prequel, Rhys's *Wide Sargasso Sea*. With its Caribbean plantation setting, its turncoat young Englishman whose clandestine 'wife' is housed in the basement rather than the attic, and in its central motif of violent renaming, *The Long Song* knowingly intervenes in the fraught critical history of these two texts, pursuing and extending the project first begun by Rhys of disrupting the embedded imperialist assumptions of Brontë's nineteenth-century novel.

Rhys's inscription of the elided history of Rochester's marriage to his first wife, Bertha Mason, has become one of the most celebrated canonical interventions of recent decades. Concerned that Brontë's novel provided 'only one side – the English side' (Rhys quoted in Smith 1997: xvii), Dominican-born Rhys determined to give voice to Brontë's inarticulately raging Creole. Depicted in her original Victorian incarnation as barely human – 'it snatched and growled like some strange wild animal' (Brontë 1992: 351) – Jane's narrative reduces Bertha to an object of horrified fascination and in doing so negates all vestiges of her subjectivity. As John Thieme notes, Brontë's Bertha is presented as 'the personification of a savage alterity that is unequivocally inimical to "civilized" English codes' (Thieme 2001: 76). In *Wide Sargasso Sea* instead, Rhys refigures Bertha as Antoinette, a haunted and haunting figure of untold narrative potential, and thereby constructs an oppositional counter-discourse to attenuate Brontë's implicit canonical and imperialist authority. As Antoinette, Bertha is humanized, and her mental instability becomes a complex consequence of multiple contributory factors, psychological and societal, rather than a congenital inevitability. With later, second-wave feminist critical analyses such as Sandra M. Gilbert

and Susan Gubar's *The Madwoman in the Attic* (1979), however, this reclamation of the Creole woman's subjectivity was eschewed in favour of
potent readings of Bertha as a metonymic figure of repressed female
rage within the nineteenth-century novel. Appropriated as 'Jane's truest
and darkest double' (Brontë 1992: 360), Bertha is reduced to an 'avatar of
Jane' (Brontë 1992: 359), enacting the Englishwoman's unconscionable
desires for violence and revenge.

A proliferation of such persuasive psychoanalytic feminist accounts
led to Gayatri Chakravorty Spivak terming *Jane Eyre*, in her hugely
influential revisionist 1985 essay, 'Three Women's Texts', a 'cult text of
feminism' (Spivak 1985: 244). In this essay Spivak charges Brontë with
bestializing Bertha to Jane's advantage in order to weaken the first
wife's moral entitlement to self-determination, and she accuses Western
feminist readings such as that of Gilbert and Gubar of sacrificing non-
Western female subjectivity in order to shore up the individualism of
Western women. This critique is also extended to Rhys's novel. While
*Wide Sargasso Sea* is conceded to challenge the colonial assumptions of
*Jane Eyre*, for Spivak it remains circumscribed by the conceptual limits
of Brontë's European text:

> In this fictive England, [Antoinette] must play out her role, act out the trans-
> formation of her 'self' into that fictive Other, set fire to the house and kill
> herself, so that Jane Eyre can become the feminist individualist heroine of
> British fiction. I must read this as an allegory of the general epistemic vio-
> lence of imperialism, the construction of a self-immolating colonial subject
> for the glorification of the social mission of the colonizer. (Spivak 1985: 251)

Spivak's analysis precipitated further critiques of Rhys's novel, and
critics such as Maria Olaussen, for example, have subsequently challenged common critical readings that equate Antoinette's patriarchal
domination with slavery as a Western feminist conceptual elision that
reprehensibly 'disregards the actual, historical institution of slavery as
experienced by black people' (Olaussen 1993: 69). It is to this charge that
Levy might be seen to address *The Long Song*. Where Rhys's novel juxtaposes Jane's white Britishness with the instability of Antoinette's Creole
identity, July's blackness locates her at a still further remove from the
imperial centre of British power. For Spivak, while Rhys at least 'sees to
it that the woman from the colonies is not sacrificed as an insane animal
for her sister's consolidation' (Spivak 1985: 251), her challenge to Brontë's
Eurocentrism ultimately fails to rewrite the predetermined script that
would forfeit the colonial other to affirm the colonizing self. As Kaplan
notes, since the publication of Spivak's essay, '"Jane Eyre" has become
a much more tarnished and controversial cultural emblem of Western
feminism's ambiguous political legacy' (Kaplan 2007: 17).

If *Wide Sargasso Sea* destabilized the Eurocentrism of Brontë's tale of
an Englishwoman's development, albeit with certain limitations, Levy's

*The Long Song* pursues a similarly revisionist project whereby the figure of Bertha/Antoinette is subject to a further, at least partial, imaginative reconstitution as Levy's July. When, with the death of Howarth – whose name perhaps carries a knowing echo of the Brontë family home – Caroline finds herself in charge of her brother's plantation, she employs the inexperienced young Robert Goodwin as overseer. The son of a clergyman, Robert arrives in Jamaica with youthful optimism, proclaiming his gratitude that 'Slavery – that dreadful evil – is at an end!' (Levy 2011: 214). As in Rhys's novel, the island works a seductive enchantment over the Englishman; overwhelmed by the heat and abundant verdure and beguiled by July's 'rare exotic beauty' (Levy 2011: 258), Robert is 'enthralled, motionless' (Levy 2011: 267) in her presence. Putatively in love but unable to conceive of an open relationship with a black woman, Robert instead marries Caroline in order to maintain July as his mistress: ' "You are my real wife," he told her. "This is my real home," he said of their damp little room under the house' (Levy 2011: 288). Relegated to the basement, July, like Bertha/Antoinette before her, is pushed to the periphery of the legitimate domestic space, haunting its edges and troubling the security of the sanctioned family narrative.

While echoing *Wide Sargasso Sea*, and thus *Jane Eyre*, *The Long Song* simultaneously works to delineate its distance from its textual precursors. July enters into her clandestine relationship with Robert willingly, flaunting her subsequent pregnancy in front of a powerless and determinedly unseeing Caroline. The lovingly furnished basement provides Robert with a welcome retreat from his sham marriage. And while the violent renaming that Antoinette undergoes in an attempt to Anglicize and thus 'civilize' her recurs in *The Long Song* when Caroline ascribes to her young slave the more refined appellation 'Marguerite', the mistress's futile persistence with the ill-fitting moniker is rendered ridiculous by the text, for 'it was only Caroline Mortimer who did look upon July's face to see a Marguerite residing there' (Levy 2011: 55). The clandestine wife of Levy's tale seems possessed of more robust strategies for resistance, and the renaming that so diminishes Rhys's Antoinette merely serves to expose the limitations of an obdurate imperial power that insists upon a crumbling omnipotence it cannot hope to sustain.

Caroline's attempt to rename July is a thoughtless act of oppression, but July's easy resistance signals an optimism within Levy's text regarding the persistence of a self-inscribed black identity unmediated by the rewritings and retellings of white history. Optimism does not preclude realism however, and Levy's young Rochester figure soon retreats to a retrenched colonialist racism, reasserting his previously disavowed racial privilege when he snaps at a devastated July: 'You heard your mistress, Marguerite. Bring some water' (Levy 2011: 326). If this renaming, in accordance with Rhys, is, after all, emblematic of an erasure of subjectivity, July's personhood is later negated entirely when Robert shouts: 'Get away from me, nigger, get away' (Levy 2011: 333). Interpellating July into an allotted object position, his words demand that she submit to his construction of her inhumanity. *The Long Song* is at its bleakest at this point, as 'all at once, July heard herself crying, "Mercy, mass, mercy," as she cringed away from him' (Levy 2011: 333). Like Antoinette in *Wide Sargasso Sea*, July experiences at this moment a psychic splitting of the self that signals the disintegration of her selfhood. Unlike *Wide Sargasso Sea*, however, this moment is succeeded, not by Antoinette's unwritten but inevitable self-immolation, but rather by the continuance of July's narrative and the reclamation of her self-proclaimed authority over her constructed identity as the 'July' of her authored text.

## Conclusion

*The Long Song* commences with the conception and birth of a daughter, and it concludes with the search for another lost daughter. In this notably matrilineal narrative, with its many echoes of *Wide Sargasso Sea* and *Jane Eyre*, and its preoccupation with female narrative authority, Levy's novel bears the marks of second-wave feminism's influence on contemporary women's writing. In its wider concerns with the legacy of empire, the novel also responds to Spivak's charge that 'the emergent perspective of feminist criticism reproduces the axioms of imperialism' (Spivak 1985: 243), and it exemplifies instead Anne McClintock's description of race, gender and class as 'articulated categories' that 'come in to existence *in and through* relation to each other' (McClintock 1995: 5). In Levy's novel, these categories coalesce around overlapping definitions of reproduction and inheritance, both biological and conceptual. In particular, the young black women in the novel are inculcated within the 'weird world of European racism' (Levy 2011b: 406) jealously guarding a complex racial schema of mulatto, quadroon and octoroon, and seeking a partner whose offspring might 'lift forward to white' (Levy 2011: 240). Fully assimilated within this racist logic, July thinks her newborn son 'the ugliest black-skinned child she had ever seen' (Levy 2011: 186). When proud claims of Scottish paternity are juxtaposed with Caroline's dismissive retort, 'Oh who on earth cares about that silliness? You are still a negro' (Levy 2011: 348), it becomes apparent that July has imbibed a cod legalistic discourse around racial purity that has only ever intended to define her otherness. Later, when plantation owners are compensated for the emancipation, 'July had been pleased with her price. Thirty-one pounds! She used to boast of it' (Levy 2011: 208). Levy's novel, while frequently optimistic in its portrayal of the irrepressible black female voice, nevertheless acknowledges in these moments and others the intractable psychological legacy of slavery.

The same pressing theme of inheritance also motivates Thomas's appended 'Afterword'. Seeking discretely to ascertain the whereabouts of July's lost daughter Emily, taken by Caroline and Robert to be raised as their legitimate child in England, Thomas realizes that his fair-skinned sister may be unaware of her African-Caribbean heritage and that 'the finding of negro blood within a family is not always met with rejoicing' (Levy 2011: 398). This image of English Emily and the revelations that await her functions, for Levy, as a figure of the penetrative reach of the British Empire. Infiltrating every strata of society, colonialism is envisioned as an intimate, disentangle-able part of British ancestry and identity, so that white Emily, who may be 'unaware of the strong family connection she has to this island of Jamaica' (Levy 2011: 398), is as much a child of slavery as her black brother, Thomas. And so the novel concludes where, according to Levy, it began: on the hoped-for capacity of the reader to discover a source of pride rather than shame in the polyphonic strands of July's wily narrative.

# CHAPTER EIGHT

# At the Centre of the Picture: Andrea Levy's *The Long Song*

## SUSAN ALICE FISCHER

**Chapter Summary:** Narrated in the voice of a former slave named Miss July, Andrea Levy's *The Long Song* (2010) imagines one of the countless voices lost from slavery in Jamaica with a view to recuperating that history. At the centre of the novel is a painting, ostensibly of the master and mistress of Amity Plantation, with Miss July proffering sweetmeats on a tray, her pose meant to signify their importance and her subservience. Yet Miss July upstages the master and mistress, and by becoming the focal point of the picture shows not only her own prominence in their story, but more broadly slavery's centrality to any history of both Britain and Jamaica.

At the centre of Andrea Levy's fifth novel, *The Long Song* (2010), is a painting of slave master and mistress, Robert and Caroline Goodwin, with their slave Miss July, placed in the picture as a possession to signify their wealth and importance. Yet, despite being relegated to the position of object, Miss July forces her subjectivity into the painting with such vigour as to become its central focus.

Andrea Levy has said that this image was suggested to her by the painting of 'Dido Elizabeth Belle and Lady Elizabeth Murray', which she saw at Kenwood House, in London (Fischer 2014: 134). The portrait by an unknown artist belongs to the Earl of Mansfield's collection and was displayed as part of the 'Slavery and Justice Exhibition' in 2007, when Levy was still working on the novel. According to the information provided by English Heritage's Kenwood House, Dido Elizabeth Belle was the 'illegitimate' daughter of Sir John Lindsay, nephew of Lord Mansfield, and of a woman of African descent who had possibly been enslaved. Dido was raised by Lord and Lady Mansfield in Kenwood House along with her cousin Lady Elizabeth Murray, and she was an important member of the household.

The painting foregrounds Lady Elizabeth, shown reading a book and holding on to the arm of Dido, who is carrying a sylvan sheaf. Dido dons a white turban and a flowing dress that highlights her dark complexion, while Lady Elizabeth wears a more highly structured and elaborate pinkish dress which blends with her light skin tones. Like Caroline's dress in Levy's novel, Lady Elizabeth's shows 'the detail of this gown, [so] that the pink silk of the garment shimmers as if the actual cloth were pasted upon it' (Levy 2010a: 21).

The iconography of the original painting suggests that Lady Elizabeth is of the world of culture and high society, whereas Dido is of the natural world and exotic. Although foregrounded, Lady Elizabeth fades into the distance, and it is Dido, with her intelligent eyes and impish face, that constantly draws the viewer. As Levy has said, 'Dido absolutely steals [the picture] by the look on her face and her demeanour. Clearly the artist was in love with her or something [laughs] – it's really very palpable' (Fischer 2014: 134).

Similarly, the painting at the centre of Levy's novel is ostensibly of the master and mistress of Amity Plantation, with July proffering sweetmeats on a tray. While her presence in the portrait is meant to 'add a touch of the exotic' (Levy 2010a: 24), July insinuates herself into the picture in such a way that she upstages the mistress, thereby showing her importance in their story, as well as the centrality of slavery and colonialism in British history.

As in the painting that inspired Levy, viewers of this one cannot take their eyes off July, who is as clever and mischievous as Dido in the original. Moreover, in the portrait, Robert gazes fixedly upon July, rather than upon his wife, and as Levy suggests of the painter of the original portrait, clearly Robert is in love with July. After considerable detail about the positioning of Robert and Caroline in the composition, Levy describes the painting thus: 'it is not the main subject "*Mr and Mrs Goodwin*"' of the picture that catches the eye, but rather Miss July, who is 'wearing a white muslin dress with a red silk turban upon her head' – evocative of Dido's headgear – which 'create[s] a pleasing counterpoint to the fair hair of the seated woman and the dark head of the upright man' (Levy 2010a: 225). The imposition of the white man between the two women with respect to the original painting highlights the power dynamics of their relations not only because Robert is the unspoken personal connection between the two women as July's lover and Caroline's husband, but also because this underlines the ways slavery is rooted in social relations based on both patriarchy and white supremacy. In the composition of the fictional picture, 'July, now sideways to her missus, leans toward her with one knee bent, proffering the contents of the tray she carries' (Levy 2010a: 225). While this is supposed to convey July's 'obedient esteem' for her mistress, 'July's countenance craftily contrives to catch the eye of the viewer with an expression that says quite clearly, "So, what you think of this? Am I not the loveliest negro you ever did see?"' (Levy 2010a: 226). This rhetorical question captures Dido's attitude in the original painting as she points to her own be-dimpled face with open pleasure.

This central image in *The Long Song* of Miss July forcing her way to the centre of the picture symbolizes how slavery must be similarly recognized as central to English culture and history, despite the ways that it continues to be sidelined. This is Levy's second historical novel and the first to take place primarily in Jamaica. It is also the first not to focus on the Windrush Generation or its offspring. Levy uses the historical novel to unearth and recuperate silenced and marginalized lives and to place these experiences at the forefront. *The Long Song* represents a continuation of Levy's preoccupation with the 'inextricably linked' pasts and destinies of Britain and Jamaica, this time going closer to the root of that relationship with an exploration of slavery and its immediate aftermath (Fischer 2010: 38). Here, Levy uncovers Jamaica's and Britain's interwoven histories, by recreating the years of slavery, 'the Baptist War 1831, the interim years of forced indentured servitude, known as the Apprenticeship, final abolition in 1838, and continued exploitation after that time' (Fischer 2010: 39). Levy thus uses historical fiction to reimagine the past with a view to changing our perception of both past and present (see Armitt and Gamble 2006: 141 on this characteristic of historical fiction).

As Levy notes in her essay 'The Writing of *The Long Song*', there are the 'potted' histories of slavery that one learns in school, as well as good scholarship on the subject, but few extant sources incorporate the voices of those that lived through it, in which 'enslaved people speak of and for themselves. Little writing or testimony has emerged that was not filtered at the time through a white understanding or serving a white narrative' (Levy 2010b: n.p.). This is the gap she has chosen to fill with *The Long Song*. As Levy writes, 'This is where I believe that fiction comes in to it's [sic] own. Writing fiction is a way of putting back the voices that were left out' (Levy 2010b: n.p.). Levy imagines what the lives of enslaved people were like by setting them against the research she did for the novel, which of necessity drew mostly upon the voices of the hegemonic culture:

> For me, reading these British settlers' accounts was a bit like gazing at an optical illusion – at first I see a candlestick, but suddenly it turns into two faces in profile. By reading between the lines of these narratives, and by tapping into our common human ways (our motives, fears and ways of coping with the hand life deals us) I found it was possible to imagine a vivid picture. (Levy 2010b: n.p.)

In re-imaging that living, Levy draws the lives of people under slavery not as mere victims of their circumstances, but as actors in their own lives – lives that were certainly complicated and included tragic events, but which they *lived* – hence the *song*. As she says, the novel 'is really a story about a person's life, a lost voice from history that needed to be heard' (Levy 2010b: n.p.).

Giving voice to this lost history, *The Long Song* takes place primarily on Amity Plantation in Jamaica and presents the story of one woman – Miss July – who manages to survive with her dignity intact despite the terrible things that slavery does to her life and those of people she lives with and loves. Levy gives the narrative over to Miss July who, at the request of her son, retells her story in 1898, as she draws towards the end of her life. July's struggle for voice – and sometimes her desire to silence the pain of slavery – structures the narrative. Although her more educated son, Thomas Kinsman, who is also Jamaica's first black printer, attempts at various points to direct the narrative, July wrests it back from him, as she tells us in the margins of the story. Ultimately, her narrative – rather than the 'official' story told from the point of view of the white slave owners – will emerge as central.

The structure of the novel rhetorically reinforces July's – and by extension black people's – movement from margin to centre, to use bell hooks' phrase (see hooks, 2000). On the one hand, the narrative is shaped by the horrible things that July's mistress Caroline does to her: she abducts July from her mother, Miss Kitty, and renames her Marguerite; she frames July's first lover, Nimrod, for a crime he did not commit, thus setting in motion a chain of events that lead to his and Miss Kitty's deaths; she marries July's lover, Robert Goodwin; and finally, she abducts July's daughter and takes her to England. Not only do Caroline's actions demonstrate the slave owners' accrual of benefits at the expense of the enslaved, but they also suggest that she is in control of the storyline of July's life. Yet at each step of the way, it is July who refuses to allow these events to destroy her and who prevails despite the pain she endures. She does this by snatching the plot away from Caroline and becoming the protagonist in her own narrative, telling it in her own way and not allowing herself to be silenced.

One way the feisty Miss July subverts the master narrative is through mischief and humour and by refusing to allow herself to be minimized by her experiences. Indeed, July throws herself into comedic performances, enacting melodramatic distress when Caroline's dress is ruined and remains confident that she will thus avoid a whipping – which she does. While Caroline attempts to make July obey and become a good lady's maid like 'a turkey seized for the Christmas table [that] had been raised, caught and stuffed' (Levy 2010a: 55), July deliberately sets the Christmas dinner table with a bed sheet in lieu of table linen to foil Caroline's attempt to impress her guests.

Levy has written and spoken about the way humour enhances an understanding of tragedy and about the necessity of claiming it as part of maintaining humanity. Moreover, she makes the point that slavery – an institution which lasted for some 300 years – created a society. As such, there were moments not only of 'the wails of anguish and victimhood that we are used to, although that is very much part of the story, but the chatter and clatter of people building their lives, families and communities' in horribly challenging situations (Levy 2010b: n.p.). Levy has also pointed out that humour is not just a form of resistance, as people born into a society, no matter how little they like it, do not spend their entire time resisting, but get on with the business of living and with being human, as much as possible. Even in dire circumstances, people may do things that are 'funny', Levy says. 'And then you start to acknowledge the real *humanity* in people. People then stop becoming just the victim of a tragedy. They become real people, and you can understand how their lives would have evolved' (Fischer 2014: 137). By making humour central to a work about a serious topic, Levy foregrounds the humanity of the people about and for whom she writes.

Miss July's tale is sandwiched between her son's foreword and afterword, which provide another otherwise silenced voice, that of a successful black man during the years after slavery. July's use of the third person to relate her tale enables her to distance herself from a story that brings her suffering back to the surface. At the margins of the novel are moments of slippage which interrupt Miss July's narrative as she periodically resists her son's prodding to continue telling her story even when it becomes too painful for her to push forward. July also puts up a fight when her son attempts to guide her writing style, though she ultimately allows him to cajole her into finishing her narrative. Yet July is most of all a spirited and feisty character bent on telling her story her own way. From the first chapter, July begins to do battle with her son so that she may tell her story as she pleases when he questions the way she begins her tale. She addresses the reader directly by telling us that she is 'a woman possessed of a forthright tongue and little ink' (Levy 2010a: 9). As her son is a printer, she clearly has all the ink she wants; yet she has few words to waste on trivial details describing the island that might round out the edges of her tale, but make it less authentic. She directs any readers desirous of that sort of writing to books containing 'the puff and twaddle of some white lady's mind' (Levy 2010a: 10).

So little regard does she have for the trials and tribulations of the 'white missus' on the island that she uses just such a volume – with its author's gnat-like 'distracting' and 'insistent buzzing' – to squash an insect 'upon [the] open book' (Levy 2010a: 10). After she has 'wiped its bloody carcass from the page' she 'continue[s] her tale' (Levy 2010a: 10). July thus points to the plethora of words that have been written about the white experience of slavery, which July reduces to a mere insect to be squashed. Her story needs to be told because the 'official' story has minimized the truly harsh experiences of those who were actually enslaved and whose story is far more central to the whole enterprise of colonialism, slavery and Empire. In reducing the white version of the story to a pesky insect whose death is insignificant, July underscores the greater centrality of the slaves' experience. The detail of the squashed insect is rhetorically similar to, and perhaps echoes, the device in John Donne's poem, 'The Flea' (1633), in which, to win his argument, the speaker of the poem first literally and figuratively puffs up the flea, only to reduce its 'murder' to naught. More to the point, perhaps, this device recalls how Chinua Achebe diminishes the white colonizer's experience in Africa to a mere paragraph at the end of *Things Fall Apart* (1958) as a direct response to the way colonialism has erased the African experience in its version of history. Thus, July quashes the insistent and vapid utterances of the white mistress while giving voice to her own experiences.

July opens her story using an almost matter of fact tone to relate the routine brutality of slavery. Her first words recount her conception during her mother's perfunctory rape while working in the field. Her mother, 'Kitty felt such little intrusion from the overseer Tam Dewar's part that she decided to believe him merely jostling her from behind like any rough, grunting, huffing white man would if they were crushed together within a crowd' (Levy 2010a: 9). Relating Kitty's rape in such a way shows how commonplace an event it was, and it also cuts the over- seer down to size by suggesting that his manhood was lacking. This is further underscored when the piece of cloth he gives her as a compensa- tion of sorts is referred to as a 'limp offering' (Levy 2010a: 9). This trope of minimizing hegemonic power, which John Clement Ball has noted as a feature of postcolonial literature (see Ball 2004), enables Kitty and July to shrink the power – at least from a psychological perspective – of those who attempt to dehumanize them through the system of slavery.

That July is born to voice her own and her mother's silenced story is emphasized in the very next episode in which July relates her birth. Tam Dewar, the overseer who is July's father, can't bear the yelling that accompanies childbirth and silences July's mother, forcing her to bite 'down hard upon the cloth within her mouth so that she would make no sound that could cause his mood to change' and thus whip her (Levy 2010a: 16). July, on the other hand, is from birth, 'a squealing, tempestu- ous, fuss-making child' (Levy 2010a: 19), who 'did yell so' and whose 'constant screeching' and 'torturous din' 'rupture[d] the ears' (Levy 2010a: 20–1). Kitty's silencing further necessitates July's story. Indeed, from the beginning of her life, July seems poised to find a way to voice her story of enslavement in Jamaica.

Despite her early boisterous confidence, July's childhood with her lov- ing mother ends abruptly when the recently widowed Caroline comes to live with her brother, John Howarth, the master of Amity Plantation. Initially afraid of 'the negroes' whom she is surprised to see at every turning, she 'find[s] herself delighted by a negro', young July, and takes her for her own 'lady's maid', renaming her Marguerite, which she deems a more suitable name than the one her mother bestowed upon her: 'only Caroline Mortimer [could] look upon July's face to see a Marguerite residing there' (Levy 2010a: 45). This renaming reiterates the imposition of the slaveholders' version of history that July seeks to undo, and July forever holds onto the name her mother gave her. It is perhaps significant that July was born in December, the month, though in a different year, in which the Baptist War that would lead to Emancipation broke out, and that she is, however, called July, perhaps to foreshadow the month in which the Emancipation was announced in 1893.

Thus embodying the period of history that needs to be recovered, July undercuts and dismisses versions of history that do not tell the truth, whether they are Caroline's or other 'official' versions. Indeed, July reiterates the gap between official histories and the lives of the people at various times in the novel. After her 'forthright' narration of how she came to be conceived – for which her son chastises her – July tells her readers that there are plenty of other books, 'wrapped in leather and stamped in gold' (Levy 2010a: 10), that gloss over such unpleasantness and tell her story from a completely different point of view, and she invites readers to close her book if that is what they are seeking. July also warns readers against the version of the Baptist War told in John Hoskin's *Conflict and change. A view from the great house of slaves, slavery and the British Empire* and recommends instead George Dovaston's account titled *Facts and documents connected with the Great Slave Rebellion of Jamaica (1832)* (Levy 2010a: 80). July claims that the former blames only Africans and 'men of God' for the Baptist War, and she again dismisses those readers that believe that version.

In the foreword and afterword that July's son pens and which bookend July's narrative, he underlines the need to tell stories that act as counterweights to the official story, and he hopes that his mother's tale will 'never be lost and, in its several recitals, might gain a majesty to rival the legends told whilst pointing at the portraits or busts in any fancy great house upon this island of Jamaica' (Levy 2010a: 3). It is for this reason that he must continue to urge July to carry on with her narration when it becomes too much for her. After relating Miss Kitty's execution and the declaration of the end of slavery in 1893, in the very next chapter, July tells us her story is at an end and she can no longer go on. Yet her son insists, knowing that there is much more to the story, starting with his own birth. At first July absurdly pretends that the story is fictional and that she may thus tell it as she pleases, a diversion her son refuses to accept. When he insists she continue, she writes that her son was born but that her 'lip curled with disgust when [she] first saw that a child of hers was as black as a nigger' so that she left him with a minister who had said 'that even ugly-ugly slaves with thick lips and noses flat as milling stones were the children of God' (Levy 2010a: 146). After attempting to deflect with such insults, July then goes on to list, in condensed and rapid succession, the horrors that she does not want to recount, asking rhetorically if she 'should find pretty words that could explain' the 'lashes', the 'howl[s]', the 'anguish', the death and the 'weeping' that accompanied the events of the Baptist War and her dream of her mother 'dangling' from a tree 'within the rustling leaves and sagging fruit [which] tasted only of Nimrod's blood' (Levy 2010a: 149). She claims that she can 'go no further' because her 'reader does not wish to be told tales as ugly as these'. More importantly, 'she has no wish to pen them [. . .] and suffer every little thing again' (Levy 2010a: 149).

Miss July thus attempts to bring her narrative to a premature close particularly when she is faced with a devastating memory. This occurs when she must relate her mother's execution, Nimrod's death, Robert Goodwin's betrayal and the loss of her children. Instead, she wishes to skip to the end, where she will claim that 'July's tale has the happiest of endings' now that she is in her son's family (Levy 2010a: 307). However, she has another memory to unearth, that of finding her son, after a period of hardship in which, living 'upon those backlands at Amity' (Levy 2010a: 307), she was reduced to abject poverty and near starvation before being brought before a court for stealing two chickens (though, as she slyly points out, she was only caught for taking only one). This is where she is reunited with her son, Thomas Kinsman, and where his history in England, where he was educated and apprenticed as a printer, is related.

July is compelled to pick up her narrative again partly in response to an 'official', printed version of a chapter of her story written by the white woman who raised her son. While July cannot relive the painful decision that resulted in her giving up her son by writing about it herself, Jane Kinsman's version tells us that July gave Thomas to her 'so the baby would not be sold' (Levy 2010a: 152). While July is relieved to read this part of her story, which justifies her motives and relieves her of the need to narrate the episode herself, she adds a few corrections. While conceding that she did 'drop to her knees' to beg the woman to raise her son, she clarifies that this was 'to get this white woman to raise her black baby' (Levy 2010a: 152). But she categorically denies that she 'said [any] such fool-fool thing' as telling the white woman that her son was not born in 'wedlock' but 'in de wood' (Levy 2010a: 152). This final part of the written record annoys her so much that she decides she 'must now return to my story with some haste, before another foolish white woman might think to seize it with the purpose of belching out some nonsensical tale on my behalf' (Levy 2010a: 152). Setting the record straight thus motivates July to carry on with her story, despite the accompanying distress.

Indeed, the place of the master narrative is questioned at various points in the novel. One of the most egregious distortions of history takes place when John Howarth, Caroline's brother and master of Amity Plantation, shoots himself after seeing the brutalities that slavery has wrought, including the tarring and feathering of a Baptist who supports the slave rebellion. His sister, Caroline, cannot let people know that her brother has died in this 'dishonourable' way, and aided by Tam Dewar, the overseer, she frames a free black man, Nimrod Freeman (who will turn out to be the father of July's son), shooting him as he purportedly 'escapes'. July tells us how, in fabricating the story to disguise her brother's suicide, Caroline turns Tam Dewar 'into her gallant knight. He took her into his arms to swear that he would move all within heaven and earth to bring the culprit of this heinous crime to justice' (Levy 2010a: 157) – none of which is true. By the time she has told the story several more times, Caroline herself becomes its 'resolute heroine' (Levy 2010a: 157). Yet throughout the novel July debunks the 'official' version of the master narrative and shows what really happened.

One of the ways that July provides versions that are 'true', even when she is not personally there to witness them or when she needs a third, impartial eye is to conjure up witnesses from the slave community. When July and Nimrod go on the run after John Howarth's suicide and in the course of events encounter Miss Kitty, who reportedly kills Tam Dewar to save her child, we do not have July's word for this alone. Rather, the novel is populated with numerous eyewitnesses from the slave community who can attest to the facts at various points.

The 'distiller-man' Dublin Hilton is one such witness, who makes several brief, but significant appearances. While he is not able to confirm that Miss Kitty killed Dewar, the novel suggests that he and the others are reliable witnesses whose version of history needs to be heard. The figure of the witness thus enables the author to recuperate lost voices from history, those unable to leave an official record, but who would have provided a more accurate picture of what happened and how people's lives were affected by slavery and its aftermath. Dublin Hilton stands in as one of the countless voices of the people most touched by these events. He witnesses key moments, from testifying to July's howling as a baby to informing the people of the rent charges that the new master of Amity, Robert Goodwin, is now levying on those working on the land after Emancipation – 'a full week's wage in rent for every acre of land worked' (Levy 2010a: 243). Dublin Hilton later moves away from Amity Plantation with some of the other former slaves to work a 'rough, squatted land' and it is he who, every morning, as he gives the call to work, reminds them that 'This is free' (Levy 2010a: 264). As one of the cast of minor characters that make up the society of slaves (and later former slaves), Dublin Hilton represents the real lives of the people and embodies the arc of history from slavery, to the Baptist War, the Apprenticeship and beyond. The figure of Dublin Hilton suggests the missing point of view that, if it could be recovered, would provide a much fuller historical picture.

Another painting towards the end of the novel reiterates the need for this perspective. One day, Dublin Hilton sees a white man near the 'great house' painting a picture of the scene before him. He stops and observes the artist at work as he paints 'the view of the lands of Amity into the background of this picture' which overlooks 'the scruffy thatched tops of the houses within the negro village' (Levy 2010a: 233). Something strikes Dublin Hilton as odd about the representation, and he asks the painter why he cannot see – and therefore why he has not included – 'the negro dwellings', insisting that 'they are there before you' (Levy 2010a: 234). The artist replies that 'no one wished to find squalid negroes within a rendering of a tropical idyll' (Levy 2010a: 234). Dublin Hilton declares that the artist is painting 'an untruth' (Levy 2010a: 234). Later, he discusses this erasure with his friends, one of whom declares 'the artist a cunning man to turn his eye blind to those run-down negro places' (Levy 2010a: 235). As a previously established reliable witness, Dublin Hilton denounces this false picture of the island. This is why Miss July must tell her whole story. Her son's hope is that her narrative will become a historical legacy that is accorded the attention it deserves.

Another way that Levy ensures that a multidimensional and 'truer' picture emerges in *The Long Song* is by connecting July's idiosyncratic character to a much broader history through allusions to other black literary characters and texts. This extends July's individual story into one that is much larger than herself and that embraces the history of the African diaspora. In addition to the allusion to Chinua Achebe's *Things Fall Apart* mentioned above, the novel also alludes to the slave narrative of Olaudah Equiano (*The Interesting Narrative of the Life of Olaudah Equiano, Or Gustavus Vassa, The African*, 1789) when July remarks upon the 'scolding eyes' in the 'portrait of the dead missus in the drawing room' that 'watched [her] all the while and did tut when July threw the missus's chair cushions upon the floor' (Levy 2010a: 100). This recalls the scene in which the young Equiano feels that the eyes of the portraits on the wall of his master's house are keeping him under surveillance. Allusions to African American women's fiction are also present. For instance, Robert Goodwin's most notable feature is that he has 'the bluest eyes' (Levy 2010a: 170), a clear reference to Toni Morrison's novel, *The Bluest Eye* (1970), in which young Pecola, brutalized by society and her father, longs for blue eyes in the belief that she will then be perceived as beautiful and worthy. In her relation with Robert Goodwin, July insists upon her 'mulatto' heritage, thinking that this will make her more appealing, and she needs his affirmation that she is beautiful, even though he will ultimately take almost all that is valuable from her. A remnant from her relationship with him, and one of her prized possessions, is a cracked blue-and-white plate, which recalls Zora Neale Hurston's *Their Eyes Were Watching God*, in which the former slave, Nanny says to her granddaughter, 'Have some sympathy fuh me. Put me down easy, Janie, Ah'm a cracked plate' (Hurston 1987: 37). Like Nanny, Miss July is doing the best she can do for herself and her descendants in the aftermath of slavery and its abuses. In her much more boisterous, though less direct way, Miss July is saying much the same to her son. Although strong, Miss July is also a 'cracked plate'. But she is intent on telling her story and finding a way to go on living. Through these allusions, Miss July's personal story acquires a connection to the larger history of the African diaspora and thus extends its reach.

The novel closes with an afterword by Miss July's son, Thomas Kinsman, which reasserts the importance of reclaiming and re-examining history. He does this by telling the reader that he has searched for his half-sister, Emily Goodwin, but that 'all trace [. . .] has been lost' (Levy 2010a: 309). He and his mother are left to wonder whether she even knows about her history and her connection to slavery. While he urges any reader who knows her whereabouts to inform him, he is also keenly aware that 'In England the finding of negro blood within a family is not always met with rejoicing' and he does not wish her to be 'unsettl[ed]' by such an announcement (Levy 2010a: 310). By ending with this reminder that a woman with a more complex history than perhaps she realizes has blended into white English society to such a degree as to be 'lost', Levy emphasizes the unbreakable connection between the intertwining histories of Jamaica and Britain, and of black and white people, through the history of slavery – a history that must be placed at the centre of the picture. As Levy remarks, people like Miss July 'did more than survive, they built a culture that has come all the way down through the years to us. Their lives are part of British history' (2010b: n.p.).

# 'Andrea Levy in Conversation with Susan Alice Fischer' (2005 and 2012)

Andrea Levy is the author of five novels: *Every Light in the House Burnin'* (1994), *Never Far from Nowhere* (1996), *Fruit of the Lemon* (1999), *Small Island* (2004) and *The Long Song* (2010). She has also written short stories, including 'Loose Change' (2005). *Small Island* won the Orange Prize for Fiction, the Whitbread Book of the Year Award, the Commonwealth Writer's Prize and others; the novel was made into a film for the BBC in 2009. While Levy's first three novels focus on the experiences of young women born in London to Jamaican migrants, *Small Island* looks back to the Windrush Generation's encounter with the 'Mother Country'. Levy's own father came to England on the SS Empire Windrush in 1948 and was joined by her mother several months later. Her fifth novel, *The Long Song*, shortlisted for the 2010 Man Booker Prize, takes place primarily in Jamaica during slavery and its immediate aftermath.

The first part of this interview is an edited version of a conversation that took place between Andrea Levy and Susan Alice Fischer on 11 July 2005 at the author's home in North London and was originally published in *Changing English: Studies in Culture and Education* (12 (3), 361–71), a Routlege/Taylor & Francis journal. That discussion touches upon a range of topics, including Levy's views of education in relation to class and ethnicity. The author also talks about her development as a reader and writer, her writing process and recurring themes in her fiction, such as migration, home and belonging, as well as about broader concerns in contemporary British culture.

The second portion of the interview is an edited conversation that took place via telephone between Andrea Levy, speaking from her home in London, and Susan Alice Fischer, in New York, on 18 May 2012. This updates the conversation by including the author's most recent novel, *The Long Song*.

\* \* \*

**Susan Alice Fischer:**   The past year must have been a wonderful year for you with your hat trick of awards for *Small Island*.

**Andrea Levy:**   It's one of those beyond-your-wildest-dreams moments, but my dreams are pretty wild. Before the book came out, I knew it was the best I could do at that time and so my biggest fear was that it'd come out to howling indifference.

**SAF:**   I've read that you started writing in your mid-thirties in the 1980s. That was a time when there was so much going on in feminist and third world publishing. Was there was any connection for you in that respect?

**AL:**   Certainly, feminist publishing was how I got into reading. All those presses, Virago, The Women's Press – those were my books; they were my people. That's where I started on the journey. Those were books that spoke of what I was going through at that time.

**SAF:**   Does anything in particular come to mind?

**AL:**   Lots of things – you can see on my shelves – the beginning of Black consciousness as well: Angela Davis, *Women, Race and Class* and *Some of Us Are Brave*, I remember that from the States. There were pamphlets at the time, and fiction as well. I remember reading things like Zoë Fairburns's *Benefits*. And of course *The Women's Room* started me off reading. It was the first book I really ever read.

**SAF:**   How did you start writing?

**AL:**   My Dad dying was the impetus. He died in 1987, and I think I just wanted to make him visible, record something of his life, and also the experience that we'd gone through with it. I actually started with an evening class to have a hobby and see if I could do it. I went to a class with Alison Fell, and it was a fabulous class. You met people, you talked, you had a nice day out in Covent Garden every week, and I really enjoyed it.

**SAF:**   I wanted to talk about the development of your body of work because it seems that each novel builds very much upon the other. With *Every Light in the House Burnin'*, you have a coming-of-age story – a young woman beginning to think about who she is – and you explore that much more fully in your next novel, *Never Far from Nowhere*, with Vivien and Olive and their duality – do I belong in England, do I belong in Jamaica? Then Faith in *Fruit of the Lemon* does have to go to Jamaica. It seems a logical step for *Small Island* to be about the previous generation since in *Fruit of the Lemon* you have just traced that history. And I just read 'Loose Change' which is about another wave of migration.

**AL:**   The first three I see as a baton race, passing the baton on to the next person. I suppose it was about exploring aspects of my life, although in fiction. I didn't research it, obviously; it was there in my head for those three books. I think you're absolutely right – with *Fruit of the Lemon*, I started that backward look, when Faith goes into her family, once I had actually asked my mum about our family and gone to history books and had a look. Before I wasn't so interested in the link between Jamaica, the Caribbean and Britain. I was much more, 'We're black British, we're here, and how are we going to move on?' And that's absolutely part of what I do, too, but I didn't think that looking backwards was so important, whereas now I think it is absolutely important and so fascinating. When you start a book you've got to write something that's going to interest you – to hold on to it for four-and-a-half years. I suppose you can just see the development of my interests. It's all pretty clear. There's no artifice there. It's how it seems.

**SAF:**  For *Fruit of the Lemon*, you interviewed your mother about your family history?

**AL:**  Yes, as far as she could tell me anything.

**SAF:**  So when you were growing up, your parents' experience wasn't talked about?

**AL:**  No, no, no, no, no. We never really discussed that. I had no idea. I had to prise it out of my mother. I can't tell you what it's like to grow up in an *incredibly* nuclear family – a nucleus – because we had nobody else at all. And then to have a sense that actually you do have family, that you have connection, that you do go back. It sounds crazy, but it's a revelation because I've just grown up in this tiny, tiny world. So when people talk about grandparents – I never knew a grandparent. When my grandmother died it meant absolutely nothing to us kids – which is incredible. Connecting with that again – I think that's where it started off. Now I want to know *everything*.

**SAF:**  What is interesting in your work is that you pick up questions that were unanswered in the previous novel.

**AL:**  I hope so. If I felt I had any answers, I would stop. As a writer, one of the big dangers is that you begin to believe what you hear. People tend to take everything that you do terribly seriously, which on the one hand is good, but when you begin to believe yourself to be some sage, instead of being inquisitive, when you are providing the answers instead of asking the questions, it is a dangerous time. I see it in writers I respect, and I think, 'Ah, you've stopped asking and started answering, haven't you?'

**SAF:**  I know you don't talk about what you're working on, but would you talk a bit about your writing process?

**AL:**  I laugh because, as I haven't written much for a couple of years, I come back to my writing process, and I think, did I manage to write a book?

SAF:   Is mulling part of the process?

AL:    Mulling is an essential part of the process. Maybe I was brought up with some sort of Protestant ethic that somehow mulling isn't work. That unless you're actually doing something, it doesn't really count. I realize that I do almost inhabit the book: when I was working on *Small Island*, anything to do with the Second World War. I listened to Glenn Miller in the car. Everything was just to keep me in that space. And now I've got a book and I'm just trying always to keep myself in that space, which is a slightly harder space to stay in. And I love it, and that is very much part of the process because the actual writing can be as little as an hour a day. And that's an outrage, isn't it? It's an absolute outrage [*laughs*].

But from a blank page to something on it – I don't like to work too long before I let serendipity in. So there's a process where I write something down and then literally I carry it round with me all evening. I put it by the side of the bed, I write something else on it, I think of it and then I come back to it the next day.

I don't like to write ten pages straight off because I know I want to be able to really think and get in deeper and deeper. That's what happened with *Small Island*. That was a slightly different process to the other three because the first three were fiction, but they were much more lived. But because I'm researching and I've got to think of all the things I've read, I've got to trust that it's all in there and it's got to come out and give it time.

Also, you're thinking yourself entirely into somebody else's existence and into somebody else's life and the way somebody else would think about things. Often the first thing when you're writing with a computer or by hand is *you*. And it's only after a while when you let it meld that you get the other person that you're trying to write. I always find the actual process of sitting down and writing can be – this is going to sound odd – the least creative. This morning I was thinking, and I know when I get to the computer it's going to go. You know, like when you write a letter and it's all sorted out and you go to do it, somehow it's not there. Sometimes it is. That's the point and you have to get past that. That takes a bit of work. So it's a very loose process.

SAF:   So you're not one of those people who sits down every day and writes for two, three hours.

AL:    No, no. I wish I could be. I really envy people like Graham Greene with his thousand words a day. I think I could write a thousand words a day, but I'd have to keep going over it. It'd be pointless.

SAF:   I suppose one of the things is to learn what one's process is and just have faith in it.

**AL:**  I have faith in it till the next time and then sit down and think, 'I can't do it, it's not coming', and it gets difficult. It does take a long time, which is why I never sell a book before I've written it. If I had somebody breathing down my neck – which I do have, but they can breathe all they like, I haven't signed anything, I owe them nothing – it might all evaporate. I might not want to carry on. I would produce rubbish. I really would. I hate even journalism for that, because I don't work under pressure at all. If you give me a deadline, I'm like a rabbit in headlights.

**SAF:**  You've said somewhere that you were particularly fond of your character Gilbert in *Small Island*. How do you go about creating a character?

**AL:**  I have no idea. I remember starting Gilbert. I start a character, and they're usually out of central casting and what happens after a while is that they remind me of someone, maybe not someone I know, but that gives it some sort of padding. Gilbert reminded me of someone, but I don't know who.

**SAF:**  So do you come up with the story first or does it all evolve together?

**AL:**  I kind of know what the character is going to be doing, and then I start writing. And they might come into a situation and then, *Oh right, that's what they do*. So with Gilbert, I'd got this central casting guy, and then one of the first things I wrote, which appears later on in the book, is his encounter with Queenie.

I remember I was walking to the petrol station, and I just heard Queenie saying 'You remind me of someone' and he saying 'Don't tell me, Paul Robeson'. And it had come. And then she said, 'You think a lot of yourself, don't you?' And I remember just sitting on the wall there writing out that little bit of speech. And that's Gilbert. And once you've got that – that's what I mean about serendipity. Then I go back and say, now I've got this guy who says that about Paul Robeson, who is sitting on a bench and someone's following him and suddenly he's got this other character, and that's kind of how it happens. That's what I mean about not writing straight out.

**SAF:**  And that says so much about him, that he would say that.

**AL:**  And then make the joke about if it were Paul Robeson he'd slide him under the door. So, yes, I can hear him now. That's as much as I know. And I just hope it happens naturally. Sometimes I worry I'll just never ever get a character.

**SAF:**  As *Changing English* is a journal for teachers of English, I wanted to talk about education. Some of the women in your books are or have been teachers. Hortense in *Small Island* had been a teacher and has a horribly rude awakening when she gets to this country that her qualifications do not count. Beryl in *Every Light in the House Burnin'* is also a teacher and does the Open University course.

AL:     These things all come up because my mother was that thwarted teacher. Being a teacher was very big in my childhood. My mother's dream for me was that I would become a teacher. I was always brought up with a rather elevated sense of The Teacher as demi-god. When I was at school, I remember that my parents' relationship to the teacher was: if the teacher says it, then it's right – whereas I liked my friends whose mums would come up to school and threaten the teacher. That was my idea of teacher relationships [*laughs*]. I always remember the 'My mum's coming up the school today', and we'd all stand around watching this mother haranguing the headmaster, and I'd think, if only my mum would do that, and I used to say, 'Why don't you go up the school' and get, 'No, if the teacher says it, then it's right'.

SAF:    Did she go back to teaching?

AL:     She became a primary school teacher. There was a problem being a teacher after the war if you were married. The men were coming back out of the forces, doing a year's training and becoming a teacher – a dreadful teacher. And then they changed it and wanted these women who had been teachers and then got married to come back into the profession. My mother, who had been a teacher and then had been sewing and bringing up kids, heard it on the radio and she said she practically ran out of the house to do this. She went back to college when she was 40 and became a teacher. So teaching is big in my horizons.

SAF:    In your work you also talk about these young girls, the second generation, and their experiences of school are not always what one would hope for. In *Never Far from Nowhere*, we see Olive encountering low expectations because of her ethnicity –

AL:     And her class. In my experience, I really enjoyed school. I absolutely loved it, but when I look back on it, with some teachers there were high expectations of me and with some very low. Whenever someone didn't know you, then they were low. Because they just took one look at you and you were boxed – therefore you went to work in a shop. But when the teacher knew you, then there was something different. And I know the difference between the schooling I had and the schooling some of my friends had, which was really very poor – and also my brother and sisters – there wasn't a great deal expected of you. I would have to say it was class almost more than ethnicity. I don't know what it is now, but it really was class. You were working class and nobody thought that you could be bright because you didn't show any of the signs of it. If you grow up in a middle-class house and you've got books, and you've read, you show signs of that. You might have gone to the theatre, you might know who Shakespeare was. And because you couldn't give all those codes to teachers, you were thick. And *that* is terrible. When I think of some of the kids that I grew up with, how bright they were, but because they didn't have those codes, they were completely dismissed and put that energy into something else, often not very healthy.

There's a deal of work to do when you take working-class kids and try to make them into the norm of intelligence. There's a whole load of cultural stuff. I grew up watching the television. It's a hell of a thing to get from there to being a person who reads books because you're not going to go through university without having to cross that. That's where the work has to be done – to cross out of the everyday, you just get into this much more difficult and rarefied world of learning. I had to make that transition, and it's a very painful one. You leave behind a lot that you know, a lot that's familiar, and it's easier by far to stay where you were. I had to change my whole peer group, and I had to go into areas where I felt like shit. Where I was then making friends with very middle-class people who had big houses and took so much for granted. It's not an easy thing to do.

SAF:   You see that with Vivien in *Never Far from Nowhere*. She's pretending to be from someplace else – and goes through that transition when she goes to college.

AL:   Yes, I did try to explore that. Maybe I'd like to go back to that whole transition because it's important to understand how that works: that leaving behind and starting to feel frustrated with that life that you know, which I tried to put forward in *Never Far from Nowhere* with Eddie. I loved Eddie, who's a sweet, lovely guy, but who just couldn't keep up with her. Just being frustrated because you know something else, you've moved on – it can be a quite painful process.

SAF:   Was the English curriculum part of the experience of exclusion?

AL:   *Oh, I'll say. Middlemarch?* [*Laughs.*] Yes, because it was something entirely different, the code was Jane Austen, George Eliot, Dickens, fabulous writers. I can see what they were getting at now, but for someone who was coming from having to watch the telly from 4 o'clock to 11 – and there were some great things on the telly – but for someone who just doesn't read, this isn't going to work. You've got to understand what reading is about before you can get into anything like that. So there was *life* – and there was this stuff that you had to do at school.

SAF:   And the connections just weren't there.

AL:   No, no. Even now, I'd still say what is the connection between me, ever having read, at the age of 15, *Middlemarch? Middlemarch?* At the age of 15? Are you kidding me? I just read it recently, and I thought I'm beginning to understand it now, but the age is crazy. Books to me were where you got bored stiff. That's what a book was. It was something to get through if you could.

SAF:   I think that's the experience of many kids in so many parts of the world. I had one student who said a book we'd done was the first she'd ever read from cover to cover and she was very proud of herself. But it was very hard work making the connections to the work and also selecting things that people might actually want to read as a way in before moving on to other stuff.

AL:    That's right, because it's a very difficult thing. You don't want to be patronizing, you've got to find the stuff and it's not always there. Being a novelist, you tend to be educated, and when you move out of your class, you tend to forget. It's very easy to slip into 'Oh, if I could do it, anyone could do it'. You wind up reading *Middlemarch* and thinking, 'This is wonderful, if only they'd read it'. You tend to forget how you got there – like any pain. I try not to. I certainly have forgotten a lot, and I know when I sometimes see some of my family who are still in that place, I'm taken aback by the gulf between us.

SAF:   Your website says that you live and work in London in the city that you *love* and use London as the setting of all your novels. What drew me to your work in the first place was that it was set in London, as I'm writing about contemporary women's London novels.

AL:    People have pointed out to me that my books are all set in London. It's just because I live in London, and London as far as I am concerned is a country and very different from the rest of Britain. I grew up here and everything I know and understand is in London, and I really value that sense of belonging I feel in London. It's really important to me, I feel like a Londoner, and I am. I love that. Having said that, my next book isn't set in London. I'm beginning to worry [*laughs*].

SAF:   In all your novels, that sense of belonging is something that your protagonists have to struggle to get.

AL:    When I was first on the shortlist for the Orange Prize, two papers said that there was only one Briton on the shortlist and that was Rose Tremain. I tell you, I nearly packed my bags. I felt very grounded in London, but as soon as that happened, I felt, actually my family have the most incredibly fleeting relationship with this place. I'm not grounded to it. My parents came here. They lived here for 30-odd years. My mum is at the moment living in New Zealand. My dad is dead. I've got a sister in New Zealand, a brother in Vietnam, very little family here. In fact my family in the next 50, 100 years, will probably no longer be here – I don't have children. And in a way it didn't matter as well. This is my home, and it's dynamic. You struggle with it all the time. There are people who would like you to piss off, but it doesn't worry me.

**SAF:** In your most recent novel, two people come to Britain thinking the doors are going to be open to them and they literally and figuratively have the doors slammed in their faces.

**AL:** People have often said to me – because that happens, because there is that sense that people don't want you here – don't you feel that you should say you belong somewhere else? Shouldn't you find your sense of self or belonging somewhere else, somewhere where people want you?

**SAF:** That seems an extraordinary thing to say.

**AL:** It *is* an extraordinary thing to say.

**SAF:** At the end of *Never Far from Nowhere* somebody asks Vivien where she is from, and she answers, 'My family are from Jamaica, but I am English'.

**AL:** That's how I feel. My sense of belonging doesn't depend on being universally loved or accepted. I don't know whether some people do have that sense, but I never really have. I'm always a bit of an outsider everywhere. When I was in Jamaica people talked about me being a Caribbean writer, and I'm sort of 'I don't think so' and people are, 'Aren't you proud of what you're doing? Why don't you want to be a Caribbean writer?' But I don't come from the Caribbean. I felt like a fraud to say I was a Caribbean writer because I don't know the Caribbean. Therefore the Caribbean isn't necessarily the thing that is informing my work, maybe it is a bit, but I don't feel like a Caribbean writer. And then I thought, why shouldn't I say I'm a Caribbean writer? I just decided to be cool about it. Passing through Birmingham – Birmingham writer.

**SAF:** Related to this notion of London spaces, of belonging at times and being excluded at others, is what constitutes home. It's in *Every Light in the House Burnin'* when the characters go to the Ideal Home Exhibition, but it's also in your most recent work where the house is emblematic of England. Though very clearly drawn as individuals, the characters also seem to represent the interaction between migrants from Jamaica and the English. And in your recent short story, 'Loose Change', there's homelessness.

**AL:** Oh yes, how interesting. Academics always have a different take – it's wonderful. When you're talking, I'm suddenly thinking I can see how home is very important. I have a tremendous fear of being homeless. My biggest fear would be to be a refugee – absolutely terrifying. I grew up in this tiny little council flat, and it was a real dive, six of us in this tiny little place and we always dreamed of a home, not dissimilar to the one you're sitting in now. And there was this programme on the telly once called *Kathy Come Home*, about homelessness in Britain, and I remember watching it, I must have been quite young – terrifying. So I think there is something about finding that space that feels yours. If you can see it in my work, then it has probably something to do with that.

**SAF:** I imagine it also has to do with being first generation in a new place.

**AL:** Yes, that's right. Because my parents had a fear of losing their home, if they were homeless for a while. If you've got a home, if you've got somewhere that you can shut the door on, you've got something solid and you are within a society. When that's taken away, you are just floating.

**SAF:** When Faith has the breakdown in *Fruit of the Lemon*, she doesn't feel she has a home anymore. And the novel opens with her parents saying they are going 'back home' and all she can think they mean is back to their council flat in Stoke Newington.

**AL:** That sense of home must have to do with having immigrant parents and a palpable sense of insecurity of being in a society where the only real sense of security is being at home. I used to dream about it. And the Ideal Home Exhibition – all my friends and I when we were young wanted a home, a nice home, it's very important. For some people, though, their home is what they carry with them; it's not necessarily a place. For me it really is a place.

**SAF:** With the experience of migration in the family, you can be in between places.

**AL:** Yes, absolutely. I grew up with a sense of insecurity about home because I was always in council housing and they can always chuck you out and so the sense of somewhere that is in your control in the middle of London, to have a house – to have control over where you can stay –

**SAF:** In 'Loose Change' – your story of the refugee from Uzbekistan who doesn't know where to sleep that night – the narrator remembers her immigrant grandmother who was given a spare bed, but then her decision at the end is very curious, very . . .

**AL:** Very Andrea Levy. The genesis of that short story, like most of my short stories, is from a dream. I remember having a dream where I woke up thinking, what would I do in that situation? Am I big enough? I often think about that with the war, would I have been a hero or would I have been one of those collaborators. If tested, if push came to shove – do I just want to fit in or could I be different? And until you're tried you never know. That's what that's about. You don't know what you're protecting. If I so tenaciously want a home, would I protect it?

**SAF:** How does your writing fit in or intersect with contemporary British writing today? Or does it?

**AL:** Time will tell. But, I think that at the moment there's a lovely sort of vibrancy about black British culture. We're having a little moment, and perhaps we may look back on this and see it. Certainly in the last year, we've had the Mastermind champion – do you get that programme in the States? It's a big quiz. We had *The Apprentice*, and he was black and British, and then we've had Zadie Smith, we've had my book, we've had Kelly Holmes getting two gold medals . . .

**SAF:** At the West End theatres, *The Big Life* and *Elmina's Kitchen* –

**AL:** And some fantastic actors. In theatre, Roy Williams's stuff is really good. Music – and in art, Chris Ofili. I'm hoping we're going to look back on it as a sort of Harlem Renaissance. But you don't know when you're going through it.

We're going to have to fight our way into the canon. I'll have to fight to get in the canon. I had this thing through the post about the classics of the future, and they wanted me to choose 15 books out of this list of a hundred books. I just looked at this list of a hundred books and I thought *Small Island*'s not on it. You've left my book off it, and there's *Captain Corelli's Mandolin* and *Birdsong*. Who chose this list of a hundred? Who's making this canon? And I wrote back saying this list is so limited. It's daft. It makes me so mad. I do think we're going to have to fight so hard to come out of this oh-that-was-lovely-dear syndrome. It's so patronizing. No, this is serious work. It's more serious than a lot of serious writing in Britain. Because you laughed, you think it's not serious.

**SAF:** Oxford University Press recently published two separate histories of contemporary British literature, one about Black and Asian literature, and one more focused on white writers, and it seemed an odd choice to keep these traditions separate. In an article called 'Literary Apartheid', Susie Thomas (2005) talks about the way publishing and marketing seem to separate these writers. She says that Maggie Gee had difficulty getting *The White Family* published because it was assumed that she couldn't possibly write knowledgeably about black characters.

**AL:** I had someone ask me how can white writers write about a black character because as soon as we do we're accused of being racist. I said, if you don't think you're being racist, then fight your corner. If you've written about a black person and someone says you're racist and you think they're wrong, then say why, so that we move on. Don't just don't do it. It makes me laugh to think people are scared to write about characters because someone says that's not right, a black person doesn't do that. If you think they're wrong, then you say. Then that's how it will break down. If you get into a big row, and it gets into a big hoopla, what the hell, this is what is dynamic about it. That sort of mindset, 'Oh we can't do that because then we'll be accused of being racist': well, if you are and you're not, then fight your corner, what's the matter with you lily-livered bastards? [*Laughs.*]

I think that some of the more established British writers are feeling a sense of threat in that it's becoming clear that writing about a modern society and a modern Britain does actually involve having to know something about other communities, and you can live in Britain and know absolutely nothing. I know about the ethnic majority, as I call them, because I live here, so that's no problem for me to write about. It's hard to make a book feel like it's dealing with a modern Britain unless it takes in the changing face of Britain.

**SAF:** How have your tools as a writer developed over the years?

**AL:** I think I'm definitely learning. At the moment I'm fixated on story-telling. I really want to be a storyteller. So I read all sorts of books by people that I wouldn't normally read, but I think they're fantastic storytellers. I really do feel like I am learning all the time and that there is a lot to learn. With each book there is something different that you're exploring and trying to learn both in terms of its content and in terms of the way you actually deliver it. I just love novels, I love stories, and when they work well, I don't think there's anything to beat it in terms of art. I don't think there's anything to beat a really finely crafted, fantastic novel.

\* \* \*

**SAF:** You and I last spoke in 2005, shortly after you'd won three major prizes – and I know there were more to follow – for *Small Island*. Since that time, the novel's been turned into a film, and you've written your fifth novel, *The Long Song*. Can you bring us up to date about how your life as a writer has changed since then?

**AL:** How has it changed? It hasn't changed a great deal. It's changed in that I have a much higher profile now. People know who I am, which is a bit odd. I was in the theatre the other day and someone recognized me, and I nearly fell over. That's slightly different. But apart from that – when *The Long Song* came out, I was straight into publicity, going round the world sort of thing. That was quite different because with *Small Island*, it was a much slower and more gradual process, whereas with *The Long Song*, it was completely full on. And I'm absolutely whacked now with travelling and speaking – I'm fed up with the sound of my voice. And so I'm back at home now, hopefully just working and having a quiet time.

**SAF:** I know you won't talk about your work in progress, but are you working on a new novel?

**AL:** Yes.

**SAF:** And is that as much as you're prepared to say about it right now?

**AL:**   *Oh, yeah [laughs]*.

**SAF:**  In 2005 you said that you felt that black literature and culture in Britain was going through a sort of renaissance moment. Do you still feel that way?

**AL:**   No, not quite so much, no. I think that literature in this country – that publishing – is going through a very difficult time. I think things have stalled a little bit. It doesn't feel like that great renaissance.

**SAF:**  Aside from the publishing industry itself, do you attribute that to anything else?

**AL:**   I don't get out much at the moment, so I can never tell whether I'm just out of touch. But I do feel that there's a sense that things have quieted down. I don't know why that is.

**SAF:**  Beside yourself, who do you see as some of the important voices writing in black Britain today?

**AL:**   Jackie Kay, Bernadine Evaristo, Laura Fish, Zadie Smith to name a few. I know I will have left people out, that's just from the top of my head. But the time I was talking to you before, it really did feel like a lot more people were working and being published and doing good work. It felt like a gathering of momentum. I don't know whether it's just that the political situation has turned towards the financial.

**SAF:**  I'd like to talk about *The Long Song* since last time you were in the process of writing it. You did hint that it wasn't going to take place in London, and of course you turned your sights to Jamaica with another historical novel. One of the images that I found most compelling in that story is the portrait that an artist paints of July's mistress, Caroline, and her husband, who's also been July's lover. You write that no matter how much the artist attempts to put Caroline and her husband at the centre, it winds up being July who takes centre stage. Elsewhere you have a part where Dublin Hilton accuses an artist of lying because he doesn't paint the poor dwellings of the black people on the island. So I think this theme of putting black experience squarely into the centre of British history and moving black experience from margin to centre is important in this work, but also in your earlier work as well.

**AL:**   Yes, it is important to me – that idea of those images that I always see when I go around museums or galleries. You see an image of Britain or of England that comes from the eighteenth or nineteenth century, and it's almost always devoid of anything other than the white, English and usually the aristocracy, and then occasionally a black servant fawning over somebody. That's the sort of abiding image that we see of Britain. I just wanted to turn that around and say, if we had had those images of how the Empire actually was, and not the idealized view, how would we feel about black people now? How would we feel about that history?

SAF:   What's so interesting about July is the way she refuses to be a mere accessory and places herself front and centre.

AL:    I was thinking about a wonderful painting of somebody called Dido Elizabeth Belle. She lived in Kenwood House. She was an illegitimate child and taken in and brought up, with a cousin of hers who was white. It's a picture of these two young women, and the white woman is at the centre of the picture, but Dido absolutely steals it by the look on her face and her demeanour. Clearly the artist was in love with her or something [*laughs*] – it's really very palpable. And I just loved that idea.

SAF:   Were you thinking of that picture when you wrote that scene?

AL:    I was thinking of that picture, really. I was just thinking of the way she stole the scene – and how charming that was in a way.

SAF:   The other scene I was referring to is when Dublin Hilton comes upon the landscape painter and essentially calls him a liar. It seems to me that what your body of work has done is put – not only put back in, as it's not just a question of adding it back in, but of re-evaluating the whole experience –

AL:    Oh, absolutely. Yes, that's what I wanted to do. When I was researching *The Long Song* and learning about the history of slavery and putting it against what I had learned in school and putting it against what I know other people know of slavery in this country, I was thinking that this really needs to be brought centre stage. This is an incredibly important event that happened. I say *event* – 300 years, if you can call that an event – and there's enormous amnesia about it in this country. We understand about abolition very well, but there's enormous amnesia about the preceding 300 years or more. This is very important to who we are as a nation, and it's very important to understand it.

SAF:   Edward Said wrote an interesting piece about the slave owner family in *Mansfield Park*, and the whole way they live is based upon the fact that they have plantations somewhere in the West Indies.

AL:    There's a lot of exciting work now being done on that period of slavery. I was at a conference here where they were talking about what happens to the 20 million pounds compensation money for slave-owners, where does it go, how was it spent, who spent it, who were these people who gained money from slavery and how did it directly affect the Britain that we live in. And all that is just music to my ear. That's fascinating stuff. And so I really hope that starts to come a little bit to the centre of our consciousness.

SAF:   Is there a particular piece of work that you're thinking of or person writing in this area?

AL:    Some work that's being done at UCL with Catherine Hall. What she's doing is getting together a website – I think it's actually live now – where you'll be able to put in the names of people and see who they were and what they got. I'm really excited about that.

SAF:   That's fascinating because the legacy is obviously still very much with us. Another thing I thought about with *The Long Song* – and you talk about this in *Small Island, Never Far from Nowhere* – is the way you address the very painful and divisive topic of colourism. I've found this particularly interesting not only in and of itself, as a sort of internalized racism, but also because I teach students either themselves from the Caribbean or of Caribbean descent, and this seems to be one of the aspects of *Small Island* which they find most compelling. Can you talk about the importance of this topic for you?

AL:    It's so much part of the experience of slavery, so much part of how racism came to us, and so important to the formation of the different societies. I'm amazed that we actually don't discuss it a little bit more. It's a very emotional subject, and it's still around today all over the world – that idea that to be lighter is to be better. It was so fundamental to the ways that the societies in the Caribbean grew up. And the funny thing about it is that when I talk about it to white people, and I say it's a pigmentocracy (and people laugh about it and say it's a strange word) that depends on the colour of your skin and you can be a mulatto or a quadroon, there's this real interest in it from people but in a sort of – it's almost laughable, it's almost funny, quaint. But actually, I have to point out this isn't black people being quaint. This has been handed to black people as a way of dividing and ruling and keeping that sort of stratification to give more privilege to some people so they help you to keep someone else down. It's a big political manoeuvre. But it comes down to something so fundamental and so human and so personal as the way that you look, the colour of your skin. I think it's a fantastic – somebody I'm sure must have done a PhD on it – it's a very important issue because it's still with us today. Because we still have skin whiteners –

SAF:   Around the world –

AL:    Absolutely, absolutely. I think I was in Hong Kong and someone was telling me that in Malaysia there were skin whiteners on the TV –

SAF:   And in India –

AL:    Yes, a lot in India. So yes – terribly important in the relationship that we have, black and white, with each other – and fascinating. Fascinating in the Caribbean because you could actually breed yourself out for white – and become legally white.

SAF:   Interesting – the United States had a very different configuration legally, with the idea of the one drop of black blood –

AL: Absolutely – but you could become legally white in Britain.

SAF: On a slightly different topic, in each of your books you have a Jewish character somewhere in the background or some allusion to Jewishness. You've mentioned this is part of your ancestry, and I'm curious about it because it's mine as well. Could you talk about the significance of this for you?

AL: All my life, people have said – Levy, must be Jewish. And I say, well, no, I come from the Caribbean, and then they think you can't possibly be Jewish, if you come from the Caribbean. There was a huge Jewish population in Jamaica –

SAF: And a very old synagogue, I believe –

AL: A lot of synagogues. There was a big Jewish population, not just a little one. The Jews were actually – somebody said to me the other day – the only people in Jamaica who were there because they wanted to be. There were African slaves who were taken there; there were white planters who were factory owners who were left there. And the Jews were actually there to settle. They came in from North Africa and from Portugal, and so there is a quite large Jewish population. So I like to keep reminding people of that – because people do seem to find it odd that I'm called Levy – and life is much more complex than we would have it.

SAF: In *Small Island* Gilbert, whose father's Jewish, is very conscious of the connections between Jim Crow in the United States, the rise of Nazi Germany and Hitler, and anti-Semitism, and of course being Jamaican in Britain and the continued legacy of colonialism and racism that he personally experiences. So would you say that making those connections of race and ethnicity – and class and feminism as well – is part of your politics?

AL: [*Laughs*] Yeah, I mean, I don't consciously go out to do those things –

SAF: No, but it seems to be an underlying ethics or politics of your work –

AL: It's me, I suppose, the things that interest me, things that I think are very pertinent. It's a way as well of confounding people's understanding of a place – so that you do make those connections more complex than we'd like. I'm always trying to do that. We're very complex societies, and so it doesn't always come down to black and white – all those things that are easy to understand.

SAF: Humour is so important in your work, and we didn't get to talk about it much last time. In *The Long Song*, you're talking about a very difficult situation –

AL: Humour, as far as I'm concerned, is part of the human condition – it's with us everywhere. I don't think I have to say, am I writing a tragedy, am I writing a comedy? That's not how life is. And I also think that when you give a novel the full panoply of human experience, that which involves humour as well as the difficult bits, they help to bring each other out. I think comedy really helps to understand the tragic, and the tragic helps you understand the comedy. So I like to always have them in the mix. And I know with *The Long Song* – a book on slavery – you would think you wouldn't have any room for anything that would make you smile. But I just thought, in all the research that I was doing, all the time these things came up that made me laugh: the way the people were actually dealing with the situation they were in. It seems incredibly funny to have slaves in a room where they're serving their masters, and every time that the wine comes around, they're sticking it out the window. It's funny. And then you start to acknowledge the real *humanity* in people. People then stop becoming just the victim of a tragedy. They become real people, and you can understand how their lives would have evolved. They become like you and me. And that's always what I try to do – so that anybody's who's reading my book would have – even though you have 200, 300 years separating you from a character – complete empathy, because you understand this person, the way they think – and you can't do that if they never give you something to smile about.

SAF:  Humour is so important for their survival as well –

AL:  Absolutely, if no one cracks a joke, it's crazy [*laughs*].

SAF:  It also shows the different forms resistance can take in a situation like that –

AL:  Yes, but the thing about it is that when you're talking about 300 years, I don't know that you're talking about constant resistance. You're talking about living. And I often say, I wonder if we'll look back on our society now and think, how did they live through such a hugely unequal society? Do you know what I mean?

SAF:  Yeah, we do it through all the different ways that we try to entertain ourselves, try to maintain our humanity in the face of whatever –

AL:  I don't think someone's who's been born into slavery thinks 'I've been born into slavery and therefore it has to be like this'. You're just born into a society, and you make the best of it. I really wanted to bring that out – that nobody thought that 'I've been born into a tragic situation'. A lot of tragedy would have come in their lives probably, but I wanted to say they're just *born*, too; they're just living – as best they can in that situation. It's 300 years of a society that's grown up under those conditions – it's a whole way of life.

SAF:  Are there any particular literary influences that have become important to you? As I read your work, I think about different people, such as Sam Selvon in *Small Island*, sometimes Zora Neale Hurston. Is there anybody in particular that you feel was important?

AL: I have no idea. I don't think in those terms. I read a lot. I love lots of books – and it has an influence, but I would never point you in any one direction – there's nobody that I could say I'm trying to be like. . . . Certainly, Sam Selvon, we have a subject in common – and I loved, I love *Lonely Londoners*. But I don't ever think like that. I try to take in things from everywhere. I do try not to think about the writing process too much. I want to keep it almost subconscious. I don't quite understand it. I'm almost scared that if I look at it too much, it'll disappear. I just carry on, seeing what happens.

SAF: You've done a lot of interviews over the years, and I'm wondering if there's something you've wished someone would ask you, but no one's had the good sense to do so.

AL: [*Laughs*]. No, no. I don't think so. I've been asked a lot of questions. Sometimes I can get frustrated with being interviewed. You want to talk about something, and you want to talk about it in your way, and you have to talk about it in the way that somebody asks you the question. So I can become a little more tongue-tied; I feel incredibly inarticulate when I do interviews. So when *The Long Song* came out, I actually wrote an essay about the writing of *The Long Song* because I wanted first of all to put out my articulate version, and then I was going to get asked a lot of questions and you were going to get the inarticulate [*laughs*]. But sometimes I get a little frustrated with that in that I know that I'm better understood in written work than I am when I'm speaking. I'm never sure whether talking to the author is a good idea when you're talking about their work. I always think they're the last person you should consult – they know nothing [*laughs*].

# References

## Works Cited by Contributors

### Introduction: 'Towards Serious Work', Jeannette Baxter and David James

Arana, R. V. and Ramey, L. (2004), *Black British Writing*. London: Palgrave.

D'Aguiar, F. (1989), 'Against Black British Literature', in Maggie Butcher (ed.), *Tibisiri: Caribbean Writers and Critics*. Dangaroo: Coventry, pp. 106–14.

Eliot, T. S. (1975 [1919]), 'Tradition and the Individual Talent', in Frank Kermode (ed.), *Selected Prose of T. S. Eliot*. London: Faber and Faber, pp. 37–44.

Fischer, S. (2014), 'Andrea Levy in Conversation with Susan Alice Fischer', in Jeannette Baxter and David James (eds), *Andrea Levy: Contemporary Critical Perspectives*. London and New York: Bloomsbury, pp. 121–38.

Knepper, W. (2012), 'Special Issue on Andrea Levy', *EnterText*, 9, 1–171.

McLeod, J. (2008), 'Some Problems with "British"; In a "Black British Canon"', *Wasafiri*, 17 (36), 56–9.

Morrison, T. (1989), 'Unspeakable Things Unspoken: The Afro-American Presence in American Literature', *Michigan Quarterly Review*, 27 (1), 1–34.

Phillips, M. (2006), 'Toward: Migration, Modernity, and English Writing Reflections on Migrant Identity and Canon Formation', in Gail Low and Marion Wynne-Davies (eds), *A Black British Canon?* Basingstoke: Palgrave, pp. 13–33.

Walters, T. L. (2011), 'Andrea Levy: Interview', *Mosaic*, 6 November, http://mosaicmagazine.org/blog/?p=1011 [accessed 3 February 2013].

### Chapter One: Unhappy *Bildungsromane*, Dave Gunning

#### Works by Andrea Levy

Levy, A. (1995 [1994]), *Every Light in the House Burnin'*. London: Headline Review.

—(2000 [1999]), *Fruit of the Lemon*. London: Headline Review.

—(2004a [1996]), *Never Far from Nowhere*. London: Headline Review.

—(2004b), *Small Island*. London: Headline Review.

#### Secondary Reading

Gilroy, P. (1993), *The Black Atlantic: Modernity and Double Consciousness*. London: Verso.

Hall, S., Critcher, C., Jefferson, T., Clarke, J. and Roberts, B. (1978), *Policing the Crisis: Mugging, the State, and Law and Order*. London: Macmillan.

McLeod, J. (2010), 'Extra Dimensions, New Routines', *Wasafiri*, 25 (4), 45–52.

Moretti, F. (1987), *The Way of the World: The Bildungsroman in European Culture*. London: Verso Books.

Perfect, M. (2008), 'The Multicultural Bildungsroman: Stereotypes in Monica Ali's *Brick Lane*', *The Journal of Commonwealth Literature*, 43 (3), 109–120.

—(2010), '"Fold the Paper and Pass It on": Historical Silences and the Contrapuntal in Andrea Levy's Fiction', *Journal of Postcolonial Writing*, 46 (1), 31–41.

Petersen, K. and Rutherford, A. (1986), *A Double Colonization: Colonial and Post-Colonial Women's Writing*. Aarhus: Dangaroo.

Stein, M. (2004), *Black British Literature: Novels of Transformation*. Colombus, OH: Ohio State University Press.

Velickovic, V. (2012), 'Melancholic Travellers and the Idea of (Un)belonging in Bernardine Evaristo's Lara and Soul Tourists', *Journal of Postcolonial Writing*, 48 (1), 65–78.

## Chapter Two: Council Housing and the Politics of the Welfare State in *Never Far from Nowhere*, Matthew Taunton

### *Works by Andrea Levy*

Levy, A. (1996), *Never Far from Nowhere*. London: Headline Review.

### *Secondary Reading*

Beider, H. (2009), 'Similar Problems, Different Solutions: Race, Housing, and Renewal in the United Kingdom and the United States', in Margery Austin Turner, Susan J. Popkin and Lynette Rawlings (eds), *Public Housing and the Legacy of Segregation*. Washington DC: The Urban Institute Press, 69–78.

Brooker, J. (2010), *Literature of the 1980s: After the Watershed*. Edinburgh: Edinburgh University Press.

Fairbairns, Z. (1979), *Benefits*. London: Virago.

Fischer, S. A. (2005), 'Andrea Levy in Conversation with Susan Alice Fischer', *Changing English: Studies in Culture and Education*, 12 (3), 361–71.

Hall, S. (1979), 'The Great Moving Right Show', *Marxism Today*, January: 14–20.

Hanley, L. (2007), *Estates: An Intimate History*. London: Granta.

Hansen, D. M., Larson, R. W. and Dworkin, J. B. (2003), 'What Adolescents Learn in Organized Youth Activities: A Survey of Self-Reported Developmental Experiences', *Journal of Research on Adolescence*. Blackwell Publishing Limited, 13 (1), 25–55.

Judt, T. (2010), *Postwar: A History of Europe since 1945*. London: Vintage.

Le Corbusier. (1967), *The Radiant City: Elements of a Doctrine of Urbanism to be Used as the Basis of our Machine-age Civilization*, trans. Eleanor Levieux. London: Faber & Faber.

Lessing, D. (1993a), 'DHSS', *London Observed: Stories and Sketches*. London: Flamingo, 64–71.

—(1993b), 'The Mother of the Child in Question', *London Observed: Stories and Sketches*. London: Flamingo, 36–42.

Levy, A. and Morrison, B. (2009), 'Andrea Levy Interviewed by Blake Morrison', *Women: A Cultural Review*, 20 (3), 325–38.

Lima, M. H. (2005), 'Pivoting the Centre: The Fiction of Andrea Levy', in Kadija Sesay (ed.), *Write Black, Write British: From Post Colonial to Black British Literature*. Hertford: Hansib, 56–85.

Self, W. (2012), 'Walking is Political', www.guardian.co.uk/books/2012/mar/30/will-self-walking-cities-foot?newsfeed=true [accessed 30 March 2012].

Sennett, R. (1978), *The Fall of Public Man*. London: Penguin.

Sinclair, I. (2002), *London Orbital: A Walk around the M25*. London: Granta.

Smithson, A. M. and Smithson, P. (1967), *Urban Structuring: Studies of Alison & Peter Smithson*. Studio Vista: Reinhold.

Taunton, M. (2009), *Fictions of the City: Class, Culture and Mass Housing in London and Paris*. Basingstoke: Palgrave Macmillan.

—(2011), 'The Flâneur and the Freeholder: Paris and London in Metroland', in Sebastian Groes and Peter Childs (eds), *Julian Barnes: Contemporary Critical Perspectives*. London; New York: Continuum, 11–23.

Teige, K. (2002), *The Minimum Dwelling*, trans. Eric Dluhosch. Cambridge, MS: MIT Press.

Timmins, N. (1995), *The Five Giants: A Biography of the Welfare State*. London: Harper Collins.

Trentmann, F. (2008), *Free Trade Nation: Commerce, Consumption, and Civil Society in Modern Britain*. Oxford: Oxford University Press.

## Chapter Three: Existing in More than One Plane of Time: Memory and Narrative Form in *Every Light in the House Burnin'*, Michael Perfect

### Works by Andrea Levy

Levy, A. (2004a [1994]), *Every Light in the House Burnin'*. London: Headline Review.

—(2004b [1996]), *Never Far From Nowhere*. London: Headline Review.

—(2004c [1999]), *Fruit of the Lemon*. London: Headline Review.

—(2004d), *Small Island*. London: Headline Review.

—(2010), *The Long Song*. London: Headline Review.

### Secondary Reading

Beyer, C. (2012), '"Or perhaps I should describe the old, wild-haired man": Representations of Ageing and Black British Identity in Andrea Levy's *Every Light in the House Burnin'* and Joan Riley's *Waiting in the Twilight*', *EnterText*, 9, 105–21.

Fischer, S. A. (2004), 'Andrea Levy's London Novels', in Lawrence Phillips (ed.), *The Swarming Streets: Twentieth-Century Literary Representations of London*. Amsterdam: Rodopi, pp. 199–213.

Fischer, S. A. and Levy, A. (2005), 'Andrea Levy in Conversation with Susan Alice Fischer', *Changing English*, 12 (3) (December), 361–71.

Perfect, M. (2010), '"Fold the Paper and Pass It on": Historical Silences and the Contrapuntal in Andrea Levy's Fiction', *The Journal of Postcolonial Writing*, 46 (1), 31–41.

## Chapter Four: The Immediacy of *Small Island*, David James

### *Works by Andrea Levy*

Levy, A. (2004), *Small Island*. London: Headline Review.

—(2009), 'Interview by Blake Morrison', ed. and introduced by Deirdre Osborne, *Women: A Cultural Review*, 20 (3) (Winter), 325–38.

### *Secondary Reading*

Attridge, D. (2011), 'Once More with Feeling: Art, Affect and Performance', *Textual Practice*, 25 (2), 329–43.

Lang, A. (2009), '"Enthralling but at the Same Time Disturbing": Challenging the Readers of *Small Island*', *The Journal of Commonwealth Literature*, 44 (2), 123–40.

Mullan, J. (2011), 'Week One: Back Story', *The Guardian*, 8 January, www.guardian.co.uk/books/2011/jan/08/small-island-andrea-levy-bookclub [accessed 1 February 2013].

Phillips, M. (2004), 'Roots Manoeuvre', *The Guardian*, 14 February, www.guardian.co.uk/books/2004/feb/14/featuresreviews.guardianreview10 [accessed 1 February 2013].

Perfect, M. (2010), '"Fold the Paper and Pass it On": Historical Silences and the Contrapuntal in Andrea Levy's Fiction', *The Journal of Postcolonial Writing*, 46 (1), 31–41.

Sandhu, S. (2004), 'A New England', *The Telegraph*, 24 February, www.telegraph.co.uk/culture/book/3612682/A-New-England.html [accessed 15 February 2013].

## Chapter Five: *Small Island*, Small Screen: Adapting Black British Fiction, Rachel Carroll

### *Works by Andrea Levy*

Levy, A. (2004), *Small Island*. London: Headline Review.

### *Secondary Reading*

Cardwell, S. (2002), *Adaptation Revisited: Television and the Classic Novel*. Manchester and New York: Manchester University Press.

Collins, J. (2010), *Bring on the Books for Everybody: How Literary Culture Became Popular Culture*. Durham and London: Duke University Press.

Daileader, C. R. (2000), 'Casting Black Actors: Beyond Othellophilia', in Catherine M. S. Alexander and Stanley Wells (eds), *Shakespeare and Race*, Cambridge: Cambridge University Press, 177–202.

English, J. F. (2005), *The Economy of Prestige: Prizes, Awards and the Circulation of Cultural Value*. Cambridge, Massachusetts; London, England: Harvard University Press.

Fowler, C. (2008), 'A Tale of Two Novels: Developing a Devolved Approach to Black British Writing', *The Journal of Commonwealth Writing*, 43, 75–94.

Fuller, D. and Proctor, J. (2009), 'Reading as "Social Glue"? Book Groups, Multiculture and the *Small Island Read* 2007', *Moving Worlds*, 9 (2), 26–40.

*Gone with the Wind*. USA, 1939. Dir. David O. Selznick.

Grmelová, A. (2010), 'From Loneliness to Encounter: London in the Windrush Generation Novels of Sam Selvon and Andrea Levy', *Litteraria Pragensia: Studies in Literature and Culture* 20 (40), 70–84.

Higson, A. (ed.) (1996), 'The Heritage Film and British Cinema', in *Dissolving Views: Key Writings on British Cinema*. London: Continuum, pp. 232–48.

Huggan, G. (ed.) (2001), 'Prizing Otherness: A short history of the Booker', in *The Postcolonial Exotic: Marketing the Margins*. London: Routledge, pp. 105–23.

Joseph, P. (2011), 'Why Wuthering Heights Gives Me Hope', *The Guardian*, 11 November, www.guardian.co.uk/commentisfree/2011/nov/11/wuthering-heights-black-actors [accessed 1 February 2013).

Lang, A. (2009), '"Enthralling but at the Same Time Disturbing": Challenging the Readers of *Small Island*', *The Journal of Commonwealth Studies*, 44 (2), 123–40.

Malik, S. (2002), *Representing Black Britain: Black and Asian Images on Television*. London: Sage.

Mead, M. (2009), 'Empire Windrush: The Cultural Memory of an Imaginary Arrival', *Journal of Postcolonial Writing*, 45 (2), 137–49.

Muñoz-Valdivieso, S. (2010), 'Africa in Europe: Narrating Black British History in Contemporary Fiction', *Journal of European Studies*, 40 (2), 159–74.

Murray, S. (2012), *The Adaptation Industry: The Cultural Economy of Contemporary Literary Adaptation*. New York and London: Routledge.

Procter, J. (2003), *Dwelling Places: Postwar Black British Writing*. Manchester and New York: Manchester University Press.

Rooney, K. (ed.) (2008), 'Jonathan Frantzen Versus Oprah Winfrey: Disses, Disinvitation, and Disingenuousness', in *Reading with Oprah: The Book Club That Changed the America*. University of Arkansas Press, pp. 33–66.

*Small Island*. UK, BBC, 2009. Dir. John Alexander.

Squires, C. (2009), *Marketing Literature: The Making of Contemporary Writing in Britain*. London: Palgrave Macmillan.

Thompson, A. (2006), 'Practicing a Theory / Theorizing a Practice: An Introduction to Shakespearean Colorblind Casting', in Ayanna Thompson (ed.), *Colorblind Shakespeare: New Perspectives on Race and Performance*. New York; London: Routledge, pp. 1–24.

Walters, T. L. (2005), '"We're All English Now Mate, Like It Or Lump It': The Black / Britishness of Zadie Smith's *White Teeth*', in Kadija Sesay (ed.), *Write Black, Write British: From Post Colonial to Black British Literature*. London: Hansib, 314–22.

## Chapter Six: Exquisite Corpse: Un/dressing History in *Fruit of the Lemon/The Long Song*, Jeannette Baxter

### Works by Andrea Levy

Levy, A. (2004 [1999]), *Fruit of the Lemon*. London: Headline Review.

—(2011a), *The Long Song*. London: Headline Review.

—(2011b), 'The Writing of *The Long Song*', *The Long Song*. London: Headline Review, pp. 405–16.


### Secondary Reading

Adamowicz, E. (1998), *Surrealist Collage in Text and Image: Dissecting the Exquisite Corpse*. Cambridge: Cambridge University Press.

Ashcroft, B. (1999), 'The Rhizome of Post-colonial Discourse', in Roger Luckhurst and Peter Marks (eds), *Literature and the Contemporary*. London: Pearson, pp. 111–25.

Buckridge, S. O. (2004), *The Language of Dress: Resistance and Accommodation in Jamaica, 1760–1890*. Jamaica, Barbados, Trinidad and Tobago: University of the West Indies Press.

Carroll, R. (2014), '*Small Island*, Small Screen: Adapting Black British Fiction', in Jeannette Baxter and David James (eds), *Contemporary Critical Perspectives: Andrea Levy*. London and New York: Bloomsbury, pp. 65–77.

Emery, M. L. (2013), 'The Poetics of Labour in Jean Rhys's Caribbean Modernism', *Women: A Cultural Review (Reading Jean Rhys)*, 23 (4), 421–44.

Kern, A. M. (2009), 'From One Exquisite Corpse (in)to Another: Influences and Transformations from Early to Late Surrealist Games', in Kanta Kochar-Lindgren, David Schneiderman and Tom Denlinger (eds), *The Exquisite Corpse: Chance and Collaboration in Surrealism's Parlor Game*. Lincoln and London: University of Nebraska Press, pp. 3–28.

Knepper, W. (2012), 'Introduction', 'Special Issue on Andrea Levy', *EnterText*, 9, 1–13.

Luckhurst, R. and Marks, P. (1999), 'Hurry up Please It's Time: Introducing the Contemporary', in Roger Luckhurst and Peter Marks (eds), *Literature and the Contemporary*. London: Pearson, pp. 1–12.

Lyotard, J.-F. (1984 [1979]), *The Postmodern Condition: A Report on Knowledge*, trans. Geoffrey Bennington and Brian Massumi. Minneapolis: Minnesota University Press.

Miller, P. D. (2009), 'Totems without Taboos: The Exquisite Corpse', in Kanta Kochar-Lindgren, David Schneiderman and Tom Denlinger (eds), *The Exquisite Corpse: Chance and Collaboration in Surrealism's Parlor Game*. Lincoln and London: University of Nebraska Press, pp. ix–xv.

Perfect, M. (2010), '"Fold the Paper and Pass It on": Historical Silences and the Contrapuntal in Andrea Levy's Fiction', *The Journal of Postcolonial Writing*, 46 (1), 31–41.

## Chapter Seven: 'I am the narrator of this work': Narrative Authority in Andrea Levy's *The Long Song*, Fiona Tolan

### *Works by Andrea Levy*

Levy, A. (2004a [1996]), *Never Far from Nowhere*. 1996. London: Headline Review.

—(2004b [1999]), *Fruit of the Lemon*. London: Headline Review.

—(2004c), 'Made in Britain', *The Guardian*, 18 September, www.guardian.co.uk/books/2004/sep/18/featuresreviews.guardianreview33 [accessed 21 February 2012].

—(2010), *The Long Song*. London: Headline Review.

—(2011a), *The Long Song*. London: Headline Review.

—(2011b), 'The Writing of *The Long Song*', *The Long Song*. London: Headline Review, pp. 405–16.

### *Secondary Reading*

Bakhtin, M. M. (1981), *The Dialogic Imagination: Four Essays*, ed. Michael Holquist, trans. Caryl Emerson and Michael Holquist. Austin: University of Texas Press.

Brontë, C. (1992 [1847]), *Jane Eyre*. Ware: Wordsworth Classics.

Genette, G. (1997), *Paratexts: Thresholds of Interpretation*, trans. Jane E. Lewin. Cambridge: Cambridge University Press.

Gilbert, S. M. and Gubar, S. (2000 [1979]), *The Madwoman in the Attic: The Woman Writer and the Nineteenth-Century Literary Imagination*. 2nd edn. New Haven: Yale University Press.

Higgins, T. E. (2001), *Religiosity, Cosmology, and Folklore: The African Influence in the Novels of Toni Morrison*. New York: Routledge.

Hutcheon, L. (1988), *A Poetics of Postmodernism: History, Theory, Fiction*. Abingdon: Routledge.

Kaplan, C. (2007), *Victoriana: Histories, Fictions, Criticism*. Edinburgh: Edinburgh University Press.

Lima, M. H. (2005), '"Pivoting the Centre": The Fiction of Andrea Levy', in Kadija Sesay (ed.), *Write Black, Write British: From Post Colonial to Black British*. Hertford: Hansib, pp. 56–85.

Lyotard, J.-F. (1984 [1979]), *The Postmodern Condition: A Report on Knowledge*, trans. Geoff Bennington and Brian Massumi. Manchester: Manchester University Press.

McClintock, A. (1995), *Imperial Leather: Race, Gender and Sexuality in the Colonial Contest*. New York: Routledge.

Mitchell, K. (2010), *History and Cultural Memory in Neo-Victorian Fiction: Victorian Afterimages*. Houndmills: Palgrave Macmillan.

Olaussen, M. (1993), 'Jean Rhys's Construction of Blackness as Escape from White Femininity in Wide Sargasso Sea', *Ariel: A Review of International English Literature*, 24 (2), 65–82.

Perfect, M. (2010), ' "Fold the Paper and Pass It on": Historical Silences and the Contrapuntal in Andrea Levy's Fiction', *Journal of Postcolonial Writing*, 46 (1) (February), 31–41.

Rushdie, S. (1992), *Imaginary Homelands: Essays and Criticism 1981–1991*. London: Granta/Penguin.

Smith, A. (1997 [1966]), 'Introduction', in Jean Rhys (ed.), *Wide Sargasso Sea*. London: Penguin, vii–xxiii.

Smith, J. R. (1997), *Writing Tricksters: Mythic Gambols in American Ethnic Literature*. Berkeley: University of California Press.

Spivak, G. C. (1985), 'Three Women's Texts and a Critique of Imperialism', *Critical Inquiry*, 12 (1) (Autumn), 243–61.

Stein, M. (2004), *Black British Literature: Novels of Transformation*. Columbus: Ohio State University Press.

Thieme, J. (2001), *Postcolonial Con-Texts: Writing Back to the Canon*. London: Continuum.

White, H. (1973), *Metahistory: The Historical Imagination in Nineteenth-century Europe*. Baltimore: Johns Hopkins University Press.

## Chapter Eight: At the Centre of the Picture: Andrea Levy's *The Long Song*, Susan Alice Fischer

### Works by Andrea Levy

Levy, A. (2010a), *The Long Song*. New York, Farrar, Strauss and Giroux.

—(2010b), 'The Writing of *The Long Song*', www.andrealevy.co.uk//content/ Writing%20The%20Long%20Song.pdf.

### Secondary Reading

Achebe, C. (1958), *Things Fall Apart*. London: Heinemann.

Armitt L. and Gamble, S. (2006), 'The Haunted Geometries of Sarah Waters's *Affinity*', *Textual Practice*, 20 (1), 141–59. Academic Search Complete. Web. 9 April 2012.

Ball, J. C. (2004), *Imagining London: Postcolonial Fiction and the Transnational Metropolis*. Toronto: University of Toronto Press.

Equiano, O. (1789), *The Interesting Narrative of the Life of Olaudah Equiano, or Gustavus Vassa, the African, Written by Himself*. London: T. Wilkins.

Fischer, S. A. (2010), 'Every Answer Raises Another Question.' Review of *The Long Song* by Andrea Levy. *The Women's Review of Books*, 27 (5) (September/October), 38–9.

—(2014), 'Andrea Levy in Conversation with Susan Alice Fischer', in Jeannette Baxter and David James (eds), *Andrea Levy: Contemporary Critical Perspectives*. London: Bloomsbury, pp. 121–38.

Hurston, Z. N. (1987), *Their Eyes Were Watching God*. London: Virago.

hooks, b. (2000), *Feminist Theory: From Margin to Center*. 2nd edn. Cambridge, MA: South End Press.

'Slavery and Justice Exhibition at Kenwood House', (2007) *English Heritage*, www.english-heritage.org.uk/discover/people-and-places/the-slave-trade-and-abolition/slavery-and-justice-exhibition-at-kenwood-house/.

## Interview: 'Andrea Levy in Conversation with Susan Alice Fischer' (2005 and 2012)

### Works by Andrea Levy

Levy, A. (1994), *Every Light in the House Burnin'*. London: Headline Review.

—(1996), *Never Far from Nowhere*. London: Headline Review.

—(1999), *Fruit of the Lemon*. London: Headline Review.

—(2004), *Small Island*. London: Headline Review.

—(2005), 'Loose Change', in M. Hamand (ed.), *Underwords the Hidden City: The Booktrust London Short Story Competition Anthology*. London: Maia, pp. 67–76.

—(2010), *The Long Song*. London: Headline Review.


### Secondary Reading

Davis, A. (1982), *Women, Race and Class*. London: The Women's Press.

De Bernières, L. (1994), *Captain Corelli's Mandolin*. London: Secker & Warburg.

Fairburns, Z. (1979), *Benefits: A Novel*. London: Virago.

Faulks, S. (1994), *Birdsong*. London: Vintage.

Fischer, S. A. (2004), 'Andrea Levy's London novels, in L. Phillips (ed.), *The Swarming Streets: Twentieth Century Literary Representations of London*. Amsterdam: Rodopi, pp. 199–213.

—(2010), 'Every Answer Raises Another Question.' Review of *The Long Song* by Andrea Levy. *The Women's Review of Books*, 27 (5), 38–9.

French, M. (1978), *The Women's Room*. London: Sphere.

Gee, M. (2002), *The White Family*. London: Saqi.

Hull, G. T., Scott, P. B. and Smith, B. (1982), *All the Women are White, All the Blacks are Men, but Some of Us are Brave: Black Women's Studies*. New York: The Feminist Press at The City University of New York.

King, B. (2004), *The Oxford English Literary History, Volume 13: 1948–2000: The Internationalization of English*. Oxford: Oxford University Press.

Kwei-Armah, K. (2003), *Elmina's Kitchen*. London: Methuen.

Said, E. W. (1993), *Culture and Imperialism*. London: Chatto & Windus.

Selvon, S. (1956), *The Lonely Londoners*. London: Alan Wingate.

Sirett, P. (2004), *The Big Life*. London: Oberon Books.

Stevenson, R. (2004), *The Oxford English Literary History, Volume 12: 1960–2000: The Last of England?* Oxford: Oxford University Press.

Thomas, S. (2005), 'Literary Apartheid in the Post-war London Novel: Finding the Middle Ground', *Changing English*, 12 (2), 309–25.

University College London. 2012, 'UCL Neale Colloquium 2012: Emancipation, Slave-ownership and the Remaking of the British Imperial World: 29th–31st March 2012', UCL. www.ucl.ac.uk/lbs/nealeconference [accessed 2012].

University College London, UCL History Department, 1999–2013. 'Legacies of British Slave-ownership', UCL. www.ucl.ac.uk/lbs/index [accessed 2012].

# Further Reading

## I Works by Andrea Levy

### Novels
Levy, A. (1994), *Every Light in the House Burnin'*. London. Headline Review.
—(1996), *Never Far from Nowhere*. London: Headline Review.
—(1999), *Fruit of the Lemon*. London: Headline Review.
—(2004), *Small Island*. London: Headline Review.
—(2010), *The Long Song*. London: Headline Review.

### Other fiction and non-fiction
Levy, A. (2000), 'This Is My England', *The Guardian*, 19 February, www.guardian.co.uk/books/2000/feb/19/society1.
—(2004), 'Made in Britain', *The Guardian*, 18 September, www.guardian.co.uk/books/2004/sep/18/featuresreviews.guardianreview33.
—(2005), 'Loose Change', in M. Hamand (ed.), *Underwords the Hidden City: The Booktrust London Short Story Competition Anthology*. London: Maia, pp. 67–76.
—(2011), 'The Writing of *The Long Song*', *The Long Song*. London: Headline Review, pp. 405–16.

### Television adaptations of Levy's work
*Small Island* (2009). Dir. John Alexander for BBC.

## II Critical Material

### Book-length studies (dedicated solely to Levy's work)
Knepper, W. (2012), 'Special Issue on Andrea Levy', *EnterText*, 9, 1–171. [A special edition of the journal devoted to Levy's work, containing an Introduction, eight essays and two creative responses.]
Flajsarova, P. (2014), *Diaspora in the Fiction by Contemporary British Women Writers*. Palacky University Press. [This forthcoming monograph largely focuses on the works of Andrea Levy, although it also explores the writings of Bernadine Evaristo and Monica Ali.]

### Book chapters
Fischer, S. A. (2004), 'Andrea Levy's London Novels', in Lawrence Phillips (ed.), *The Swarming Streets: Twentieth-Century Literary Representations of London*. Amsterdam: Rodopi, pp. 199–213.

Lima, Maria H. (2005), ' "Pivoting the Centre": The Fiction of Andrea Levy', in Kadija Sesay (ed.), *Write Black, Write British: From Post Colonial to Black British Literature*. Hertford: Hansib, pp. 56–85.

### *Journal articles*

Beyer, C. (2012), ' "Or perhaps I should describe the old, wild-haired man": Representations of Ageing and Black British Identity in Andrea Levy's *Every Light in the House Burnin'* and Joan Riley's *Waiting in the Twilight*', *EnterText*, 9, 105–21.

Brophy, S. (2010), 'Entangled Genealogies: White Femininity on the Threshold of Change in Andrea Levy's *Small Island*', *Contemporary Women's Writing*, 4 (2), 114–33.

Courtman, S. (2012), 'Women Writers and the Windrush Generation: A Contextual Reading of Beryl Gilroy's *In Praise of Love and Children* and Andrea Levy's *Small Island*', *EnterText*, 9, 84–104.

Casagranda, M. (2010), 'How Many Women Were on the *Empire Windrush*? Regendering Black British Culture in Andrea Levy's *Small Island*', *Textus*, 23 (2), 355–70.

Ellis, A. E. (2012), 'Identity as Cultural Production in Andrea Levy's *Small Island*, *EnterText*, 9, 69–83.

Fischer, Susan A. (2004), 'Contested Spaces in Monica Ali's Brick Lane and Andrea Levy's *Small Island*', *Critical Engagements: A Journal of Criticism and Theory*, 1 (1), 34–52.

Githire, N. (2010), 'The Empire Bites Back: Food Politics and the Making of a Nation in Andrea Levy's Works', *Callaloo*, 33 (3), 857–73.

James, C. (2007), ' "You'll Soon Get Used to Our Language": Language, Parody and West Indian Society in Andrea Levy's *Small Island*', *Anthurium: A Caribbean Studies Journal*, 5 (1), n.p. http://anthurium.miami.edu/volume_5/issue_1/james-language.html.

Gui, W. (2010), 'Post-heritage Narratives: Migrancy and Travelling Theory in V. S. Naipaul's *The Enigma of Arrival* and Andrea Levy's *Fruit of the Lemon*', *The Journal of Commonwealth Literature*, 47 (1), 74.

Lang, A. (2009), ' "Enthralling But at the Same Time Disturbing": Challenging the Readers of *Small Island*', *The Journal of Commonwealth Literature*, 44 (2), 123–40.

Laursen, O. (2012), ' "Telling Her a Story": Remembering Trauma in Andrea Levy's Writing', *EnterText*, 9, 53–68.

Lima, M. H. (2012), 'A Written Song: Andrea Levy's Neo-Slave Narrative', *EnterText*, 9, 135–53.

Machedo Saez, E. (2006), 'Bittersweet (Be)Longing: Filling the Void of History in Andrea Levy's *Fruit of the Lemon*', *Anthurium: A Caribbean Studies Journal*, 4 (1) n.p. http://anthurium.miami.edu/volume_4/issue_1/saezbittersweet.html.

Marquis, C. (2012), 'Crossing Over: Postmemory and the Postcolonial Imaginary in Andrea Levy's *Small Island* and *Fruit of the Lemon*, *EnterText*, 9, 31–52.

Medovarski, A. (2006), ' "I Knew This Was England": Myths of Return in Andrea Levy's *Fruit of the Lemon', MaComère: Journal of the Association of Caribbean Women Writers and Scholars*, 8, 35–66.

Murphy, A. (2012), 'Stranger in the Empire: Language and Identity in the "Mother Country"', *EnterText*, 9, 122–34.

Pérez Fernández, I. (2010), '(Re)Mapping London: Gender and Racial Relations in Andrea Levy's *Small Island', Interactions*, Special Issue: 'The Role of Female Voices in Constructing Fictional Maps of Contemporary Britain', 19 (1–2), 25–40.

Perfect, M. (2010), '"Fold the Paper and Pass It on": Historical Silences and the Contrapuntal in Andrea Levy's Fiction', *The Journal of Postcolonial Writing*, 46 (1), 31–41.

Pready, J. (2012), 'The Familiar Made Strange: The Relationship between the Home and Identity in Andrea Levy's Fiction', *EnterText*, 9, 14–30.

Toplu, S. (2005), 'Home(land) or "Motherland": Translational Identities in Andrea Levy's *Fruit of the Lemon', Anthurium: A Caribbean Studies Journal*, 3 (1), n.p. http://anthurium.miami.edu/volume_3/ issue_1/toplu-homeland.htm.

## III  Select Interviews and Profiles

Allardice, L. (2005), 'The Guardian Profile: Andrea Levy', *The Guardian*, 21 January, www.guardian.co.uk/uk/2005/jan/21/books.generalfiction.

Anon (2010), Interview with Andrea Levy, *Scotsman*, 11 February, www.scotsman.com/news/interview-andrea-levy-writer-1–473985 [accessed 18 April 2013].

Barringer, N. (2010), 'Andrea Levy and *The Long Song', The Interview Online*, www.theinterviewonline.co.uk/library/books/andrea-levy-interview.aspx [accessed 14 September 2012].

Brace, M. (2004), 'Notes from a Small Island', *The Independent*, 12 June, www.independent.co.uk/news/people/profiles/andrea-levy-notes-from-a-small-island-6167726.html [accessed 14 November 2006].

Burns, C. with Andrea L. (2004), 'Off the Page: Andrea Levy', *Washington Post*, 24 June, www.washingtonpost.com/wp-dyn/articles/A52272–2004Jun18.html [accessed 12 July 2004].

Ciabattari, J. (2010), 'Giving Voice to Slaves: An Interview with Andrea Levy', *BookBeast*, 8 June, www.theinterviewonline.co.uk/library/books/andrea-levy-interview.aspx [accessed 23 March 2011].

Ezard, J. (2005), '*Small Island* Claims Whitbread Prize', *The Guardian*, 26 January, www.guardian.co.uk/uk/2005/jan/books.whitbreadbookawards2004 [accessed 23 October 2005].

Fischer, S. A. (2005), 'Andrea Levy in Conversation with Susan Alice Fischer', *Changing English: Studies in Culture and Education*, 12 (3), 361–71.

Gerard, J. (2004), 'Every Inch an English Woman: Jasper Gerard Meets Andrea Levy', *The Sunday Times*, 13 June, www.thesundaytimes.co.uk/sto/news/article109351.ece [accessed 28 July 2006].

Jamieson, T. (2007), 'The Author Andrea Levy on Racism, Rejection and Writing', *The Herald Magazine*, 6 January: 9–11.

Morrison, B. (2009), 'Andrea Levy Interviewed by Blake Morrison', *Women: A Cultural Review*, 20 (3), 325–38.

Prasad, R. (1999), 'Two Sides to Every Story', *The Guardian*, 4 March, www.guardian.co.uk/world/1999/mar/04/gender.uk [accessed 15 April 2013].

Walters, T. L. (2011), 'Andrea Levy: Interview', *Mosaic*, 6 November, http://mosaicmagazine.org/blog/?p=1011 [accessed 3 February 2013].

Young, K. (2011), 'Desert Island Discs', BBC Radio 4, 12 June.

Younge, G. (2010), 'I started to realise what fiction can be. And I thought, wow! You can take on the world', Andrea Levy interviewed by Gary Younge, *The Guardian*, 30 January, www.guardian.co.uk/books/2010/jan/30/andrea-levy-long-song-interview [accessed 15 April 2010].

## IV Websites

www.andrealevy.co.uk [Andrea Levy's official website. This site provides excellent resources – interviews, reviews, bibliography, biography, news and events.]

www.literature.britishcouncil.org/andrea-levy [Provides a very useful Critical Perspective by James Proctor.]

www.litencyc.com/php/speople.php?rec=true&UID=12626 [Critical Overview by Michael Perfect. Requires subscription.]

www.en.wikipedia.org/wiki/Andrea_Levy [Provides useful links and a bibliography.]

# Index